IDEAS OF HOME

IDEAS OF HOME
LITERATURE OF ASIAN MIGRATION

GEOFFREY KAIN
CONTRIBUTING EDITOR

MICHIGAN STATE UNIVERSITY PRESS
EAST LANSING

Copyright © 1997 Geoffrey Kain

All Michigan State University Press Books are produced on paper
which meets the requirements of American National Standard of
Information Sciences—Permanence of paper for printed materials
ANSI Z23.48–1984

Printed in the United States of America

Michigan State University Press
East Lansing, Michigan 48823–5202

05 04 03 02 01 00 99 98 97 1 2 3 4 5 6 7 8 9 10

Library of Congress Cataloging–in–Publication Data

Ideas of Home: literature of Asian migration / Geoffrey Kain,
          contributing editor.
          p.   cm.
          Includes bibliographical references (p.   ) and index.
          ISBN 0-87013-466-3 (alk. paper)
              1. American literature—Asian American authors—History
and criticism. 2. Emigration and immigration in literature. 3. Asian
Americans in literature. 4. Immigrants in literature. 5. Home in
literature. 6. Asia—in literature.   I. Kain, Goeffrey
PS153.A84I34   1997
810.9' 995073—dc21   96-53669
                                                  CIP

FOR LISA, WHO IS HOME

CONTENTS

Acknowledgments

I am grateful to Dr. Fred Bohm, director of the Michigan State University Press, for his interest in this project from its earliest conceptual phase. Thanks to Deborah Schafer, Laura Robbins, Kathleen Citro, and Jane Beckman of the Embry-Riddle library staff for their assistance, and to Warren Stuart and Al Brust who came through more than once when I badly needed technical assistance. Special thanks to Carol Liptak for her cheerful and reliable service in helping prepare this manuscript. Thanks, also, to artist Martin Hoffman for his advice in preparing the dustjacket illustration. And, of course, warm thanks to all the contributors to this collection whose correspondence and patience during the long period of creating and organizing this project is greatly appreciated; hopefully the wait has proven worthwhile.

Notes on Contributors

Fakrul Alam is chairperson of the Department of English and director of the Centre for Advanced Research in the Humanities at the University of Dhaka, Bangladesh. Author of *Daniel Defoe: Colonial Propagandist* (University of Dhaka Publications, 1989) and *Bharati Mukherjee* (New York: Twayne Publishers, 1995), he has also published essays on Defoe, Melville, Kipling, Lawrence, Rushdie, R. K. Narayan, and Nirad Chaudhuri. From 1989 to 1991 he was Fulbright scholar in residence and visiting associate professor at Clemson University.

Rocio G. Davis received a B.A. in English from the Ateneo de Manila University, Philippines, and an M.A. and Ph.D. from the University of Navarra in Pamplona, Spain. She has been serving as Professor of English and American Literature at the University of Navarra since 1989, and served as Visiting Professor at the Ateneo de Manila University in 1994. In 1992, she served as Visiting Scholar at the University of Illinois in Chicago. Her chief research interests are in Asian American literature and the new literatures in English. She has published essays on Maxine Hong Kingston, Sui Sin Far, Amy Tan, Kazuo Ishiguro, Michael Ondaatje, and others.

Samir Dayal formerly taught in the English Department at Franklin College, Indiana, and currently serves as assistant professor of English at Bentley College, Massachusetts. His primary interests are in postcolonial and cultural studies. Recently, he has published on the work of figures associated with the Indian subcontinent such as Salman Rushdie, Bharati Mukherjee, Sara Suleri, and filmmaker Mira Nair. Other essays are forthcoming in several collections of essays. He is completing a book on Rushdie and is editing another entitled *Postcolonial Diasporas*.

David Goldstein-Shirley teaches American and ethnic studies at the University of California, Irvine. He has published on American ethnic history, culture, and literature.

John C. Hawley received his Ph.D. from the University of Pennsylvania and currently serves as associate professor at Santa Clara University, California. He has edited *Reform and Counterreform* (Mouton, 1994), *Writing the Nation: Self and Country in the Postcolonial Imagination* (Rodopi, 1995), *Through a*

Glass Darkly (Fordham, 1995), and *Cross-Addressing: Discourse on the Border* (SUNY, 1996). His essays have appeared in *Ariel*, *Research in African Literatures*, and elsewhere.

Feroza Jussawalla is associate professor of English at the University of Texas at El Paso. She is coauthor of *Interviews With Writers of the Postcolonial World* (University Press of Mississippi) and author of *Family Quarrels: Toward a Criticism of Indian Writing in English* (New York: Peter Lang). She has edited *Excellent Teaching in a Changing Academy* (Jossey Bass) and the *Holt Guide to Writing Across the Curriculum*. She has published numerous scholarly and newspaper articles and one short story entitled "AIDSwallah" in *Her Mother's Ashes* (Toronto: South Asian Press).

Geoffrey Kain serves as associate professor and associate chair in humanities at Embry-Riddle University, Daytona Beach, Florida. He has also taught at Idaho State University, University of Wisconsin-Marinette, and served as foreign expert in English language and literature at two universities (Fuzhou and Xiamen) in the People's Republic of China, 1984-88. He has published numerous essays on a wide range of topics and authors, including Hemingway, Hawthorne, R. K. Narayan, Bharati Mukherjee, Louis Chu and Cao Xue Qin, and edited *R. K. Narayan: Contemporary Critical Essays* (Michigan State University Press, 1993).

Amy Ling is professor of English and director of the Asian American Studies Program at the University of Wisconsin, Madison. She is the author of *Between Worlds: Women Writers of Chinese Ancestry*, the groundbreaking history of Chinese–American women writers, and *Chinamerican Reflections*, a chapbook of her poems and paintings. She is editor or coeditor of seven books, including the *Heath Anthology of American Literature* and the *Oxford Companion to Women's Writing in the United States, Imagining America*, and *Visions of America*. She has published numerous articles on Asian American literature and given talks nationally and internationally.

Clayton G. MacKenzie was born and educated in Africa, furthering his studies at the University of Glasgow in Scotland. He has been a visiting researcher at universities in the West Indies, Malta, central Africa, and China; and he has worked in teaching and administrative capacities at university institutions in Britain for ten years, including four years as assistant dean of St. Mary's University College in London. He joined the staff of Hong Kong Baptist University in 1993. His publications include novels, several edited books, and numerous articles on Shakespeare, postcolonial literatures, and contemporary theater.

Dolores de Manuel is an assistant professor in the Department of English at Manhattan College, where she has taught since 1990. She received her Ph.D. from Fordham University; her dissertation was on self-reference in British poetry. She has a master's degree in Philippine literature from Ateneo de Manila University. Her publications include essays and reviews in scholarly journals and anthologies, as well as works of short fiction.

Sheng-mei Ma received his Ph.D. from Indiana University and is currently Assistant Professor of American Thought and Language at Michigan State University. His book *Immigrant Subjectivities in Asian American and Asian Diaspora Literatures* is forthcoming. His essays have appeared in journals such as *Journal of American Culture, Modern Language Studies,* and *Holocaust and Genocide Studies,* as well as collections such as *English Studies/Culture Studies: Institutionalizing Dissent* (University of Illinois Press) and *Rage* (New York University Press).

Pushpa N. Parekh is an assistant professor of English at Spelman College in Atlanta, where she has taught comparative, international, and women's literature courses, including "New Immigrant Women's Literature in the United States." She has also published a number of articles and chapters on Asian and Asian-American literature.

Ismail S. Talib is senior lecturer in English language and literature at the National University of Singapore, and is associate editor of *World Literature Written in English.* His essays have appeared in journals such as the *Journal of Narrative Technique,* the *ELT Journal,* the *Journal of Multilingual and Multicultural Development, Guidelines, Social Semiotics,* and in critical anthologies such as *Words in a Cultural Context* (ed. A. Pakir), and *Language, Education and Society in Singapore* (eds. W. Ho, et al.). His essays written in Malay have appeared in *Dewan Sastera, Dewan Behasa,* and *Linguistik Melayu* (ed. Zaharani Ahmad).

James A. Wren has spent much of his life moving from "house to house, city to city, country to country." Having undertaken graduate study on three continents, Wren specializes in twentieth-century Japanese literature, Asian American literatures, and East-West literary relations. His most recent publications include a study of stylistics in contemporary Japanese prose as well as an article on Japanese narrative scrolls. At work on a book-length manuscript on the original dramatic works of Mori Ogai, he holds a research position in modern Japanese literature in the Graduate School of Modern Culture and Society at Niigata University, Niigata, Japan.

Yuan Yuan is currently associate professor of English at California State University San Marcos. He received his M.A. from Shandong University, China, and his Ph.D. from the University of Wisconsin-Milwaukee. His research interests are in critical theory, modern and postmodern fiction, ethnic studies, and postcolonial discourse. He is the author of *The Discourse of Fantasy: Theoretical and Fictional Perspectives* (Hollowbrook Press, 1995). In addition to publishing articles on psychoanalysis, Marxism, translation, postmodern fiction, and ethnic literature, he has also served as guest editor of *Journal of the Fantastic in the Arts*.

Niaz Zaman is professor of English at the University of Dhaka, Bangladesh, where she teaches drama, American, and Commonwealth literature. She has coedited *Other Englishes: Essays on Commonwealth Writing; Infinite Variety: Women in Society and Literature*; and *Migration, Migrants, and the United States*. She is also interested in folklife and has published a translation of Bengali tales, *Princess Kalabati and Other Tales*, as well as a book on women's folk art, *The Art of Kantha Embroidery*. She is editor of the *Bangladesh Journal of American Studies*. From 1981 to 1983 Zaman served as the educational attaché at the Bangladesh Embassy in Washington, D.C.

INTRODUCTION

An eyebrow may be justifiably raised on first coming to a text titled *Literature of Asian Migration*, chiefly because of the nearly audacious inclusiveness of such an identifier as "Asian," a heading which obviously embraces a tremendous breadth of peoples, cultures, languages, etc.[1] To narrow the subject field to East Asian or South Asian or Central Asian does not allow one to evade this great diversity, just as Chinese or Indian does not, nor for that matter Szechuanese or Goan. So, clearly, to collectively address so variegated a subject field will inevitably lead to the exclusion of numerous peoples, many of whom are represented by significant literary achievement that is in keeping with this volume's thematic focus.

And it is the thematic focus with which I am primarily concerned and which defines this essay collection's genesis and binding force. I have initiated this project because I perceive a need for it. While there are a number of excellent works centering on Asian American, Asian Canadian, or Asian British literature, they only occasionally (though inevitably) cross into direct exploration of the topic or theme of immigration and the subsequent quest for "home," as they tend to be organized around the principle of ethnicity exclusively—that is, as "Asian American" or "Asian Canadian" rather than according to a specific thematic thread or common topic addressed in the literature. *Ideas of Home: Literature of Asian Migration*, however, has evolved around a specific point of thematic interest: recent literature that explores challenges to the Asian immigrant's sense of self and conception of home. The experience—and the description of it in literature—of leaving home and arriving in a new place is naturally a very ancient one which has always encouraged or demanded some degree of self-redefinition, and a complex of factors have always had to be resolved (or at least have presented or clarified themselves) before the new place—or perhaps new place(s) as well as place of origin—may be sincerely embraced as "home." Among the Asian migratory population, a network of causes for this relocation is found, from political oppression to poverty to political upheaval to war . . . the so-called "push" factors; as well as the so-called "pull" factors of (real or perceived) economic opportunity in the West, greater educational opportunities for children, (in some cases) greater personal liberties, etc. The adjusted sense of self that follows from relocation and the necessarily new interaction of self and environment are the points of interest for this collection of essays, as is the impact on the people and place left behind as a result of emigration; these are essays which explore prominent literature that evokes for us the experience of characters (and frequently also authors) who have removed from nations in Asia and have settled in the West.

The literature of Asian immigration/emigration is, I believe, among the most excellent and important now being written. Vibrant, poignant, and exciting, this body of literature expresses and explores the soul of an entire complex of vital, broad-based contemporary experiences and social issues. Social or sociopolitical context nearly always illuminates our understanding and appreciation of literature,[2] and the literature of Asian migration should certainly be approached within this context or perhaps even as a most faithful revelation or most definitive facet of the larger context—a context which finds itself bound to or serving as some of the most central fibers of contemporary life in the West. The issues raised by the literature and the realities giving rise to and expressed through the literature are central to/tied to some of the most dynamic forces driving the evolution of modern culture.

In the introduction to their collection of essays *Migration: The Asian Experience*, Judith M. Brown and Rosemary Foot impress upon us the historical and cultural significance of large-scale movement out of Asia:

> Human migrations are a significant force in historical change. Large-scale migration, of Asians, Africans and Europeans, was central in fashioning the world of the nineteenth century, its world-wide empires and the establishment of global and political dominance by people of European origin. Twentieth century migrations have been just as important, particularly in the creation of a post-World War and post-imperial world order. Asian peoples have been among the most central in these processes. By the last quarter of this century about nine million South Asians (Indians, Pakistanis, and Bangladeshis) and over 30 million Chinese are to be found living outside their country of origin as a result of migration or birth within a migrant community. . . . Asian migration is, therefore, not only an important aspect of Asian history and the life experiences of people from that continent, but is also part of the creative contribution of Asia and its peoples to the contemporary world. (1)

The creative contributions of Asian peoples to many nations outside of Asia have been realized in almost every field and institution of culture—in literature and the arts, science and technology, education, business and finance, family and community affairs, etc.—and these contributions continue to impress themselves more deeply and more overtly on the public consciousness.

Yet this contribution has not been made without a continuing struggle against prejudice and resistance, and general public recognition and acceptance of Asian "belonging" in Western societies has been slow in coming, as much of the modern and contemporary literature of Asian migration makes clear, and as the essays in this volume generally reflect. Widespread concern over immigration levels in the United States, for example, often vents itself in hostility toward Asian immigrants or, perhaps worse, toward citizens (many of them second- or third-generation "natives") of Asian descent. The post-1965 (following upon reform of immigration policy in the Immigration Act of 1965) influx of immigrants is, indeed, the heaviest since the great European migrations to the United States during the latter nineteenth and early twentieth centuries. And while European immigration to the States has slowed to a trickle, approximately 45 percent of recent immigrants have come from the nations of Asia, making it the most fertile current source of immigrants to the United States (North America—i.e., Mexico, Cuba, Haiti, etc.—being secondary). As Morrison Wong points out, by comparison with this current level only seven percent of immigrants to the United States in the early 1960s were Asian; the years 1965-81 saw a tenfold increase over that level (154). The Asian American population was well over seven million by 1990, compared with approximately three million in 1980 and about a million and a half in 1970 (Daniels, 95). In Canada, people of single Asian origins (South Asian, East and South East Asian) made up 5.1 percent of the total population in 1991, up from 3.5 percent in 1986 (Renaud and Badets, 20); although more than half of Canada's immigrant population lives in Ontario, one in nine individuals now living in British Columbia is of Asian ancestry (11 percent of the total population in 1991, up from 8 percent in 1986); and more than 19 percent of Vancouver's population is now of Asian ancestry (Renaud and Badets 22).

The new immigrants to North America are thus providing a tangible demographic shift and are serving as catalysts for the evolution of culture. As novelist and short story writer Bharati Mukherjee puts it, "We' re not on Ellis Island any more" (3). True—and some (often rather vocally) would it were not so. In her study "Asian Immigration and American Race Relations: From Exclusion to Acceptance?" Sharon M. Lee writes the following:

Besides questions of economic adaptation, there is the tangled relationship between immigration, nativism, and racism. Rose[3] referred to "old nativists" and "neo-nativists," whose targets include Asians. For the first group, increased Asian immigration has revived the spectre of unassimilable aliens threatening to change the complexion of American society. . . . Neo-nativists include other deprived minorities, in particular, blacks, who resent the diversion of dwindling social welfare funds to foreigners (the Southeast Asian refugee assistance-programmes have been especially galling). As long as nativism and racism remain part of American culture, Asians, immigrant and native-born alike, risk the prejudice and discrimination that follows. (386-87)

In a recent article published in the *Atlantic Monthly*, "The Coming Immigration Debate," as an example of "old nativist" critique, Jack Miles provides a thorough review of Englishman Peter Brimelow's new book *Alien Nation: Common Sense About America's Immigration Disaster* (Random House), in which Brimelow articulates some frequently introduced concerns of the dominant culture regarding the "tidal wave" of new immigrants to the States. As Brimelow remarks, in 1990 alone 1.5 million *legal* immigrants were admitted to the United States,

> . . . of whom only eight percent came from Europe, including some enroute from Asia or the Caribbean by way of Europe. In 1960 the U.S. population was 88.6 percent white. By 1990 the percentage of whites had dropped to 75.6, and the Bureau of the Census forecasts a further drop, to 64 percent by 2020 and to 53 percent by 2050. (132)

These are facts and projections; why would they be concerns? (In response to anxiety over the "darkening of America," one would do well to contemplate the plethora of facts and statistics regarding Asian immigrants' levels of education, employment, family income, receipt of social services, divorce rates, etc., provided in Morrison Wong's excellent article "Post-1965 Asian Immigrants: Where Do They Come From, Where Are They Now, Where Are They Going?") Brimelow looks to history, to precedent, and argues that the United States' post-1965 openness to immigration is unprecedented and unparalleled, and the likely consequences—though unknowable—are ominous. As Miles summarizes Brimelow's position,

. . . America will indeed be different—not just different from what it has been but different from every other nation in the world in its radical openness to immigration. No other nation, as Brimelow's queries make clear, permits immigration by the hundreds of thousands annually on criteria no more compelling than "family reunification." None would dream of countenancing a tremendous demographic transformation for that reason alone. (132)

The fear Brimelow presents is, simply put, that while in the past the vast majority of immigrants to the United States "took on American history as their own," with "numerous poems and short stories [having] been written over the years about the comedy and poignancy of this process," the latest newcomers (including Europeans) tend to

> evince little enthusiasm for what Lincoln called the "unfinished work" of building a nation on "the proposition that all men are created equal." They hold or divest U.S. citizenship on the basis of tax-savings yield just as some native-born Americans have done. Their attitude bodes ill for the United States as other than a business arrangement. . . . (132)

Miles notes that while "perhaps a few Americans formally espouse the view that their country is not truly a nation but only a political system," he wonders what the future will be for a nation that is committed to heavy immigration and yet "can no longer assimilate new groups because it has itself become no more than a group of unassimilated, contending cultures" (132).

Perhaps in part as a result of the demographic shifts in the United States and other Western nations, the value of cultural assimilation is itself being called into question. As Feroza Jussawalla argues in "South Asian Diaspora Writers in Britain: 'Home' versus 'Hybridity,'" the first essay in this volume, for Asian immigrant writers (for a variety of reasons that she details in her paper) "the notion of home is that of a place many thousands of miles away." The "Black British" are never fully accepted by the dominant culture (and parallels are drawn with experiences in the United States—and could be drawn with experiences in Canada and elsewhere) and cultural hybridity is not allowed. Professor Jussawalla poses an important question:

> Should we just give up any notion of "home"? It is argued that in the global village we call home, there isn't room enough for separate locations, for separate cultures, and that communication highways and travel at superspeeds have altered cultures so that we

are all hybrids. What accounts then for the rise in Islamic fundamentalism, Hindu fundamentalism, neo-Nazism, "American nativism," Hawaiian indigenousness, and various such searches for the culturally perfectly located "homes"—the platonic ideas, as it were, of "home"?

"Is there," she asks, "a binary opposition between 'hybridity' and 'indigenousness'"?

Michael Lind, senior editor at *Harper's* magazine, explores similar ground and comes to some different conclusions in his article "Reinventing America," calling into question a number of the assumptions that he characterizes as contemporary zeitgeist—that zeitgeist being, essentially, the prevailing belief that we are witnessing a rapid movement toward the simultaneous strengthening of both the global and the local (or "tribal") as we witness the disintegration of the nation-state. Global integration continues apace even as ethnic, religious, and political "tribes" isolate themselves from other local groups. Across the Western world, most notably in the United States, as the predominant view has it, we are experiencing the balkanization of culture. While global integration and interdependence in the spheres of manufacturing, technology, and finance are now largely taken for granted, "there remains the supposed global resurgence of ethnic identity, which, the Spirit of the Age would have us believe, threatens to tear established nation-states apart" (79). In response to the assumption that ethnic divisions and broader xenophobia are gaining strength, Lind argues that

> . . . the collapse of imperial and federal structures in the Soviet Union, Yugoslavia, and Czechoslovakia is thought to be, not merely a one-time-only response to the crumbling of a particular empire, but a harbinger of runaway fragmentation throughout the world. The problem with this view is that most of the ethnic conflicts that are usually linked to post-Soviet disorder, like the Palestinian-Israeli conflict, the Northern Irish problem, the Basque conflict, and so on, are generations old and for the most part indefinitely containable. They are different things, not different versions of the same thing. Irish and Basque and Kurdish national struggles are not part of a "global" resurgence of ethnicity; they have been simmering away all along. (79)

Lind goes further in his assault on claims of cultural balkanization by maintaining that we risk losing touch with reality altogether when we apply the metaphor of "Balkanization" to various racial and social problems in the United States. This misconceived analogy—"America Herzegovina"—has been invoked most often for three different kinds of conflict: moral debates, racial divisions, and controversies over immigration and assimilation. (80)

Regarding immigration and assimilation, Lind argues that "balkanization" is certainly a misleading analogy and that more useful comparisons will be drawn between the United States and the democracies of Western Europe, "which began admitting large numbers of immigrants from former colonial provinces or adjacent Third World areas around the same time that America implemented its present policy, or nonpolicy, of family reunification, permitting ever-escalating mass immigration from Latin America and Asia" (81). The ethnic enclaves to be found throughout the nations of the West—the Chinatowns, Koreatowns, Little Indias, etc.—"tend merely to be temporary way-stations on the road to the complete acculturation of immigrants" (81). So far as the situation in the United States is concerned, Lind feels that

> the assimilatory power of American vernacular culture is so great that the fears of nativists and the hopes of multiculturalists will almost certainly be confounded as today's so-called Third World immigrants become tomorrow's bland, conventional Middle Americans only incidentally named Ramirez and Wong. The eligibility of Latin American and Asian immigrants to participate in a racial spoils system devised initially for black Americans will not slow their acculturation, though it may give them a material incentive to affect an ethnicity that they may have for the most part lost. (81)

But is that ethnicity truly "for the most part lost"? And does the literature of Asian migration tend to reveal a loss of ethnic identity in lieu of a full sense of identification with the "new" culture as "home"? Shirley Geok-lin Lim, like Feroza Jussawalla, dismisses the idea of the immigrant as cultural hybrid. Considering the field of American literature exploring immigration and ethnic identity, she writes,

> . . . minority writers, especially first-generation immigrant writers, the ones straight off the boat or the Boeing 747, contain within themselves this double perspective; as in an optical illusion, their identities encompass more than one figure simultaneously, like the figure that is both the image of a delectable young female and the

> horrid witchy profile of an old woman. This double, even triple or
> multiple perspective exists simultaneously . . . . Human sight
> cannot hold both contradictory visions in one glance. So too with
> the identity of alien and American. For while immigrants are both
> simultaneously alien and American, they are conscious of only one
> or the other at a given time. (22)

Professor Lim maintains that the contemporary immigrant author thus
explores and exudes, perhaps even celebrates, this bifurcated (though not
"hybrid") identity as both alien and native, of being the native foreigner, of
posing for culture at large a problematized definition (or adjusted/expanded
connotation, at least) of the concept of "home":

> The immigrant and minority writer who is identified as such is
> immediately suspicious as to the intentions of that identification.
> The historical fact of foreign birth, once it is in your hands, can be
> used for all kinds of purposes, ... This knowledge of my other-
> origin allows you to deny me entry into your society on your
> terms, brands me as an exotic, freezes me in a geographical
> mythology.
>
> Yet I am proud of my origin. Should you proceed to treat me as if I
> were not different, as if my historical origin has not given to me a
> unique destiny and character, I would also accuse you of
> provincialism, of inability to distinguish between cultures. (18)

Assimilation, she therefore argues, is an ambiguous realization, certainly not
simply an either/or prospect. Without question, certain elements tied to one's
nation of origin are retained in the rhythms of daily life (whether food,
clothing, traditional modes of family relationships, etc.), while other aspects
of the original culture are either consciously abandoned or suppressed, or are
simply lost, as they are replaced or displaced by the ways and ideas of the new
culture. Conflict between these modes and between ways of seeing—or
conflict between individuals (whether husband-wife, siblings, etc.) or between
generations embracing more or less of the original or the more newly
encountered ways or ideas—become the centerpiece of much Asian immigrant
literature, while the easier complementarity of otherwise alien ideologies
serves as an organizing principle of other Asian immigration literature.[4]

Certainly the bulk of Asian immigration literature investigates the
experience of cultural ambiguity, an ambiguity that is explored in various
essays in this volume. In my "The Enigma of Departure: The Dynamics of
Cultural Ambiguity in Rohinton Mistry's *Swimming Lessons and Other Stories*

from Firozsha Baag," I trace Mistry's skillful rendering of the fluid process of departing/arriving and the subsequent ways in which the ambiguities of "self" and "home" present themselves; and in David Goldstein-Shirley's "Home(s), Family(ies), and Identity(ies) in Mukherjee's *Jasmine*," he calls the novel "supremely American" because as an immigrant novel in a nation of immigrants it reveals as much about the nation as it does about the immigrant's quest to comprehend and control changes in self; and in Amy Ling's "Maxine Hong Kingston and the Dialogic Dilemma of Asian American Writers" she investigates the ambiguous American/Chinese identity of Kingston's central character, as she perceives herself and is perceived by others, as well as the "cultural tightrope" Asian American writers are forced to walk because their work is often not considered either "American" or accurately descriptive of "native Asian" (criticism directed at Kingston for confusing Chinese mythology, or at Amy Tan for mistranslating some Mandarin Chinese words, are cases in point) or even conscientiously "Asian American" (the Asian American writer often being criticized by the minority culture for "not telling the story right" or not accurately revealing the essence of their experience, or perhaps pandering to the dominant culture's thirst for the exotic). As Amy Ling has pointed out, this essay confronts the dialogic dilemma which is "implicitly another way of being between worlds and not quite at home anywhere."

Shirley Geok-lin Lim further clarifies this ambiguous identity and its contribution to contemporary culture:

> In a nation of immigrants, there must therefore always be already that straining against the grain, the self that is assimilated and the self that is unassimilatable. This self that escapes assimilation, I believe, renews American culture, making it ready for the future. Even as each new generation of immigrants casts away its old selves in the fresh American present, so American culture casts away its old self in the presence of new Americans. This political and cultural dialectic has presented to the modern world many of its models of dynamism and continues to invigorate despite its many corruptions and oppressions in every other nation and culture in the world. (19)

"Home" is revealed to be a highly complex intellectual/spiritual locus as the individual or family departs, for whatever reasons, is thus separated physically from what has been home, only to discover in many/most cases widespread prejudice or, at least, a reluctance to accept among the dominant culture in the new land—and so "home" will become, on the one hand, an idea of what was—no doubt tinged with some nostalgia, however difficult the circumstances of departure—and a (despite the hardships of arrival) hopeful image of what might be . . . here and now, as well as in the future. Home, therefore, just as the assimilated and/or unassimilated self, becomes a highly ambiguous reality; it is both/and while it is neither/nor.[5] In her recent autobiographical essay, "Whose America Is It?" Amy Ling offers us excellent insight into this phenomenon. She cogently recounts her experience, as Chinese immigrant growing up within the United States' educational system, living the personal contradictions and ambiguities of being both American and Other:

> What is my work in Asian American literature today but an effort to make a home, a comfortable place, for myself in this still too often hostile land. The educational policy of the United States when I was growing up was totally homogenizing and assimilationist. The prevailing national self-concept was Israel Zangwill's metaphor of the large melting pot, where all peoples of the world would be mixed together and come out WASP, celebrating Columbus Day and Thanksgiving from the Pilgrims' point of view; Memorial and Veteran's Day and the Fourth of July, waving the red, white and blue. I was not supposed to notice that in the three decades of my developing and maturing years, the United States fought three wars in Asia against people that looked like me: in the Forties against the Japanese, in the Fifties against the Koreans and Communist Chinese, and in the Sixties against Vietnamese, Cambodians and Laotians. It's extremely difficult and totally confusing to feel American and to look like the enemy, to think myself at home and be asked where I come from, to be a professor of literature and complimented on my good English. (28)

And yet, despite the difficulties, despite the confusion, she finds herself asking, like so many others,

> How can I say we must close the door to others like me longing to take part in the American Dream? How can I agree with Garrett Hardin's cold and logical "lifeboat ethics"? On the other hand, now that I'm on this side of the "golden door," wouldn't I lose if the door were opened to everyone? (27)

The impact on self and family of being construed as "native foreigner" is also investigated in depth, and very powerfully, in James Wren's contribution to this volume, "'Half Fish and Half F-o-u-l': Kibei Youth, Conflicting Iconographies, and Japanese-American Internment Experiences." By turning not only to literary evocations of World War II experiences of Japanese Americans within the United States , but also to numerous accounts from the interned individuals themselves, he pointedly exposes the problematized sense of self (for individual and culture) realized by second generation Japanese Americans as a result of their ignominious ordeal.

Ways of coping with uprooting, migrating, and working to become rooted again are explored in this volume by various contributors. Sheng-mei Ma, in "Postcolonial Feminizing of America in Carlos Bulosan," reveals how the Philippine immigrant Bulosan depicts his strong attraction to and repulsion from America as homeland through the icons of white female (erotic attraction) and white male (repulsive power of the male-centered dominant culture). In her essay "Imagined Homecomings: Strategies for Reconnection in the Writing of Asian Exiles," Dolores de Manuel traces how the act of writing becomes itself a method for building bridges "that span the geographical, social, and cultural distances that they and their families have travelled"; the authors, by writing, "perform an act of reinscribing themselves within a new world . . . creating for themselves a fresh mode of relation toward their present and their past, a way of seeing themselves within a new order."

These issues/themes are further pursued by Pushpa Parekh in her essay "Naming One's Place, Claiming One's Space: Literature About Immigrant Women," in which she explores some recent literary treatments of female experiences of migration, exile, the crossing of boundaries, and individual subjectivity "located at the sites of convergence of multiple places and cultures, . . . the reworking of female migratory identity across geographical and national boundaries." Paired with Parekh's essay, and consistent with the puzzle posed by others in their discussion of Asian migrant literature, John Hawley in his "Gus Lee, Chang-Rae Lee, and Li-Young Lee: The Search for the Father in Asian American Literature" asks, "Who, [the immigrants] must ask, are they expected to be, who are they allowed to be, who do they choose to be?" And in keeping with the personal difficulty and confusion attested to by Amy Ling in "Whose America Is It?" Hawley points out that the "anxiety ramifies in the lives of many Asian ethnic groups, who frequently enough become lumped together in the view of white Americans as 'our' enemies from the Second World War, the Korean War, or the Vietnamese War." Hawley investigates works by several Asian American male writers he feels "embody the classic struggles of Oedipus and Telemachus, seeking to discover their fathers without killing them in the process or losing a secure sense of themselves as significant individuals."

To characterize the complex and problematic reality of assimilation and to attempt to describe the change in self-definition and understanding of just what "home" means is to inevitably deal in generalization which, like treatment of "Asian," will ignore so much variation and cross-identification. Most usefully, then, Niaz Zaman's contribution to this collection, "Old Passions in a New Land . . . ," compares the very different treatment of the immigrant experience provided by two authors, Bharati Mukherjee and Bapsi Sidhwa, and contrasts their depiction of this experience with the expatriate's sense of rootlessness and alienation discovered repeatedly in the works of V.S. Naipaul. While Mukherjee has moved from the "aloofness of expatriation to the exuberance of immigration," Sidhwa (a more recent immigrant to the U.S.) focuses instead on the marginalization of women and on the nature of the Pakistani woman's present as marked by persistent memories of violence against women. As she investigates Sidhwa's story "Defend Yourself Against Me," Zaman notes that for these immigrants "only in this home away from home . . .can the past be confronted . . . and finally exorcised."

The presence of the past is central to the nature of virtually all immigrant literature, and the significance of this theme is explored variously by several other contributors to this text. The impact of the Old World on the consciousness of the second-generation, "new world natives" is essential to the widely read works of both Amy Tan and Maxine Hong-Kingston, and in "The Semiotics of 'China Narrative' in the Con/Texts of Kingston and Tan," Yuan Yuan investigates the question of just how "native" the immigrants' narration of "China experiences" really are when related against the background of American society and within American culture; that is, how is "home" as "place of origin" transformed through recollection and telling, on the one hand, and through hearing and imagination, on the other? Just how is the original culture made manifest to the younger listeners (daughters, in these cases) at home in American culture?

The presence of the past and the power of the present to evoke the past (even a past that has been transformed by memory into the idyllic) is likewise explored by Fakrul Alam in his essay "A House for Mr. Chaudhuri," in which Professor Alam pursues the question of just where the aged Nirad Chaudhuri is truly at home, having left his native Bengal many decades ago and taken up residence at Oxford in 1970. Alam argues that Chaudhuri has spent most of his life attempting to regain the sense of pastoral bliss he remembers of his native village, Kishoreganj, and which he irrevocably lost when his family uprooted during the rise of Indian nationalism. The closest he has come to regaining his idyllic, bucolic home has been in Oxford and its surrounding countryside, nurturing images of an older, literary England of the imagination, apparently unaware (unlike Naipaul) of his/the diasporic

[Chaudhuri] had first learned to appreciate Kishoreganj because of his feel for English landscapes, he can now find peace in an English landscape because it evokes Kishoreganj for him." Similar to Chaudhuri's effort to look back to, reclaim, or recreate a perhaps "imaginary homeland" (to use Salman Rushdie's phrase) is, according to Rocio Davis in her contribution to this collection, Jessica Hagedorn's depiction of the Philippines in her novel *Dogeaters* and Ninotchka Rosca's depiction of it in *State of War*. Both writers, she argues, provide literary recreations of Philippine culture made possible only by their experience as immigrants to the United States. Their perceptions of their Philippine homeland are "made profound and complex because they are formed by examining the past with what Rushdie has designated 'stereoscopic vision . . . a kind of double perspective: because they, we, are at one and the same time insiders and outsiders in this society.'"

Clearly, then, a considerable number of the essays in this volume are bound to one another by their focus on the problematic and yet highly valued immigrant experience of seeing with "stereoscopic vision"—and of being seen, also, from a dual perspective: that of belonging/not belonging. Samir Dayal, in his essay "Splitting Images: *The Satanic Verses* and the Incomplete Man," considers Rushdie's treatment of the "incompleteness of the socially and politically marginalized postcolonial subject," his exposition of the postcolonial subject's curse to be his condition of rootlessness and exile—that is, of being clearly without "home."

The discussion to this point has centered primarily on literary treatment of and concern with arrival, assimilation, and perception of self, as well as on ways in which home (as place of origin—or of parents' origin) is re-created or made manifest through language once the émigré has relocated to the new culture. It is significant, then, that two of the essays in this collection specifically ask us to focus instead on the act and impact of departure. Rather than emphasize the personal or familial, Ismail Talib investigates the impact of emigration on a nation as a whole in his "Emigration as a Resistant Factor in the Creation of a National Literature: Rex Shelley's *The Shrimp People*," in which he explores the complexities of reading Shelley's novel as the closest model to date of "THE Singaporean novel" (which it has been called) when the very identity of postcolonial Singapore itself —because of the flux of immigration/emigration—as nation state is complex and resists being conceptually "fixed." Talib ties his discussion to the larger postmodern question of just what can be meant in this postcolonial, migratory world by "national literature" and "nation state."

The significance of departure is further considered by Clayton MacKenzie in "Butterflies at Sea: The Theme of Migration in Contemporary Chinese Poetry." Professor MacKenzie traces the persistent theme of

The significance of departure is further considered by Clayton MacKenzie in "Butterflies at Sea: The Theme of Migration in Contemporary Chinese Poetry." Professor MacKenzie traces the persistent theme of departure in contemporary Chinese verse (a theme that has enjoyed an important place over the long course of Chinese literary history), emphasizing that rather than simply providing literal explications of departure and odyssey, contemporary poems of migration frequently offer symbolic representations of departure that allow the poet to "explore some of the less accessible recesses of contemporary Chinese life," often providing veiled or subliminal social and political commentary.

The theme of migration is naturally central to the literary traditions of many cultures, but given the global significance of Asian migration in the past century—and especially over the past several decades—a collective, multinational discussion focused on the literary treatment of migration, such as the collective discussion represented by *Ideas of Home*, is certainly warranted and will, hopefully, encourage further attention to the literature and lead to further studies along these lines. The increasingly prominent literature of Asian migration can be valued simply for its own inherent artistic excellence, but it also serves to encourage in all of its readers—whatever their ethnic heritage—a deeper understanding of the sojourner bereft of and in quest of Home, and it asks all of us to consider again (and again) just what the nature of Home is, what its boundaries might be, and what our place and role within it might possibly be and become.

Notes

1. Indeed, as Joann Faung Jean Lee has quoted a man named Phil Nash (of Japanese Irish English descent) as saying, "This whole notion of an Asian is a European derived concept. . . . People eat rice; they eat pilaf. It's really this grab bag of people who are . . . about sixty percent of the world population" (121).

2. The body of sources listed in the select bibliography for this volume is intended to reflect the relationship of the literature to its sociocultural or sociopolitical context.

3. See Peter I. Rose, "Asian Americans: From Pariahs to Paragons" in *Clamor at the Gates: The New American Immigration,* ed. Nathan Glazer. (San Francisco: ICS Press, 1985), 181-212.

4. I have explored this topic previously in my essay "'Suspended Between Two Worlds': The Fusion of Hindu and American Myth in Bharati Mukherjee's *Jasmine,*" *Journal of South Asian Literature* 28, no. 1 (spring/fall 1993): 150-58 .

5. On a more personal, less strictly academic note—yet, I think, an excellent "flesh and blood" (some might say rather typical) example of the larger complex theme being addressed by the collective literature of Asian migration—this tension was further brought home to me this past month during a visit from a friend my wife and I had come to know during our years in the mid-1980s in China. This man has now been in the United States for four years, separated from his wife and five-year-old son. Although he is fully determined to stay in the U.S. (and has now established himself in a good position in business) and to become an American citizen, his wife is very much bound to extended family, neighborhood, and city in China and is not interested in life in the States. However, both parents feel strongly that the child needs his father, and that the nuclear family is (still) the essence of home. Mother and son will soon join husband/father. The poignant mixture of joy and bitterness, dread and anticipation, individual will and personal acquiescence, unwillingness to leave and need to effectively "arrive"—of apparent certainty and yet anxious confusion over the very nature of "Home"—is nowhere, to me, in the immigrant literature quite so immediately manifest as I am witnessing it unfold in this situation.

References

Brown, Judith M., and Rosemary Foot, eds. *Migration: The Asian Experience.* New York: St. Martin's Press, 1994.

Lee, Joann Faung Jean. *Asian American Experiences in the United States: Oral Histories of First to Fourth Generation Americans from China, the Philippines, Japan, India, the Pacific Islands, Vietnam, and Cambodia.* Jefferson, N.C.: McFarland, 1991.

Daniels, Roger. "The Indian Diaspora in the United States." Pp. 83-103 in *Migration: The Asian Experience,* eds. Judith Brown and Rosemary Foot. New York: St. Martin's Press, 1994.

Lee, Sharon M. "Asian Immigration and American Race-Relations: From Exclusion to Acceptance?" *Ethnic and Racial Studies* 12, no. 3 (July 1989): 369-90.

Lim, Shirley Geok-lin. "The Ambivalent American: Asian American Literature on the Cusp." Pp. 13-32 in *Reading the Literatures of Asian America,* eds. Shirley Geok-lin Lim and Amy Ling. Philadelphia: Temple University Press, 1992.

Lind, Michael. "Reinventing America." *World Policy Journal* 11, no. 4 (winter 1994): 77-84.

Ling, Amy. "Whose America Is It?" *Weber Studies* 12, no. 1 (winter 1995): 27-35.

Miles, Jack. "The Coming Immigration Debate." *Atlantic Monthly,* April 1995, 130-40.

Mukherjee, Bharati. "Immigrant Writing: Give Us Your Maximalists!" *New York Times Book Review,* 28 August 1988, sec. 7, pp. 3, 28-29.

Renaud, Viviane, and Jane Badets. "Ethnic Diversity in the 1990s." *Canadian Social Trends* 30 (autumn 1993): 17-22.

Rushdie, Salman. *Imaginary Homelands: Essays and Criticism 1981-1991.* London: Granta Books, 1992.

Wong, Morrison. "Post-1965 Asian Immigrants: Where Do They Come From, Where Are They Now, Where Are They Going?" *Annals of the American Academy of Political and Social Science* 487 (September 1986): 150-68.

1

SOUTH ASIAN DIASPORA WRITERS IN BRITAIN: "HOME" VERSUS "HYBRIDITY"

Feroza Jussawalla

The idea of "home" for South Asian diaspora writers in Britain can best be defined in contrast to theories of "hybridity." Much has been said recently about the notion of hybridity—of the fluidity of race and nationality, the letting go of "home" to become absorbed elsewhere—"beyond ethnocentricity," or "deterritorialization," as Homi Bhabha postulates in *The Location of Culture*. According to him, the cultural hybridity of the borderline conditions of migrants and diasporic peoples enables them to "translate" or to reinscribe themselves into new cultures; therefore, "home" becomes irrelevant. But as I would like to show here, despite diasporic conditions such as birth and nationality in another country and absorption into another culture's ways of being—language, habits, even the "superfluities of clothing and styles of living," or, in Simon During's words, "domination of the life-world by style and civility" (Bhabha, 5)—the notion of "home" is that of a place many thousands of miles away. Home for these writers, and even for the generation born in Britain or America, is usually the South Asian subcontinent. In fact, as Hanif Kureishi—probably the most hybrid of the South Asian diaspora writers in Britain—shows, the South Asian immigrant and his children are not allowed to make the country they have immigrated to their own. In Hanif Kureishi's *The Buddha of Suburbia* (1990), there are two teenagers growing up in Britain, Jamila and Karim. Jamila's parents are both Muslim immigrants from pre-partition India. Karim has an English mother. Of what their senses of identity were Karim says:

> Yeah, sometimes we were French, Jammie and I and other times we went black American. The thing was we were supposed to be English, but to the English we were always wogs and nigs and Pakis and the rest of it. (53)

In a climate where hybridity is not "allowed," so to speak, it remains inapplicable. Let us take the recent example of the aftermath of the Oklahoma City bombing. An immigrant who had been a citizen of the United States for five years was flying "home" to Jordan—his actual "home" being in Oklahoma City. This American, because of his name, Ahmad, was searched and questioned as all of America jumped to the conclusion that the act had been perpetrated by Muslims—foreigners, in the American heartland, in the American "home." "What kind of cultural space is the nation with its transgressive boundaries and its interruptive interiority?" asks Homi Bhabha in his *Nation and Narration* (5). After the xenophobia expressed in the search for the bombers, we can only say that "the nation," whether America or Britain or any other for that matter, is bounded by "interiority." After being released by authorities in Chicago, the American Mr. Ahmad was shackled by British authorities who doubted his American passport and led him through Heathrow airport. He was thus exposed to what the British notion of what his "home" appropriately is. This is the England that is debating joining the European Union and whose junior trade minister Charles Wardle resigned because its borders were already too open. The United States of America had a second generation immigrant Mexican–American chief of the border patrol, Sylvester Reyes, who would like to build a wall along the Texas–Mexico border. The "nation's" borders laid out long ago are not immediately "transgressive" but are indeed bounded by "interiority."

This is not a new phenomenon sparked by crazed American–Christian fundamentalists (re)creating an America of freedom and liberty for the white man whose supremacy and freedoms must be respected. Japanese–American writer Mitsuye Yamada, a second–generation resident of Hilo, Hawaii, writes the following:

> Many of us are now third and fourth generation Americans, but this makes no difference: periodic conflicts involving Third World peoples can abruptly change white Americans' attitudes towards us. We found our status as true–blooded Americans was only an illusion in 1942 when we were singled out to be imprisoned for the duration of the war by our own government. . . . (71)

Yamada has written a poem on a familiar theme, a theme Maxine Hong Kingston mentions several times—that of being asked, "Where are you from?"

People keep asking me where I come from says my son.

Trouble is I'm American on the inside and Oriental on the outside

No Doug

Turn that outside in

THIS is what America looks like

However much Bharati Mukherjee might proclaim "I am American now," "home" is in the eye of the beholder, and she knows this. She has written poignantly of her years in Canada when she was spat on and discriminated against. For the South Asian diaspora writers, theorists, and immigrants in general, "home" is to be defined for them as their place of origin by their features, appearance, and accent. After twenty three years in America, people still ask me, "Where are you from?" While teaching in London I was asked where I was from, and my answer, "America," was met with incredulousness. My features, skin color, and accent didn't spell American. "But where are you originally from? Where is your home?" are all questions that follow. During my last week in London when I expressed some anxiousness and readiness to go "home," a student at a postgraduate seminar at the Institute for Commonwealth Studies posed the theoretical question: "Where is home?" The metropoles and non–metropoles, London or El Paso, will not allow the metropolitan intellectual, let alone the ordinary immigrant, "hybridity." Back "home" standing in line at an art fair to buy German potato salad sold by Las Cruces, New Mexico's German sister city's delegates, the gentleman behind me said how nice it must be to visit that sister city. I told him that one of my students on such a visit had been spat on, mugged, and robbed. He immediately turned on me and said, "What! Are you from Israel or something? You look Middle Eastern." I said, "No, I'm from Las Cruces; I've lived here for fourteen years." "Hybridity" is *not* allowed. Nor is it allowed from the liberal or radical intellectuals: if you speak for indigenousness, then you must dress or look "native"! An Indian woman speaking about indigenousness must be wearing a sari. These expectations are imprinted almost like DNA imprints on our consciousness, particularly in cross-cultural situations. Anthropologist Ann Stoller said to me at a women's studies conference, "Surely you must be from a wealthy Indian background or how else could you be here?" While Trinh Minh–ha will repeatedly claim that the "personal is the political," she refuses to discuss the mitigating circumstances of her origins or her being in the United States, though she quotes all others' experiences. The project of "deterritorialization" to attain or achieve hybridity would need massive (re)education.

Our contemporary critical theorists/literary theorists/cultural theorists have proposed "hybridity" as the binary opposite of "home," "authenticity," "indigenousness," "nativeness," and "nationality" without taking into account the specifics of actual situations. In a talk at New Mexico State University describing the "exilic consciousness," Trinh Minh-ha said that the "achievements of exile are a crippling search for home." The effort of diaspora writers in describing "home," according to her, is to free themselves from the homeland: "When they open the doors of the abode they have freed themselves again from the homeland." She believes in deterritorialization: "Home is wherever one is led to in one's movements." And so she asks us to reject authenticity, nativeness, or "nativist interpretations." She quotes from Joanna Harumi Sechi, "I was made to feel that cultural pride would justify and make good my difference in skin color while it was a constant reminder that I was different." So she urges us to give up "cultural pride." For her, the nativistic position of "cultural pride" or pride in home is a form of co-optation. Trinh Minh-ha writes, "On the one hand, I play into the Savior's hands by concentrating on authenticity, for my attention is numbed by it and diverted from other important issues" (89).

She sees "planned authenticity" as a product of hegemony and a remarkable counterpart of universal standardization: "It constitutes an efficacious means of silencing the cry of racial oppression" (89). So she urges us into a "hybridity" (which, as I will show, is a form of universal standardization) and to give up "pure origin" and "true self" (90) because, as she said in her talk (which she did not permit to be taped), there are "different arrivals and different departures." "*I* am not; can be you and me"(italics mine) she writes in *Woman, Native, Other* (90). If "*I* am not," then I also not only lack identity but also individuality—selfhood, subjecthood. But as I have already shown, the "you" has to allow the "me" to merge with it and when this does not happen, when the "me/I" has to urge itself onto the "you" through devices such as "political correctness," through urging on racial equality by force, the result is an enhancing of separation and difference, as in the contemporary "angry white male" phenomenon. So should we then simply become hybrid because we have no individuality, selfhood, cultural pride left? Should we just give up any notion of "home"? It is argued that in the global village we call home, there isn't room enough for separate locations, for separate cultures, and that communication highways and travel at superspeeds have altered cultures so that we are all hybrids. What accounts then for the rise in Islamic fundamentalism, Hindu fundamentalism, neo-Nazism, "American nativism," Hawaiian indigenousness, and various such searches for the culturally perfectly located "homes"—the platonic ideas, as it were, of "home"?

It is because of the contemporary turn inward toward "our cultures," "our locations" that I postulate that hybridity remains what I have come to call Bhabha Babooisms. The Babooism is an unfortunate term of colonialist discourse to describe the utterance of the Bengali railway clerk attempting to speak in "His Master's Voice" or "His Master's Language" in order to impress the hegemonic power center—the British sahib. In the contemporary situation, "hybridity" fits into the liberal white American agenda as embodied in certain academic centers and certain power centers not only in the Clinton administration but among the conservatives who like to see "mainstreaming" and assimilation and other forms of "universal standardization." In recent developments, even radical theories of difference simply became co-opted into the white liberal ACLU "political correctness" now being dismantled by angry white male legislators and American "nativist" bombers—spurring on nativeness. It is indeed true, as Audre Lorde wrote: "How many, already, have been condemned to premature deaths for having borrowed the master's tools and thereby played into his hands? The master's tools will never dismantle the master's house" (80). How quickly the white males have responded to the mixing and merging of affirmative action and canonization of multiculturalism. Indeed, the master's tools will dismantle the master's home. Contrarily, "hybridists" would claim that nativistic positions form "a kind of perverted logic, they work toward your erasure while urging you to keep your way of life and ethnic values *within the borders of your own homelands*." While this may have been true of South Africa as Trinh Minh-ha showed, this is not true of the indigenous culture movements that are originating from India to Iran to Hawaii to the U.S. mainland.

I believe that "Babooism" as a trope to describe hybridity is appropriate in this context because like the babooism it serves as a meaningless absurdity to placate the masters. The Baboos loved the British colonizers, just as our current academic centers love European theories, particularly left-leaning ones. The Baboos tried to (re)make themselves in the colonizers' image—as Frantz so aptly put it in the Black context, to put white masks on black skins—just like our theoreticians like to put on the garb of German, French, and British theories. And the British love(d) the Baboo just like the American academic intellectuals love the Third World postcolonial critic, stuttering like Caliban in a language that bears no resemblance to reality. But the Baboos were and are kept in their place. In Britain there is still "no admission" to the club. The attempt to find "home" has to be (re)located in America. There is the famous joke of the sign at the Poona club where the Englishman played on his own stereotype: "Mad dogs and Indians not allowed." The same is true of the most assimilated of the South Asians in Britain or America today. Therefore, while some American intellectual centers have been welcoming of theories of hybridity, the reality not subject to interpretation is embodied in the public backlash to aspirations of hybridity. "Untouchable" caste status has been ascribed to the diasporans. Whether theoretician, writer, or immigrant, the South Asian diasporan remains the monolithic stereotype, and hopes of hybridity remain babooisms—empty utterances that may beguile or please the master temporarily but who has a concretized image of the diaspora etched on his consciousness. There is a wonderful passage in Hanif Kureishi's *The Buddha of Suburbia* where the theatrical director Shadwell is asking the character Karim to sound like a proper Bengali, with whom of course the feigning yet pompous Indian English style has become forever associated:

> "Karim, you have been cast for *authenticity* and not for experience."
>
> I could hardly believe it. Even when I did believe it we discussed it several times, but he wouldn't change his mind.
>
> "Just try it," he kept saying as we went outside the rehearsal room to argue. "You're very conservative, Karim. Try it until you feel comfortable as a Bengali. You're supposed to be an actor, but I suspect you may just be an exhibitionist."
>
> "Jeremy, help me, I can't do this."
>
> He shook his head. I swear, my eyes were melting. (italics mine; 147)

The hybrid must remain and portray the stereotypical Baboo. Therefore for me the "notion" of the Baboo who wants to achieve "hybridity" and the notion of Babooisms are tropes for the role of contemporary theory and its ways of defining "postcolonials" and their "homes" as being mobile, migratory, deterritorialized. This is what Kipling's Haree Babu attempted to (re)construct himself as: English. And since Kipling's Kim, Haree Babu has become the archetype of the notion of the servile, stuttering, Bengali Baboo, attempting to speak English obsequiously, flatteringly, and sprinkled with malaprops. The obsequiousness was meant to be endearing. But Kipling shows us how the "the Europeans" in general kept "the hybrid" at bay. Neither Kipling's Haree Babu nor countless other baboos were rewarded with a home in England. In fact, Kipling's voice condemns the European, particularly the Russian intelligence officers who criticize Haree Babu for embodying "the monstrous *hybridity* of the East and West" (214). Homi Bhabha and colonial discourse critics criticize Kipling for creating a hybrid character who they presume Kipling is making fun of but with whom Kipling and his character Kim actually sympathize with and heroize. And yet the same colonial discourse critics have made out of what they consider Kipling's term of monstrousness, "hybridity," a badge of honor? Babooism is the exact term that describes Bhabha's notion of hybridity because it denies the plausibility of "home" and it does so in the theoretical language that purports to please the hegemonically dominant centers of literary studies in America. These centers of literary study, though couched with Marxist, neo–Marxist, and post–Marxist veneers, have long held the "melting pot" theories of U.S. culture and would like to see the Hispanics and the Blacks all disappear into this "melting pot," in much the same way that Macaulay in his 1832 minute on English education in India wanted to (re)make India in the image of England to create the lasting Empire on which the sun would never set. "Hybridity" works perfectly for this. And yet it is interesting to see that the younger generation of "postcolonial" writers who ought really to be able to claim hybridity either by virtue of being born in England or being raised in England, much like Kureishi's character Karim, find themselves turning inward to their indigenous selves. This is because the writers know the reality of the immigrant and diasporic situations.

In fact, Hanif Kureishi's character Karim in *The Buddha of Suburbia* comes to his indigenous self, his realization of his ethnicity and his authenticity, upon realizing that his earlier stance of seeing himself as an assimilated Briton did not work:

> But I did feel, looking at these creatures now—the Indians—that in some way these were my people, and that I'd spent my life denying or avoiding that fact. I felt ashamed and incomplete at the same time, as if half of me were missing and as if I'd been colluding with my enemies who want Indians to be like them. (212)

In fact, for his audition for the part in which he has to play the proper Bengali, Karim had chosen to play Changez, a Muslim young man especially imported from India to be Jamila's husband. Changez is monstrous: a crippled arm, an Indian English accent, a greed for the material and for Arthur Conan Doyle novels. The radicals in the theatre group had objected to his portrayal as not being "politically correct." Yet they had pushed Karim towards the portrayal of "the proper Bengali." Both were monstrous hybrids, but "the proper Bengali" remained the monolithic crowd pleaser.

What Karim says is true of his father and his father's friend Anwar becomes true of Karim and seems also to be coming true for Kureishi himself, as evidenced in his last *New Yorker* story, "My Son the Fanatic." When hybridity cannot be achieved, the turn is inward to Indianness or Muslimness:

> Maybe there were similarities between what was happening to Dad, with his discovery of Indian philosophy and Anwar's last stand [which was going on hunger strike to be able to arrange a marriage

for his daughter Jamila]. Perhaps it was the immigrant condition living itself out through them. For years they were both happy to live like Englishmen. Anwar even scoffed pork pies as long as Jata wasn't looking. (My dad never touched the pig, though I was sure this was conditioning rather than religious scruple, just as I wouldn't eat horse's scrotum. But once, to test this, when I offered him a smoky bacon crisp and said, as he crunched greedily into it, "I didn't know you liked smoky bacon," he sprinted into the bathroom and washed out his mouth with soap, screaming from his frothing lips that he would burn in hell.)

Now as they aged and seemed settled here, Anwar and Dad appeared to be returning internally to India, or at least to be resisting the English here. It was puzzling: neither of them expressed any desire actually to see their origins again. "India's a rotten place," Anwar grumbled. "Why would I want to go there again? It's filthy and hot and it's a big pain–in–the–arse to get anything done." (*Buddha*, 27)

It was said critically of the older generation of South Asian diaspora writers in Britain that they rejected "hybridity" or even assimilation, that they kept themselves apart and wrote of "home"—India and Indian themes—much like the current mood of separatism and indigenousness. This older generation of writers included Kamala Markandaya, Raja Rao, and Mulk Raj Anand, though the last two had lived in England only for a short while while studying. Kamala Markandaya is probably the only true example of a writer of the South Asian diaspora writing from Britain about Indians though she quickly took to writing about the culture contact, and *The Nowhere Man* tackles the notion of hybridity versus home long before it became critical terminology. Twenty-three years ago (1973, when *Nowhere Man* was published), Kamala Markandaya articulated the condition so fashionable in discourse now—of whether to lay down roots in England or whether to make one's way back. Vasantha in the novel says:

> At last we have achieved something. A place of our own, where we can live according to our rights although in alien surroundings: and our children after us and after them theirs.

Srinivas, her husband, "experienced no such emotions":

> He did not feel like a founding father. It seemed to him that what they had done was to shackle themselves to bricks and mortar and

> it filled him with misgiving. So long as they were mobile, he liked
> to believe the way back to India . . . lay open. (20)

The older and younger generations of South Asian diaspora writers—the
foreigner and the native-born hybrid Asian—agree on the immigrants' desire
to leave the door to home open. Hanif Kureishi's Jamila in *The Buddha of
Suburbia* "deconstructs" all that her family has built up—their corner grocery
store, their hopes for a dynasty. For her, indigenousness does not work—the
arranged marriage is a disaster. She continues to cast about for a place, while
Karim embraces "this emerald isle, this England" as it were "in the centre of
this old city that I loved, which itself sat at the bottom of a tiny island." But
the generational gap between the characters and the writers closes at the point
of "no entry" from the British themselves. Changez is assaulted by neo-Nazis
who carve their initials in his belly. Neo-Fascist groups operated outside the
schools and colleges and football grounds like Millwall and Crystal Palace:

> At night, they roamed the streets, beating Asians and shoving shit
> and burning rags through their letter-boxes. Frequently, the mean,
> white, hating faces had public meetings and the Union Jacks were
> paraded through the streets, protected by the police. (56)

"Get back in yer rickshaw" (67), they shouted at the subcontinentals. The
character who is Karim's father (referred to as Dad in *Buddha)* has this
response when told by his friend Anwar to get a promotion:

> "The whites will never promote us," Dad said. "Not an Indian
> while there is a white man left on the earth. You don't have to deal
> with them—they still think they have an Empire when they don't
> have two pennies to rub together." (27)

Elsewhere in the book, he says, "We old Indians come to like this England
less and less and we return to an imagined India" (74).

Kamala Markandaya, who belongs to the elder generation of South
Asian immigrant writers, reconfirms this. When asked about hybridity she
said, "The British wouldn't allow it." Hanif Kureishi's work shows that
despite attempted assimilation, as with the generation born here, the South
Asian Indians and Pakistanis remain outcasts, "cockney Asians," a term
Kureishi himself used in describing his characters. And though Farrukh
Dhondy writes an English cultural tradition in his *Black Swan*, making
Southwark his own, he remains rooted in his own Indian and Parsi culture

even as Tom Stoppard remains British when writing *Indian Ink* or John Irving remains American when writing about Parsis in *Son of a Circus*. The fact that Mr. Dhondy writes Shakespeare's and Marlowe's Southwark should not denigrate the work as attempting to appropriate a culture not his, but rather show that it is possible for a writer to write from the inside of another culture without losing "identity." Hanif Kureishi, however, questions the notion of identity. In a lecture in my class at the University of London, 2 April 1995, he called it "a tag, everyone's claiming one." But, in fact, both Hanif Kureishi's work and Farrukh Dhondy's work show that the more rooted the writer in his own indigenous culture, the better he can understand/interpret/ represent the other culture (in Dhondy's case Southwark, and in Kureishi's the London of "white" and hybrids) and also portray his own particular and immediate locale/"location" with mastery. Therefore despite mixing and merging, like a martini in a cocktail shaker, (1) the writers do not become hybrids or "mongrels," and (2) we do not need a median point along the "scale" or "cline" of authenticity to alienation indicating "hybridity." An old-fashioned Shakespearean idea, "to our own selves be true," comes to mind as I think of how well Han Suyin puts it in her foreword to the stories of Aamer Hussein, a true South Asian diaspora writer recently emerging. She defines "new literature in English" and writes:

> Asians, Africans and other non-English non-American writers using the English language to express their own ethnic backgrounds, cultures and traditions. This is achieved not by striving for uniformity, but on the contrary, by using to the full their own cultural diversity, bringing into focus contrast and conflict, traditional ways and the impact of change upon them, alienation and the fashioning of enlarged personality. It was the Swiss poet Ramuz who, back in 1906, was to tackle the issue, at that time considered very important, of "new" literature and "international" literature. Ramuz stated that one is all the more international for being thoroughly "local," grounded in one's own language traditions, capable of conveying the essential traits of one's own culture and making them accessible, familiar. . . . The stronger the writer's roots in his (or her) own cultural ethnicity, the more original, and enriching, his contributions to literature and to real life as well, for real life is also and always literature. (Foreword to *Mirror to the Sun* 11)

In Trinh Minh-ha's 1983 film *Surname Viet, Given Name Nam*, one of the Vietnamese émigrés says something to the effect of "we must assimilate," an emotion turned into a slap in the face to the Asian community in Los Angeles during the recent Los Angeles riots when the Blacks and the Chicanos burned Asian property because the Asians were too assimilated, too successful, and seen as exploiters of the blacks and Chicanos. To some extent, this feeling exists in England. Zerbanoo Gifford gives many examples of this in *The Golden Thread: Asian Experiences of Post–Raj Britain*. But more important, the most poignant of her examples shows that when a community, white or not, elects an Asian woman she is distanced even by the Labour Party. This ties into my argument about the politics of current literary theory as it confirms my point that leftist positioning or posturing does not necessarily come from solidarity. In her chapter aptly titled "Brownie Points," Zerbanoo Gifford gives the example of Thrity Shroff:

> She won a safe Labour seat. Thrity's reception from the Labour group on the council was the cold shoulder. She puts this down not only to losing a seat Labour thought was "theirs," "but more importantly they couldn't accept, despite their claptrap about promoting the black cause and supporting the ethnic minorities, that the local community might want an Asian as their representative." (101)

In Kamala Markandaya's 1973 book *The Nowhere Man*, when Srinivas (an émigré) builds his home in a South London suburb he is spat on and hit in the forehead with Fred Fletcher's shovel. Laxman, the mainstreamed, successful son with whom Vasantha had envisioned living in this house in a happy joint family situation in his elegant Bond Street appurtenance (258), thinks after his father's assault:

> But Them and Us?
>
> As he drove he glanced now and then at the hands on the wheel, his hands, not even brown but the finest, palest Brahmin, or elephant, ivory.
>
> But regarded, apparently, as black. Black Them doing white Us. (269)

Hanif Kureishi's *The Buddha of Suburbia* shows how the sense of Black British develops as solidarity for the Asian teenagers with the movements of the sixties and seventies. For Jamila her identification with Angela Davis, for instance, becomes her focal point and hence the coming together with the other oppressed groups as Black British. In my interview with Buchi

Emecheta in *Interviews with Writers of the Post-Colonial World*, she felt that the Asians were seeking recognition by suddenly seeing themselves as "Black British." In fact, the experience of the younger generation of South Asian diaspora writers shows that this is actually a distancing device that has been placed on them. In fact, however much they try to portray themselves as assimilated and in the "in-groups" as Mr. Rushdie does—going to the "write [right] parties" and befriending British writers such as Martin Amis—the distancing does in fact take place even for the so-called archspokesman of the new hybrid generation. It is in association with *Satanic Verses* and its migrants that we most often hear the term "hybridity." But listen to the most recent voices of criticism. In an *Atlantic Monthly* article noting the fifth anniversary of the fatwa against Salman Rushdie, Geoffrey Wheatcroft quotes Auberon Waugh who had said,

> Just how much should we exert ourselves as deeply stained white imperialists to protect [Rushdie] from his own people? (*Atlantic Monthly* [March 1994], 24)

And this after *The Satanic Verses* purports to show the hybrid nature of the grey-suited bowler-hatted Salahuddin Chamcha—the assimilated immigrant who makes fun of "his own kind" in Brick Lane and Southall. Despite his kippers-eating incident, Rushdie saw himself as perfectly assimilated, as British as Julian Barnes and Martin Amis—his British contemporaries—though he did take the occasional swipe at the Thatcherite government. But it is the occasional swipe that has stuck. Again, Geoffrey Wheatcroft quotes Lord Tebbit, a Tory politician and a close colleague of Mrs. Thatcher, as follows:

> His public life has been a record of despicable acts of betrayal of his upbringing, religion, adopted home and nationality. Now he betrays even his own sneers at the British establishment as he cowers under the protection of a government, a police force, and a society he once denounced as racist and undemocratic.

While Lord Tebbit can be denounced here as being racist toward Rushdie, denying him the freedom of speech to criticize the government—a right, which is certainly granted to most white Britons and therefore one Rushdie takes for granted as an assimilated "white"—the issue at hand is whether the assimilated, hybrid immigrant can find a place in his/her adopted home, a place as equal as that for those who are considered "natives."

This is not just a matter of the postcolonials adapting in colonizer Britain. It is the condition of cross-cultural hybridity. Growing up a Parsi in India, I was subject to being called a "mongrel" by my Hindu and Muslim friends, not because of having mixed blood but for being Anglicised and Westernized. Bhabha, who at MLA in 1994 tried to argue that the Parsis were a marginalized minority, but was shouted down by Indians claiming Parsi wealth and power, finds himself in a doubly hybrid position—that of a Parsi immigrant in Britain and now in America. It is apparent that the book *The Location of Culture* and its ideas are deeply rooted in the location of Homi Bhabha's culture as a Parsi, a diasporic immigrant community in India that frequently adapted to its changing masters like "sugar blending with milk," a concept the Parsis liked to promulgate as evidence of their extreme adaptability. With this cultural framework so shaping his conceptual framework, Homi Bhabha seems to be urging us to give up ethnic locations and the binaries of authenticity and indigenousness, or location versus metropolitan cosmopolitanism, to aim for hybridity.

In *The Location of Culture*, however, Bhabha never really gives a definition of his concept of "hybridity." In the opening chapter, "The Commitment to Theory," he tells us that the radical contribution of theory lies in the translation of theory into practice: "The emphasis on the representation of the political, on the construction of discourse is the radical contribution of the translation of theory" (27). So in effect he wants the current "construction of discourse," which in effect tells the writers and critics what they ought to do, to be taking off from theory. If I understand his dictum correctly, he wants us all to move toward "hybridity":

> The representation of difference must not be hastily read as the reflection of pre-given ethnic or cultural traits set in the fixed tablet of tradition. The social articulation of difference from the minority perspective is a complex, on-going negotiation that seeks to authorize cultural *hybridities* that emerge in moments of historical transformations. (2)

When the Parsis first arrived in India in approximately 1300 A.D. from Persia as a result of Muslim persecution, the first "boat people" said to the Raja of Gujarat that they will mix with the Hindus like "sugar mixes with milk." At this moment of historical transformation, they agreed to give up much of their fixed tablets of tradition to adopt Hindu religious practice and culture. And when the British came, the Parsis renegotiated their cultural practices again. This renegotiation process is the ironically fixed tablet of tradition that Homi Bhabha comes from, and he expects Hindus and Muslims with more firmly held cultural histories to engage in these renegotiation processes which entail constant change and adaptability. Bhabha dismisses the Serbian situation in his *Location of Culture*, saying that the idea of a pure "'ethnically cleansed' nationalist identity can only be achieved through death."(5)

Hybridity for Bhabha comes from living on the borderlines of the present (1). Yet we find increasingly all over Eastern Europe as well as in America and Britain a growing sense of nationality–not melding exiles whose "exilic consciousness" gives rise to "spurious desire," according to Trinh Minh-ha, but an increasing desire to belong to a group or a nationality. And writers such as Hanif Kureishi, Salman Rushdie, and Farrukh Dhondy have given voice to this reinscription into nationalism into indigenousness for which Bhabha only has contempt as "a nativist and nationalist atavism" (207). This probably results from Bhabha's Parsi alienation from Indianness and a typically Parsi contempt for Indian nationalism embodied in the ordinary upper-class Parsis of Bombay, though there were exceptions such as Dadabhoy Naoroji. Indianness today equals fundamentalist Hindu India. For example, the Shiv Sena want Pakistanis to leave Bombay and to reclaim Bombay as Mumbai though Bombay itself stands on reclaimed land.

At such a historical moment when ethnic cleansing seems to be the way in which each individual and group searches for a location, we need to examine whether we need a concept such as "hybridity" to govern our writers and our senses of selves. Or do we need to go back to a celebration of "located" multiplicities? Is there a binary opposition between "hybridity" and "indigenousness"? Or again, is there a binary opposition between authenticity and metropolitanism? Though Bhabha would disagree that hybridity itself has become a binary, the way he describes it as "a moment of panic" is directly opposed to the fact that it is for many writers such as Aamer Hussein, a moment of "joy," a moment of reinscribing their hybridities into their indigenousness and proclaiming themselves rooted in the fixed tablets of their cultures. Bhabha seems to see in hybridity a conflictual touch: "The margin of hybridity, where cultural differences 'contingently' and conflictually touch, becomes the moment of panic which reveals the borderline experience. It resists the binary opposition of racial and cultural groups, sipahis and sahibs, as homogenous polarized political consciousness" (207). Two factors emerge here: one is that Bhabha is seeing the current moment of historical transformation still in terms of "sipahis and sahibs," subalterns and rulers, a situation that has changed in contemporary London, though the British attitude not of the sahibs but of the "Cockney" working class remain distinctly racist; the other is that hybridity is wishful thinking in London as it is in Los Angeles, for as the writer Kamala Markandaya said to me recently, "The powers that be won't allow it." Even the most hybrid of characters that make up the bulk of Hanif Kureishi's work seem not to want to express their hybridities but express their quintessential selves which are rooted in their ethnicities, and I will give examples of these. New distancing tactics originate. The postcolonials are not "natives" anymore but "Black British," and Hanif Kureishi's term "cockney Asian" has been readily adapted.

The climate into which a generation is being born, and in Britain has already been born, is one of the *native foreigner* born British (increasingly now born American) and yet not British or American enough. Nina, the teenager in Hanif Kureishi's "With Your Tongue Down my Throat," says, "I have a sister the same age, living in another country" (23). Her mother's reply follows:

> "Your father had a wife in India," Ma says, wincing every time she says *father*. "They married when they were fifteen, which is the custom over there. When he decided to leave me because I was too strong a woman for him, he went right back to India and right back to Wifey. That's when I discovered I was pregnant with you. His other daughter Nadia was conceived a few days later but she was actually born the day after you. Imagine that darling. Since then I've discovered that he's even for two other daughters as well."

Both in England and in the United States, collectives of writers and critics of South Asian descent are becoming more numerous. This is a newer pattern in Britain where the previous generation of writers, such as Kamala Markandaya, were Indians who immigrated to Britain or were simply students there. Raja Rao tells me often that I ought to do a collection of interviews with writers of his generation who were resident in England simultaneously—himself, Mulk Raj Anand, etc.—the writers who preferred to see themselves as Indo-Anglian writers with their nationality being distinctly Indian. And yet almost contemporaneous with them is/was a writer such as V. S. Naipaul who is just a generation ahead of the native-born foreigners in contemporary England—a British subject just like these contemporary Black British writers. The Naipaul experience should be instructive to this younger generation of writers. Assimilated and successful, having cut across the barriers of class and race, Naipaul did maintain his "Indian" identity though he was one generation removed from it. And the "enigma of his arrival" finally seems to be in knowing where he belongs—not in Jack's Garden in Salisbury but in the familiar Indian "ceremonies of farewell." He hasn't rejected his India, but explored it and returned to it time and again with the arched perspective of seeing Indians as others see them and telling them how they are perceived. In this manner, both his work and Rushdie's *The Satanic*

Verses are love letters to their communities, like letters that your grandmothers would send back to you with your mistakes marked in red. Yet it is the mocking tone of Rushdie's work that raised the ire of so many of his own while those who read Naipaul nod their heads in assent. You will hear them say in railway compartments: "V. S. Naipaul is right—we have wasted our money on those funny shoe-like scythes!" There seems to me a definite difference—it is the insider's perspective, the author's positionality as one among them. And I believe that this is what is going to have to be the voice of "native foreigners" as they try to be both natives and foreigners in two lands at once.

In essence we are speaking of three generations of South Asian diaspora writers: The first generation consists of writers such as Kamala Markandaya who emigrated to Britain in the 1940's; the second is an in between generation of South Asian diaspora writers via the Caribbean, born British like V. S. Naipaul, and Sam Selvon—but of Asian extraction; and the most recent generation—born in Britain—from which we have to exclude those whom we used to call the "younger writers" (Salman Rushdie, Farrukh Dhondy, etc.)

I asked Farrukh Dhondy about this in 1988. "You're obviously first-generation Indian, but then you are writing about people who are second or third generation and a whole group of younger writers are emerging labelled Black British. So what's emerging?"

> Dhondy: It's very difficult to say. I can give you the end product, or my convictions, and that is that there are going to be Brown and Black Britishers. There are already. And there are several reasons for that. There's no denying that what makes people is not their genes, is not their nostalgia, it's their interactions of daily existence. And Britain is a very stratified society. More so than America, I think, in its stratification. You go to a particular kind of school, you are seen, you are perceived by the world as somebody who fits into niches, professional or romantic, stylistic, whatever. And teenagers (the subjects of Dhondy's books) get classified very fast in Britain, because of British culture, you don't escape it. It's tighter than Indian caste, religion and regionalism. Back in India, you could say, "Here is a teenager, a 17 year old female from Kerala, of so and so caste, and she comes from the borders of a town, therefore she is going to have that kind of life. It is almost as stratified as that in Britain."

> The difference is this: in India, nobody is brought up to believe that they can move out of it. There is an atmosphere which says that very very few of you will be meritocrats, will progress by your education or whatever. The rest of you are halted. Halted by

to change the name of the American dream. It is a Western Dream. All the class system of Britain has been laid off by several layers of meritocracy. You can get there by going to Oxford or Cambridge. You can get there by education, by dint of mind, by making money in the city, you can do something, you can get loads of money. . . . The class distinctions of Britain have been fluid since the fifties. And one was ruled by a Conservative Party that has absolutely nothing in common with the Tories of the 20s. They had a grocer's daughter who was virtually the Queen. A miner's son is in charge of the Labour Party. And this has not penetrated the minds of the immigrants. And the second generation, about whom I write, is bewildered. The central facet of these characters is bewilderment. They don't quite know where they fit, because they have come from nowhere. They come from outside it. And they're decultured by their parents and by the histories that they've dragged into the body politic of Britain Indian history, maybe, or West Indian or Africa. And they don't quite know where they belong because their parents always wanted to go back home. The Punjabi always wanted, somewhere in his own little heart, to go back home. And didn't think the kids would be generated and give rise to grandchildren and so forth. But it's happened and it's happened without plan.

To my question, "What's the future of these people?" Dhondy said:

Despite what people will say to you, I actually believe that they do have a future. Yes. Some people say and they make a profession of saying it, they indulge in the politics of complaint to further themselves in a sense. They believe that Britain is endemically racist, overall whites are stultified, and so forth. I don't believe that. I think there is a percentage of bullies, a percentage of bigots. But by and large Britain lives by a liberal democratic tradition of live and let live and let's not interfere.

The word "liberal" in Farrukh Dhondy's interview brings me to some recent conversations I had with V. S. Naipaul. I was lucky enough to be working in the McFarlin Library in Tulsa soon after the purchase of the Naipaul papers when on the spur of the moment, I got invited to lunch with Naipaul by Sid Hatner, the director of special collections there. Liberalism is the word that emerged repeatedly in answer to my questions. I asked about "my hybridity"—not Mr. Naipaul's. I explained that though I am westernized, I had returned to India for a Tenure Tonsure at Tirupathi Tirumalai.

What explains that? Is it *excess baggage* as it was seen in *An Area of Darkness?* Mr. Naipaul replied, "It is our 20 layers of self" (he would never call them *excess baggage*, he tells me). "When you scratch the surfaces" he replies, "the selves show." You retain those selves—maintain those identities as I've said before in this paper. The pundit self of Mr. Biswas remains in the vegetarian V. S. Naipaul, despite the voyages around the world. "One doesn't question these selves," he says. "One accepts them." To question them is to be self-important—"The question is flawed" was a repeated answer to my questions. "One mustn't ask what one can do for one's country." I asked, "Must we go back? Must we change things?"—That is self-centered, egotistical to think the world evolves around you." I must have been scratching one of those twenty-layered selves because a very distinct Raja Rao-like Brahminical renunciatory self seems to be emerging in the modern Mr. Naipaul who, despite keeping strident pace with a fast changing world—the fall/s of communism[s], the increase of ethnic "*tribalisms*"—seems to be putting out a much more Brahmin consciousness, acceptance, detachment while yet being tapped into the changing energies (my word here—drawing on the Brahminical image I am creating) of the world. Richard Murphy, the Irish poet (who was also present at lunch), mentioned that Terry Eagleton accuses *writers* of not scratching the sound-proofing of their study walls. Mr. Naipaul quickly countered that we as academics have not scratched the sound proofing of our study walls, that we are ten years out of touch with a world where issues of colonialism and its consequences on race, class, and gender are totally out of date. And yet the issues of race and class—especially as you walk the streets of London—are not out of date. There are hybrids, cockney Asians who speak no Indian language and say "wot" when addressed in an Indian language. But these are NOT hybrids. They are Indians who have sadly lost their senses of "home." They are marked by their skin color and often by their names. As the writer Aamer Hussein so aptly said in interview with me, "Hybridity smacks of biological blending of plants." I know that I am clearly marked by my name in England in ways that I'm not in the U.S. or in the U.S. Southwest though I am marked by my colleagues who know I am not U.S. born.

My hybridity is not accepted by my cultural studies colleagues either. Recently, a cultural studies Chicana colleague of mine took me to lunch to ask me why I was interested in minority issues. She sized me up—up and down—and said, "Aren't you white?" I said, "No. I'm from India—I'm an Asian." "But you're not Asian like the Chinese," she said. "You don't look Asian!" "Aren't Indians Aryans?" she said. Since she is a great cultural studies aficionado, I asked her about the ancestry of one of cultural studies' third world icons, Homi Bhabha. "But he is dark skinned," she said. I pointed out that there were dark and light skinned Parsis as there are dark and light skinned Hispanics and in thirty minutes gave her a short history of

Zoroastrian migrations and diasporas. The "personal is the political," Trinh Minh-ha says while she adamantly refuses to talk about *her* personal, obscuring it with the voices of various other hybrids such as Elaine Chang, quoting only the "As an Asian-American, I." But it is in situating the *personal* within the context of the political of our adopted homelands whose borders we have crossed that we find, despite Vice President Al Gore's rhetoric about the global village, the crossing of boundaries and frontiers by internets and information highways, that true hybridity cannot be achieved because those who would most speak for hybridity most want to retain their essentialisms— the natives, the insiders of cultural studies, those who feel they best represent the postmodern condition and can speak for it. To play on the Elaine Chang/Trinh Minh-ha quotation, "As an Asian American I / As a Chicana I" only translates into "As an Asian American I resent white woman travelling and writing poetry about Cambodia," or "As a Chicana I resent Asian American woman teaching Chicano/a Literature." We cannot put the personal under erasure. We do not. When driven to, we turn inward to our indigenousness and try to do battle out of our "homes."

If we had hybridity, the fluidity of race and nationality . . . if exiles, émigrés, and vagrants (as Raymond Williams has called them) are merging across borders and boundaries, why the sudden surge in nationalisms and ethnic identities? As we sit here and theorize, Serbs, Muslims, Jews, and Palestinians are being killed by a wide variety of murderers from Hindu nationalists to Zionists and the "native foreigners" are being exorcised by the neo–Nazis and the skinheads. On the border where I live, which is not the margins anymore but the center, Hispanicity has degenerated into Chicano/a, Mexicano, Mexican-American, and all of Mexico is disintegrating into Mestizo, Castillano, PRI, and PAN. In *The Location of Culture*, Homi Bhabha writes about Guillermo Gomez-Pena, a performance artist in Arizona, quoting from his act as follows:

> hello America
>
> this is the voice of Gran Vato Charollero broadcasting from the hot deserts of Nogales, Arizona
>
> zona de libre cogercio
>
> 2000 megaherz en todas directiones

Bhabha calls it "the cultural hybridity of their borderline conditions to 'translate' and therefore reinscribe, the social imaginary of both metropolis and modernity." Naipaul is right—our Marxist cultural studies wallahs need to scratch the soundproofing of their study walls. The absurdity of the "cultural hybridity" of the borderline condition strikes you only if you know the context, live it, see it, and you can see that the Mexican–American immigration officer wants a wall on the border, and the Mexican laborer does not want to be hybrid, does not want NAFTA. Even as we talk about hybridity, the Indians in Chiapas want sovereignty and the *Mexican Americans* (note my use of terms) want the border closed. The move for a wall in Santa Teresa, alongside the road I drive to work and back every day, is coming from a Mexican American border patrol chief, Sylvestre Reyes, hailed by Mexican Americans in one voice along the Rio Grande for his bold stand. Mexican Americans, who are second generation, born American, don't want any more immigrants, nor do the "native foreigners" like the British. Britain has its own Sylvester Reyes, Charles Wardle, a junior trade minister who resigned because he was powerless to prevent thousands of illegal entrants and is opposed to the European Union.

At such a time we need to give up our Bhabha Babooisms, which are meaningless. But however we may try to become pukka sahibs by speaking in the language of the Terry Eagletons or the postmoderns or the hybrids, we will not make it. The brown skin and the shocks of curly black hair will remain. Is our refuge, then, to be sought in academic chairs in America because we can speak so well the language of the colonizer but the colonizer will not have us as a hybrid in his/her native country? The generational difference is that we used to protest against the oppression and segregation and hope that through our writing the injustices would be seen. But now we want to be assimilated/considered hybrid/mock our own in order to be made one. The answer is to assimilate and yet to keep our distinctness, our senses of nationality.

References

Bhabha, Homi K. *The Location of Culture*. London: Routledge, 1994.

———. *Nation and Narration*. London: Routledge, 1990.

Dhondy, Farukh. Unpublished interview with the author conducted 3 June, 1988 at Channel 4 offices, London.

Gifford, Zerbanoo. *The Golden Thread: Asian Experiences of Post-Raj Britain*. London: Grafton, 1990.

Hussein, Aamer. *Mirror to the Sun*. London: Mantra, 1993.

Kipling, Rudyard. *Kim*. 1901. Reprint, New York: Bantam, 1983.

Jussawalla, Feroza and Reed Dasenbrock, eds. *Interviews with Writers of the Post Colonial World*. Jackson: University Press of Mississippi. 1992.

Kureishi, Hanif. *The Buddha of Suburbia*. London: Faber & Faber, 1990.

———. "My Son the Fanatic." *New Yorker* (28 March 1994): 92–96.

———. "With Your Tongue Down My Throat." *Granta* 22 (autumn 1987): 19–60.

Lorde, Audre. "The Master's Tools Will Never Dismantle the Master's House." Pp. 80–105 in *This Bridge Called My Back: Writings by Radical Women of Color*, eds. Cherrie Moraga and Gloria Anzaldua. Watertown: Persephone, 1981.

Markandaya, Kamala. *The Nowhere Man*. London: Allen Lane, 1973.

Minh-ha, Trinh. *Woman Native Other*. Bloomington: Indiana University Press, 1989.

Parry, Benita. "Signs of Our Times: A Discussion of Homi Bhabha's *Location of Culture*." *Third Text* 28/29 (autumn/winter 1994): 5–24.

Yamada, Mitsuye. "Asian Pacific American Woman and Feminism." Pp. 70–75 in *This Bridge Called My Back: Writings by Radical Women of Color*. Eds. Cherrie Moraga and Gloria Anzaldua. Watertown: Persephone, 1981.

2

IMAGINED HOMECOMINGS: STRATEGIES FOR RECONNECTION IN THE WRITING OF ASIAN EXILES

Dolores de Manuel

In surveying the range of topics represented in stories and poems of Asian and Asian American writers in the United States, readers come to a quick awareness of an issue addressed and analyzed in many of these works: the dimension of exile. Whether these writers consider themselves as Asians in exile or as Asian Americans reflecting on their separation from their ethnic roots, they reveal in their work a need to construct bridges that span the geographical, social, and cultural distances that they and their families have traveled. Through this act of writing, they perform an act of reinscribing themselves within a new world, not merely assimilating to their environment in America, but rather creating for themselves a fresh mode of relation toward their present and their past, a way of seeing themselves within a new order.

While many commentators on the writing of exile focus on its expression of the deep psychic pain of what Edward Said calls its "unhealable rift" (357), and while Asian American literature itself has been summed up as "a child born of uprootedness and transplantation" (Yun 79), many writers also attempt to explore forms of healing, of taking new root, and of finding new possibilities for growth. The manifold burdens and wounds of exile, whether the departure from the homeland is voluntary or not, result not only from the separation from home, but also from the unfamiliarity and otherness imposed by life in the new land, with its alien codes. The fear of finding defeat and complete separation from the homeland in exile is present in this writing, but at the same time the energy to go on, sustained by the imagination, is presented as a mode of relation to the past that many writers find necessary. This is evident in the work of the prolific Filipino American fictionist Bienvenido Santos, one of the first writers to record the experience of Filipino immigrants; among the best-known of his stories is one of his earliest, "Scent of Apples." Santos has been an active writer for more than five decades, demonstrating in much of his fiction the complex process of the exile severing and then finding ways of recovering ties to the homeland.

"Scent of Apples," set during the Second World War, shows the nostalgia of a Filipino who has slowly realized that he has become a stranger to his people. Celestino Fabia, who calls himself "just a Filipino farmer" (180), has left his country, disowned by his family as a young man, and has made a new life for himself in the heartland of the Midwest. Away from other Filipinos for many years, he is elated to find a "first class" compatriot (184), a scholar coming to lecture at a nearby university. The story focuses on Fabia bringing the Filipino lecturer to visit his farm and reminiscing on the past, "telling his story for the first time in many years" (185).

As Fabia tells his story, it becomes apparent that although his emotional links with his homeland are strong, he has no actual connections left there, and even his memories are tenuous. He treasures a photograph of a Filipino woman, but does not know who she is, as he found the picture in Chicago, by chance. While it was once "a young face and good," now it is faded and blurred with age, "yellow and soiled with many fingerings" (188). In the same way, Fabia's memories are blurred; he knows that he and his story have been forgotten by his hometown. His picture of home is not so much a real memory as an imaginary construction that enables him to connect with a world that no longer has any kind of objective existence for him.

At the same time Fabia finds a connection with home in his marriage to Ruth, an American woman he praises by saying she is like "our own Filipino women" (189). Ruth knows nothing of the Philippines, exclaiming with disbelief when Fabia tells her he is bringing the lecturer home for a visit, "Quit kidding, there's no such thing as first class Filipino" (184). Fabia, however, recognizes in her the values of the old country, particularly her simplicity, her hard work, and her willingness to sacrifice herself for him. Elaine Kim has observed that while in Santos's stories "Filipino women can represent the homeland left behind long ago," American women, in contrast, signify "the goodness and purity of American ideals, offering friendship and acceptance to the oppressed" (71). The promise of the white woman, like the promise of America, "makes bearable the loneliness and labor that was the Filipino immigrant experience during the prewar years" (72). When Fabia hears the lecturer speak at the university, he is anxious to find out whether Filipino women still embody the ideal of virtue and self-giving that he remembers; when he is told that though they may look more modern, their essential nature has not changed, he is touchingly reassured: "'I'm very happy, sir,' he said, in the manner of one who, having stakes in the land, had found no cause to regret one's sentimental investment" (182). When Fabia introduces the lecturer to Ruth, he is proud to retell the story of her heroic efforts to save him from death, carrying him through a snowstorm to find a way to get him to the hospital, even though she is several months pregnant. The story is widely anthologized in the Philippines, probably owing its popularity to its portrayal of an American woman willing to heroically offer her life for her Filipino husband. Not only does it reverse the prejudice of interracial relationships, it also offers some form of reparation for the exploitation of the American colonizers in the Philippines and bosses of migrant workers in the United States. The acceptance that Ruth can give Fabia in America seems less important to him than the connection with his homeland that he can imagine through her; the highest praise Fabia can give Ruth, an American woman, is to compare her to the tradition of "our own Filipino women" (189).

Fabia also strikes a blow against the marginalization of Asian men as creatures not entitled to sexual expression: "In the peculiarly American tangle of race and gender hierarchies, the objectification of Asian Americans as permanent political outsiders has been tightly plaited with our objectification as sexual deviants: Asian men have been coded as having no sexuality" (Kim 69). Fabia reclaims his male identity by affirming his fatherhood. He expresses his pride in his young son Roger, who is not only "a nice boy," but also embodies Fabia's hopes for the future: "He'd be tall. You'll like him" (183). The child has a touching faith in his father: "'I laugh at him, your Daddy ain't first class. Aw, but you are, Daddy, he says. So you can see what a nice boy he is, so innocent'" (184). The boy's pride is an answer to his father's feelings of inferiority; though Fabia dismisses it as childish naiveté, it is at the same time a confirmation of the power of fatherhood.

At the end of the story Fabia sounds defeated when he speaks of home, realizing that "nobody would remember me now" (190), but although his own country and people have rejected him, it is clear that he has created for himself an unfading picture of a country whose image sustains him in his exile. He has remade in America, in the person of Ruth, a Filipino system of value to uphold him in his present life. The features of the Filipino woman in the picture he cherishes are blurred, but Ruth's are clear, and they are Filipino to him.

Another Santos short story finds a similar picture of imaginary sustenance supporting the exile. "The Day the Dancers Came" is set in the 1950s, showing a later stage in the history of immigrants and exiles. Fil, an elderly expatriate, is proud to be an American citizen and to have served in the armed forces; in this way he is happy to have assimilated. At the same time, he eagerly looks forward to the visit of a troupe of dancers from the

Philippines. Away from home, his family all dead, he has constructed for himself the picture of an ideal Filipino culture of great warmth and closeness and has made elaborate, lengthy plans to offer unstinting hospitality to the young dancers. Like Fabia, he idealizes Filipino women as the source of the motherland's warmth; when he goes to the hotel where the dancers are staying, and sees Filipino women again, he is carried away by their beauty: "He thought he would swoon in . . . fragrance long forgotten, essence of *camia, ilang-ilang* and *dama de noche*" (12).

As Fil stands in the lobby, however, trying to invite them to his apartment, the dancers avoid and ignore him. He admires their Filipino features but also notes their worldliness and sophistication, and realizes that they must have been forewarned about first–generation expatriates like him: "beware of the old-timers, the Pinoys. Most of them are bums" (16). He has been rejected by the younger generation of Filipinos, who have adapted to another standard of values and are no longer the compatriots he remembers; they now owe allegiance to a more westernized, hybridized culture. This is ironic, considering that it is Fil who lives in America, while the dancers live in the Philippines; his version of his native land exists outside of space and time.

Fil has been marginalized by his status in America; the first wave of Filipino immigrants, to which he belongs, being limited by racism to work on the lowest rung of the ladder. His own compatriots have rejected him because of this identification created by an alien system, the younger generation seeing him as a person who cannot fit into their world. Fil's name makes this rejection particularly ironic, being suggestive of a Filipino identity that they deny. Oscar Campomanes, in commenting on Filipinos writing in America, has noted "the incommensurable sense of nonbeing that stalks many Filipinos in the United States" (50), creating a "literature of exile and emergence . . . whereby life in the United States serves as the space for displacement, [and] suspension" (51). Fil's rejection by the young dancers has rendered him a nonbeing, displaced from life in spheres of both American and Filipino life.

Nevertheless, the idealized picture of the homeland that Fil has built for himself is strong enough to sustain him in spite of his disappointment. With a portable tape recorder, he goes to the theater where the dancers are performing, records their music, and returns home eager to listen. Santos has published two versions of the story; in one, Fil accidentally erases the tape of the performance music, while in the other he thinks he has erased the tape but then finds out that it is still intact. In both versions the loss of the tape, whether real or imagined, and the actual rejection of his attempts to connect by the young dancers cannot overcome the strong ties that Fil has built in his own mind, or remove him from the idealized homeland of light, warmth, and song where he has sited himself. Although this system of value is not visible to anybody but himself, it is nonetheless a vital one.

Paul Stephen Lim's "Flight" is the story of Wing, a young Taiwanese Filipino brought up in a home that follows the traditions of China and who is eager to enjoy a new freedom in America. Set in the 1960s, it portrays a younger, more educated and more westernized immigrant than those in the Santos stories; in a way, Wing and his family are already exiles, as part of the Chinese diaspora in Asia. But, while the circumstances are different, the connections between the exile and his culture retain their strength. Leaving home to go to college, Wing strives for assimilation, describing his trip and himself in terms of American pop culture: "I'd walk! Like Dorothy in *The Wizard of Oz*, down THE YELLOW BRICK ROAD. Yellow, that's me" (1). He is glad to shake off family obligations, and to have put a distance between himself and his patriarchal father and devoted mother, "far away from the whole bloody lot of you!" (1). He has no plans to ever return home—"*never*, if I can help it" (3). When he has been in the United States for two years, his father dies; he offers to go back for the funeral but his mother advises against it. Instead, Wing finds himself returning home in the life of his memory and emotions, and realizes that the distance he had tried to create is smaller than he thought: "It was really quite foolish of me to have thought that I could leave *everything behind*" (8).

Wing's father's death reminds him of expectations and ties with home and family that he had preferred to put aside. He realizes that his achievements in America do not count for much without the grounding of those ties: "I cried because the one person to whom I had wanted to show my college diploma in June—was now dead" (25). Unable to feel as much emotion as he knows he should, he represents this self-alienation in the discourse of pop culture and otherness: "Yellow, that's me. Cowardly and unfeeling" (17). Despite his sense of alienation, Wing finds a visible and literal link with the past in his father's watch, a treasured possession which he had received with surprise two years earlier when he left home: "I could not imagine my father without his old calendar watch" (6). His father's parting words, the last Wing ever hears him speak, are an admonition to change the date upon crossing the international date line. Wing has disregarded his father's words, so when he looks at the watch after hearing of his father's death he realizes that it shows the wrong time and date. Because of the difference between time zones, the hour of his father's death has not been recorded on the watch yet: "Technically speaking, my father was not yet dead. . . . Soon the luminous hands of my father's old calendar-watch would indicate that it was ten minutes past midnight, in mid-America. My father was going to die all over again, for my benefit—in Kansas!" (12). This dislocation of time and place is reminiscent of Edward Said's observation that "exile . . . is fundamentally a discontinuous state of being" (360); however, while the watch shows Wing the space and time through which he has travelled, its reminder of his exile is also a marker of continuity.

Wing uses the watch in a number of different ways: he prefers to signify the distance between himself and his father by not wearing it; he exhibits a form of self-assertion and rebellion against his father by not following his orders to change the date. And when he discovers that it displays another date and time it makes him imagine that he is living in two time zones simultaneously. The watch represents for him an inescapable connection to his origins of which he has just become aware. He thus inhabits two sites, geographically and emotionally: his present life in the United States, where he relishes his independence and his opportunities for autonomy and growth, and his past life and roots with his family, from whom he cannot disconnect as cleanly as he had hoped. His acts of distancing have not been as successful as he imagined, as he finds when he goes through the involuntary process of reconnection. When he looks at the watch and sees the time he finds out that in some ways he is still living at home. His attempts to rewrite his emotional location must be tempered by his realization that he is bound by ties too strong for him to break.

The strength of the exile's ties to the homeland, rather than their weakness, is a constant in much of this literature. Truong Anh Thuy's poem "The First Day of School" is a further chapter in the writing of exiled Asians, showing the conflict of the recent immigrant when confronted with the world of institutions and with prejudice. The poem is from the 1989 collection *War and Exile*, reflecting the experiences of Vietnamese exiles in the 1970s and 1980s, their lives disrupted by war. As they confront the changed circumstances of their new lives, the characters in the poem attempt to preserve a difficult balance in the process of needing to let go of home while at the same time holding on to it. In the poem, the mixed feelings of a parent taking a child to school for the first time are compounded by cultural differences. The parent clearly empathizes with the child's fear and confusion in confronting a world unfamiliar in several ways, in its new rules and inhabitants, and in its language. But the parent feels a responsibility to stress the need for the child to enter into the new culture. The parent feels ambivalence at having to encourage assimilation, and pain in scolding the child for wanting to stay home, retain his own culture and Vietnamese language.

To comfort the child, the parent tries to find ways to show the positive aspects of living between two cultures and of retaining the Vietnamese identity that the child's schoolmates deride, pointing out the advantages of superior knowledge: "They speak one language / But you will speak two" (Nguyen). The greatest consolation for both child and parent comes from remembering their pride in their separateness and reaffirming their Vietnamese history and heritage. The parent tells the child:

> You are different from the class
> Because you are Vietnamese
> That's what we have been
> For thousands of years. (226)

This need to acknowledge the importance of the past and the homeland in the face of exile has been noted as one of the recurring features of this literature: "The struggle to remain bicultural, to bring Vietnamese culture to America, is a theme that runs through most of Vietnamese American literature" (Christopher 259). Accordingly, the parent goes on to remind the child of the heroes of ancient Vietnam, of the familiar names and exemplars of behavior from myth and legend:

> Your ancestors are Nguyen Trai
> Le Loi and Quang Trung...
> Remember the story of Hoa Lu and Thanh Giong?
> The shining examples of Trieu and Trung? (226)

The child understands the lesson that the parent is trying to teach and responds eagerly with an expression of the same respect and admiration for their folk tales, history, and culture:

> Suddenly you shook my arm:
> "Yes! I remember now
> "The story of the Rush Battle
> "And Phu Dong who went to the sky
> "I will tell them all
> "So they won't dare . . . laugh." (226)

Both the parent and the child derive strength from retaining their connection with the past and in recognizing their ethnic identity. As Edward Said comments about the nationalism of exiles, "It affirms the home created by a community of language, culture and customs; and, by so doing, it fends off exile, fights to prevent its ravages" (359). Significantly, this poem was originally written in Vietnamese, not in English, substantiating Said's idea of "the community of language." The parent and child in the poem have reclaimed and reconstructed their history into an empowering force to help them defend themselves against the hostility of those who do not understand them, using the homecoming to fortify them in their struggles in an unfamiliar land. Their otherness and their difference from those around them, instead of signifying marginalization, weakness, and shame, become a source of pride, endurance, and determination.

In writing of the balance between the exiles' physical departure from home and their imaginary returning there, Asian writers in America are working out a pattern of action, tracing a dynamic movement between closeness and detachment, assimilation and distancing. Through this movement, the characters in their works have made for themselves a variety of strategies that reaffirm all the types of sustaining connections between themselves and their homelands that they can find. The experience of living as Asians in America has shown them their need to maintain some kind of bond with their origins and their past, at the same time as they break those ties by becoming assimilated into a new culture. As they remember their families, their ancestry, their ethnic identity, their culture, and values, they create bridges to span the many forms of distances that they have traveled. When they examine themselves as Asians in America, they recognize their otherness, and through this recognition see a need to reinscribe themselves into the new world that they inhabit. In this action, Asians writing in America come to a definition of their experience of exile that contains their rootlessness, provides them with emotional and imaginative nurturing, and reconnects them with a necessary ground of their being.

References

Campomanes, Oscar V. "Filipinos in the United States and Their Literature of Exile." Pp. 49-78 in *Reading the Literatures of Asian America*, eds. Shirley Geok-Lin Lim and Amy Ling. Philadelphia: Temple University Press, 1992.

Christopher, Renny. "*Blue Dragon. White Tiger*: The Bicultural Stance of Vietnamese American Literature." Pp. 259-270 in *Reading the Literatures of Asian America*, eds. Shirley Geok-lin Lim and Amy Ling. Philadelphia: Temple University Press, 1992.

Kim, Elaine. "'Such Opposite Creatures': Men and Women in Asian American Literature." *Michigan Quarterly Review* 29 (1990): 68-93.

Lim, Paul Stephen. "Flight." Pp. 1-28 in *Some Arrivals, But Mostly Departures*. Quezon City, Philippines: New Day, 1982.

Nguyen, Ngoc Bich, ed. *War and Exile: A Vietnamese Anthology*. [Vietnamese PEN Abroad, East Coast USA, 1989.]

Said, Edward. "Reflections on Exile." Pp. 357-66 in *Out There: Marginalizations and Contemporary Cultures*, eds. Russell Ferguson, et al. Cambridge, Mass.: MIT Press, 1990.

Santos, Bienvenido N. "Scent of Apples." Pp. 179-90 in *You Lovely People*. Manila: Bookmark, 1991.

———. "The Day the Dancers Came." Pp. 1-22 in *The Day the Dancers Came*. Manila: Bookmark, 1991.

Yun, Chung-Hei. "Beyond 'Clay Walls': Korean American Literature." Pp. 79-96 in *Reading the Literatures of Asian America*, eds. Shirley Geok-lin Lim and Amy Ling. Philadelphia: Temple University Press, 1992.

3

A HOUSE FOR
MR. CHAUDHURI

Fakrul Alam

I

On the surface, Nirad Chaudhuri seems intent on impressing everyone with the comfort and elegance in which he lives in England. Duncan Fallowell's 1991 piece "Nirad C. Chaudhuri: At Home in Oxford" seems aptly titled and describes a man obviously in his elements: the timeless Britain that surrounds him in north Oxford—"landscape, country houses, claret, Shakespeare, cathedral towns, bespoke tailors, Oxford bells" (242)— obviously sustains and energizes this ninety-plus man. Indeed, it is impossible to imagine that Chaudhuri would title a book about his coming to England *The Enigma of Arrival*. V. S. Naipaul's unique mixture of poise and tension on coming to England is not for him: if anything the vignettes Chaudhuri gives us of his arrival in England and his idyllic Oxford could almost be viewed as the feelings of an *arrivé* if one did not know him better.

Nevertheless, at one level, Naipaul and Chaudhuri come together in the way that they are able to root themselves in a kind of unchanging England created for them by their reading. There is, after all, much in the English landscape for these writers which appear to be timeless. To Naipaul, not a few of the people and places he encounters reflect characters and settings met in Shakespeare or Wordsworth or Keats. As he puts it in the opening section of *The Enigma of Arrival*:

> So much of this [the English countryside] I saw with the literary eye, or with the aid of literature. A stranger here, with the nerves of a stranger, and yet with the knowledge of the language and history of the writing. I could find a special

kind of past in what I saw; with a part of my mind I could admit fantasy. (Naipaul, 22)

In his first visit to the country, recorded in *A Passage to England* (1959), Chaudhuri, too, sees England and the English as embodiments of the land and the people created in his mind by his embrace of English culture in his reading:

> I thought today's England was very much like the history of England and perfectly consistent with it. (6)

> In no case was the idea of England I had gained from books contradicted by anything I saw, it was on the contrary completed, and that is why I can no longer recover the original bookish idea. (15)

But while Naipaul may behold the English scene with the gaze of someone steeped in the nation's history and literature, he is acutely aware of being an expatriate; of being someone with "the nerves of a stranger." In contrast, Chaudhuri apparently feels no sense of difference, no misgivings about his presence in the English landscape. If, as one commentator has observed, Naipaul never lets his readers "forget that the narrator is a stranger in a familiar–unfamiliar world" (Zaman, 127), and if he is intensely aware that it is a world which is continually changing in one sense while remaining immutable in another, Chaudhuri goes out of his way to tell us that "the traditional aspects of English life and civilization" are the "only ones that deserve attention in their own right" and that these had given "a sort of momumentality" to the English people (*Passage*, 186).

Nevertheless, Chaudhuri will admit from time to time what Naipaul, much more clear–eyed in these things, describes unequivocally as the "ruin and dereliction" of the English countryside (Naipaul, 127). In his first visit to England in 1955, Chaudhuri notes the diffidence with which the English reacted to praise of their land, but dismisses this by observing, "If I did not know how proud they were of the appearance of their country I should have thought that they were interested only in finding fault with it" (*Passage*, 89). At one point in the trip he has to acknowledge the existence of an English working class, the hardships of whose life he can sense, but he does not want to dwell on them or focus on their problems: "to go out to study the English workers, between whom and me flowed a wide river of class–consciousness, would have been too much like social research or visiting for my taste" (131).

In 1955, it was easy for Chaudhuri the wide–eyed and enthusiastic tourist to avoid looking at England negatively; by the 1980s it was impossible for the resident to ignore the tell–tale signs of decay in a country which is very different from the timeless England created by his reading. *Thy Hand, Great Anarch!* (1987) reflects fully Chaudhuri's disquiet at the way things were going in the land that he had by then irrevocably committed himself to as his home. Although this mammoth book is about what its subtitle details—1921–1952—in the context in which he is writing it, he realizes with some misgivings that the "decadence" he had attempted to evade by quitting India was now all around him. In fact, the whole West is to him now a "moral swamp" (xxv), and England, too, a prey to that foul fiend, Anarch. No longer could he pretend to ignore the working class, for in the country in which he had opted to end his life "class hatred" had become a fact of life. *Thy Hand, Great Anarch!*, then, is not only what it purports to be—an elegy for the decline of India with the demise of the British Raj; it is, implicitly, a lament for "the passing away of the greatness of the British people" (753) with the collapse of the British Empire. Everywhere in contemporary England Chaudhuri sees signs of defeatism and corruption of the will. The abandonment of the Puritan virtues that had built an empire troubles him as much as the way the English have given themselves up to popular, American, "pop" culture.

Nirad Chaudhuri, then, may be at home in Oxford, but he is not completely at ease in contemporary England. Although he would not perhaps be willing to admit as much, in this too there is a certain resemblance between his predicament and that of V. S. Naipaul's. In Sara Suleri's shrewd diagnosis of the "profound ideological ambivalence" of the Trinidadian–Indian writer in *The Rhetoric of English India*, the problem afflicting him stems from "a perspective that knows its time is done even before it has had the chance to be fully articulated," a perspective trapped at the intersection of colonialism and postcolonialism which has "no choice but to register its own bewilderment at the relation between education and empire, seduced as it was into the quaint belief that literature could somehow provide a respite from what it means to gain consciousness in a colonial world" (150). The persistent elegiac strain in Chaudhuri's writing, first heard in *The Autobiography of an Unknown Indian* (1951) and almost as a refrain in *Thy Hand, Great Anarch!* (1987), is no doubt due to his sense that the values he treasures are doomed to obsolescence despite his efforts to revive them. This idea, and the idea that there is an indissoluble link between arrival and disappointment for someone of their generation, link these otherwise different writers.

II

If Chaudhuri's arrival (and residence) in England has its share of enigmas, even if not as fraught with them as Naipaul's, Chaudhuri knows, as does the other great "Commonwealth" writer, that there is no going back for him to the country of his birth. This is because Chaudhuri, like Naipaul, is aware that a man's upbringing, especially when based on the values of another culture and imbibed from its books, can make him ultimately unfit for his own country. This situation is particularly galling for Chaudhuri because these values once seemed to have been taking root in Bengal and had given him the hope of becoming a fixture in it. What spoiled the show, of course, was nationalism, for in the end it made sure that the seeds of western civilization which once seemed to have been implanted in the minds of all educated Bengalis (and by extension, Indians) would come to naught in freedom–drunk India. That is to say, Chaudhuri had gone through a cycle of arrival and disappointment once before, for he, like many others in his generation, had felt himself set on the course of enlightenment laid out in the canonical texts of Western literature. The values they had absorbed from their reading of authors such as Shakespeare had noticeably fertilized the Bengali mind and led to the Bengal Renaissance of the second half of the nineteenth century. As far as Chaudhuri was concerned, these values seemed to have undergone a naturalization process in his homeland, but the good that had come from the movement toward enlightenment was being undone in the twentieth century by the nationalists who were agitating for the freedom from what they—unlike Chaudhuri—perceived as the imperial yoke.

What Chaudhuri will only half-admit, however, is that he had been carrying the germ of disappointment in him even when he seemed to be secure in his native land. From the moment his parents' generation of Indians embarked on a path of westernization through a regime of reading, they had begun to alienate themselves from their fellow Indians. Once more, in a similar situation, Naipaul is much more clear–sighted, for he knows that the moment his family adopted the English language as its own, and pursued "a particular kind of education" (Naipaul 52), they had split themselves off from the India of their forefathers irrevocably.

It is in a section of the *Autobiography* where Chaudhuri is discussing the religious culture into which he was born and the devotional songs that he had absorbed in his childhood that we can first intuit a key source of Chaudhuri's lifelong sense of difference. A song that he had learned from his mother, "certainly a very unusual song for a boy of six or seven to like," is one of a group of songs that will come to haunt him in later life with a feeling of estrangement from the material world (208). The opening lines of this traditional Bengali song (in Chaudhuri's translation) are:

> "What has thou done by illusions drawn?—strayed from home to
> dark, deep woods; o'er foreign countries roamed."

It is only when we remember the epilogue to *Thy Hand, Great Anarch!* In which Chaudhuri describes himself as "an apostate to Hinduism" (940) and offers us his secular faith that we can grasp the anguish of abandonment induced by his pursuit of enlightenment ideals. Surely, it is the pain of irreversible separation from one's native religious culture that gives the passage in the *Autobiography* in which Chaudhuri describes the impact of these devotional songs such pathos and an epiphany–like quality.

Two recent critiques, Cynthia Abrioux's "A Slow Alienation: Nirad Chaudhuri's Bengali Childhood in *The Autobiography of an Unknown Indian*," and Margery Sabin's "The Beast in Nirad Chaudhuri's Garden," have attempted to deconstruct his early work to show how even Kishoreganj—the remote small town in what was then Bengal and is now part of Bangladesh—where Chaudhuri was born and grew up, a town which he often describes as if it were paradise, was doomed to be lost to him because of his upbringing. As Abrioux points out, the enlightenment ideals of Chaudhuri's father ensured that Nirad would be gradually alienated from his fellow Bengalis, even when he seems to be bonded to the physical elements in Bengal. It is as if "all the dark forces of ignorance, hysteria, destruction and superstition which his education and example had made him reject had materialized before his eyes" in the shape of the mobs of the nationalist movements; "so, inevitably, rejection, solitude and alienation were the natural consequences thereof" (Abrioux, 24). What Chaudhuri will not directly acknowledge, Sabin implies, is that his family's reformist orientation had made him "eclectic and hybrid" (29). In Sabin's incisive reading, the *Autobiography* is rife with "conflicts and ambiguities" (43) caused by Chaudhuri's increasing uncertainty about his location in the world in which he is born, a world where there is a "beast" in the "garden," no matter how dimly Chaudhuri perceives it at first.

Chaudhuri's first book is thus really a narrative of a double disappointment: he and the family are first estranged from the Kishoreganj that they had rooted themselves in and then he finds himself alienated from his Calcutta setting. The immediate cause of the first uprooting is the hysteria induced in his mother by a series of catastrophes and is, Chaudhuri would like us to think, the decisive one, even though there is a whole complex of causes traceable to the ambivalence created in the family's psyche by their embrace of reformist ideals. In any case, while leaving his ancestral home, the autobiographer as a young man already has the feeling that he was destined "for ever to trudge for ever along a public road" (*Autobiography*, 251). Or as Chaudhuri puts it so wistfully later in the story of his life, "I suppose to be once *deracine* is to be forever on the road" (258).

The Calcutta sections of the *Autobiography* are dotted with accounts of his feeling of homesickness and even *Thy Hand, Great Anarch!*, mainly an account of his adult years in Calcutta, would have us believe that he kept pining for Kishoreganj in the imperial city and never felt at home in it. But while there is no reason to doubt the sincerity or the depth of his feelings about his lost Eden, it should also be emphasized that in Calcutta, too, Chaudhuri went through what to the reader is by then a familiar cycle of excitement and joy upon arrival and ultimate disappointment.

Chaudhuri and his family's great expectations from Calcutta thrilled them as they prepared for the city: "The prospect of coming away from a small and rustic place like Kishoreganj to live in Calcutta seemed to open out endless vistas of ambition before us" (*Autobiography*, 250). Once in Calcutta, Chaudhuri relishes the city, takes pride in its monumentality, and is smug in the belief that "to belong to Calcutta is not to be just anybody" (255). Chaudhuri confesses at this juncture of his autobiography that it was only after twenty years of residence in it that "the city began to lose hold" over him, for he had gloried in its intellectual culture and delighted in the sights and sounds created for "the Second City of the British Empire." True, Chaudhuri goes on to say in the next few pages that Calcutta never became a part of him as did Kishoreganj and never nurtured him as did his native habitat, but it is quite obvious that Chaudhuri protests too much about the level of his estrangement from the city. Indeed, on occasions, he even identifies himself with "the men to whom Calcutta belonged by birthright" (267)!

The fact is that both Kishoreganj and Calcutta put Chaudhuri in a similar bind. Margery Sabin's deconstruction of his account of Kishoreganj makes it a story not only of bliss but also "of tainted inheritance, confused identity, and impotent anxiety in the face of ancient malice" (45). Likewise, pages on Calcutta too can be seen as split between his celebration of its heritage and his conviction that the city itself was in the viselike grip of the evil forces of nationalism. For example, he sometimes found life in Calcutta "stifling," but "despite being the center of all intellectual activity among Bengalis, it eroded sensibility and feeling" (*Thy Hand*, 204), and, remembering "the Bengali Diaspora" which has spread (Hindu) Bengalis first all over India and then around the world, he will affectionately call the city their Zion (398).

Chaudhuri himself became part of the Hindu Bengali diaspora in 1942 when he left Calcutta for Delhi. He would live in the city until 1970, the year when he finally left India for England. From the time Chaudhuri moved to Delhi, he knew there would be no going back for him to Bengal. He had finally come off unhinged, and on this occasion there could no longer be any excitement of arrival. He cannot connect to the Delhi landscape, nor work up any enthusiasm for anything in it except its ruins and monuments. Significantly, on arrival he finds that in Delhi "even before it was noon I could not look out of the windows without discomfort" (*Thy Hand* 684).

Significantly, too, "the Delhi sand pricked but did not stick. . . . the over-all impression was of desertion and forlornness" (686). In Delhi, the present can only be a version of a wasteland for him.

Not surprisingly, it is in Delhi that Chaudhuri discovers his true vocation, that of a prophet in print warning Bengalis of the hole they had been digging for themselves by their rejection of their enlightenment heritage. It was in this city that Chaudhuri's bitterness and disillusionment at the road taken by his fellow Bengalis grew and made him Job-like in his pronouncements. The last straw for Chaudhuri was the partition of Bengal in 1947. That division meant that Chaudhuri's entry into independent India would also be the moment of the utmost frustration for him. Now the only acts of arrival he could find solace in were those stored in his memory; the remembrances of scenes past stored in his consciousness would console him during this period and help him get through it. These scenes he would recreate imaginatively in his description of Kishoreganj in the opening pages of the *Autobiography*. The act of writing was thus absolutely crucial for him; like Eliot he could almost say, "These fragments I have shored against my ruins." Lest the reference to *The Waste Land* appear to be a gratuitous one, let us note here Sabin's comments on the way in which both Eliot and Chaudhuri went to the dirges of Webster and Shakespeare for their works because Chaudhuri, like Eliot, "is drawn to a lyric like Webster's dirge at least in part for the tension that already makes its expression of solace uncertain" (39).

III

The narratives of Chaudhuri's life, the *Autobiography* and *Thy Hand, Great Anarch!*, make clear that except when in prelapsarian Kishoreganj and completely fallen Delhi, Chaudhuri's life has followed a similar pattern: initial joy felt on arriving at a place followed by gradual alienation from it. The Kishoreganj that he is born into in 1897 is not the same town that his family abandons in 1910 soon after the advent of nationalism; the Calcutta he becomes a part of that year is nothing like the city he finds himself so estranged from in 1942. To Delhi, he can connect only as a sojourner, externally, he will be in the city but will never be part of it. As we have seen, in England, too, he will go through the cycle of initial enthusiasm for the country created in his memory by his reading to a kind of recoil from its present.

And yet Chaudhuri is at home in Oxford and eager to impress this on anyone who has read his work or has talked to him in recent years. In an essay that he wrote in Bengali for Calcutta's leading literary periodical, *Desh*, a few years ago, a piece which in English can be titled "Why I Am Living in England," Chaudhuri offers some cogent reasons for his adoption of Oxford as a home: the climate suits him, he likes English food, he can use the libraries of the city for his work, he has easy access to his publishers, and England's system of health and social welfare makes life easier for someone in his nineties and gives him the leisure to write as he wishes. England may be in a state of decline and most things in contemporary England may disgust him, but Oxford can provide him mental and physical comforts which he would not have in India. He could have easily added to his list what we have gleaned from *A Passage to England*: living in Oxford, he is as close to "timeless England" as he can be.

At one point in *The Enigma of Arrival*, Naipaul writes about the suburban estate into which he had settled in England: "In that unlikely setting, in the ancient heart of England a place where I was truly alien, I found I was given a second chance, a new life, richer and fuller than I had anywhere else. . . . The years passed. I healed" (96). Chaudhuri, of course, would not ever admit to being "truly [an] alien" in England no matter how estranged he felt from the contemporary scene, and some of the wounds inflicted by his Indian experience may never really have healed, but he could have said everything else Naipaul says in the quote. Elsewhere in *The Enigma of Arrival*, Naipaul describes how soothing are the walks he takes in the English landscape and how in the "wild garden and orchard beside the water meadows I found a physical beauty perfectly suited to my temperament and answering besides, every good idea I could have had, as a child in Trinidad, of the physical aspect of England" (52). Here again, it is striking how the Trinidadian–English writer comes so close to his "Commonwealth" colleague in the way their nerves have been cured in their adopted homes in England. In "Why I Am Living in England," for example, Chaudhuri, after describing the pleasures of gardening, tells how he would go out on morning walks:

> What is most worth commenting on were the cornfields which began at the edge of the Park. I would get out of the Park and take the walks across the cornfields for three–four miles. At the end of these walks I would reach the Charwell River and stand on a bridge on it to watch as I did on the banks of the river in Kishoreganj forests of tall reeds and ducks on the water. Now I cannot go so far, but what I saw then still sustains me mentally and emotionally.
>
> Let me describe what I saw then. In some places fields of unripe corn, young and green at first, but in July–August turning golden. But always wave-like in the wind. In others, fields of rye and barley. I had read once in Tennyson:

On either side the river lie
Long fields of barely and of rye
That clothe the world and meet the sky. . .
That is really what I saw. (107)

The region near Stonehenge can be home for Naipaul and the vicinity of
Oxford can be Chaudhuri's dwelling because their mind and body find repose
here and they know they are amidst the scenes they had made part of
themselves through their childhood reading. Here, also, they can begin to
look at the world with equanimity, the serenity of the surroundings making it
possible for them to feel tranquil. Thus, *The Enigma of Arrival* and all of
Chaudhuri's autobiographical works are to some extent versions of the
pastoral in the sense that they "represent withdrawal from ordinary life to a
place apart that is close to the elemental rhythms of nature, where the
protagonist achieves a new perspective on a former mode of life amid the
complexities and conflicts of the social world" (Abrams, 142).

Naipaul, however, is a writer with too ironic a consciousness and too
much awareness of the present to be placed in the pastoral tradition. He is
thus sensitive to the way in which his presence in the English scene represents
the contemporary global diaspora of "third world" people. Ironically, by
"arriving" in England he has altered it significantly, for he can make a place
for himself here only at the expense of others—people such as his landlord and
his writer-friend Allan. As he describes it, the appearance of someone of his
color and background in the English landscape is "something like an upheaval,
a change in the course of the history of the country" (132). He is a reminder
that England has entered the postimperial phase, that the dismantling of the
empire has already taken place, that England is being reshaped by a
contemporary diaspora.

In contrast, Chaudhuri ignores totally the effect his presence—real or
symbolic—has on England and the English. What makes him so different
from Naipaul also is that far from noting the phenomenon of diasporic
populations in Britain, Chaudhuri is not interested in registering his impact
on the English landscape but on influencing his Indian readers with the unity
of his vision. The crucial point about the view from the bridge on the River
Charwell that inspires him in his Oxford walks, he would like his readers to
understand, is that it grips him so because it reminds him of the Kishoreganj
river scenes of his childhood, of his Eden before his family exiled itself from
it. It is important also to remember that he is communicating the effect the
scene has on him to his readers in Bengali; unlike Naipaul, he has not ceased
to write in his mother tongue and for his fellow Bengalis. He may be
describing Oxford and its environs, but there is a specific point he wants to
make to his Bengali readers about the appropriateness of his scenic location.

Oxford has allowed him to go back to prelapsarian Kishoreganj and he would like them to appreciate this fact as much as the other reasons he offers for living in England in his essay in Bengali on that subject. In other words, Chaudhuri has decided to house himself in Oxford because it allows him to relive his past and to recapture the feeling of love and peace and oneness with nature that was lost when nationalism reared its ugly head in Kishoreganj. He is at home in Oxford if not at ease in England because he can get back to the world of lost innocence, to the pre-Fall paradisal life when he blended harmoniously with his environment.

One remembers here how in the *Autobiography's* splendid opening book, Kishoreganj and the other places in Bengal where Chaudhuri spent his childhood are "interwoven" with the England of his imagination (257). One also remembers the section in Chaudhuri's second book about his first visit to the continent, *A Passage to England*, in which he describes how in England and France he would forget "the immediate past in a fit of amnesia" and go "back to the waters" of his childhood, as when standing on one of the Seine bridges at dusk, as on the Charwell river bridge, he "recovered, across the decades that had come in between, the peace" he "used to feel only by the rivers of East Bengal" (33). In Chaudhuri's imagination, then, this prelapsarian Kishoreganj and the timeless England (and France) epitomized in Oxford have a metonymic relationship—to someone who has read his works carefully the one will inevitably evoke the other.

It is evident that Chaudhuri's way of seeing Kishoreganj itself was shaped very early by his exposure to English culture. Thus if the Charwell (or Seine) river scene makes his mind wander to Kishoreganj, he remembers the last sunset he witnessed in Kishoreganj in terms of a Constable landscape. Even though he had at that time no firsthand experience of the English scene, he "confirmed the impression after seeing the Constable country" later in his life (*Thy Hand*, 210). The enlightenment ideals which ensured that his education would have a large dose of English literature in it also ensured that he would forever view natural scenery in terms of the images he had picked up from his excursions into English romanticism.

Indeed, the passage in *Thy Hand, Great Anarch!* in which Chaudhuri compares the Kishoreganj sunset to a Constable one is in its larger context a discussion of how when educated Bengalis "acquired a feeling for the beauties of nature they showed it by a vicarious enjoyment of those described in the source of their new feeling, namely English literature" (*Thy Hand*, 207–8). The reason Chaudhuri can appreciate the beauties of the Kishoreganj sunset, he suddenly realizes, is because of his enjoyment of the Constable one. The reason why this and other Kishoreganj scenes can continue to sustain him in his exilic state is the one which allows Wordsworth to find even "'mid the din/Of Towns and Cities" and in times of stress "sensations sweet,/Felt in the blood, and felt along the heart" stimulated by the remembrances of the "beauteous forms" of the Tintern Abbey landscape (*Thy Hand*, 214–15). In other words, finding a home in Oxford has allowed Chaudhuri to complete a circle: if he had first learned to appreciate Kishoreganj because of his feel for English landscape, he can now find peace in an English landscape because it evokes Kishoreganj for him.

IV

Nirad Chaudhuri, then, has ample reason for feeling at home in Oxford. But now in his late nineties, he still finds himself bothered by the morass he has always felt his fellow Bengalis put themselves into by abandoning their enlightenment heritage and succumbing to the spirit of nationalism. The author as a nonagenarian feels compelled to address them and explain in essay after essay written in Bengali why he has chosen to have his house in England and how he can still lead the life of a Bengali there. Unlike V. S. Naipaul with whom we have been comparing and contrasting him throughout the essay, Chaudhuri would like to keep a lifeline to the country of his origin through his writing. Moreover, some instinct in him seems to drive him even now to defend himself against imputations of betrayal by Bengali readers. Far from being guilty of disloyalty, he implies, the good health and the leisure and the means to write that have resulted from his residence in England have allowed him to carry out his mission of telling them that they are still capable of getting out of their stupor and renewing their fallen light.

As Chaudhuri sees it, being in Oxford actually allows him to fulfill his destiny—a destiny he first intuited from his reading of Matthew Arnold's poem, "The Scholar Gipsy." As he puts it in his first book: "I . . . fell so headlong in love with the idea of being a scholar gypsy after reading Matthew Arnold's poem that this love marked its trail on all my subsequent worldly career" (*Autobiography*, 143). In the second part of his autobiography, Chaudhuri acknowledges that it was this poem that helped him find his vocation in life at a critical juncture in his career (*Thy Hand*, 76). Reading it then, he decided that he would give up a permanent job rather than sacrifice his instinct to write and project his ideas about himself and his world to his readers.

Arnold's celebrated poem is, of course, about an Oxford scholar who, because of poverty, leaves his studies and joins a band of gypsies because he is "tired of knocking at preferment's door." One day, years later, he meets some of his college friends and tells them that he intends to communicate the secret of the art of the gypsies to them after he has mastered it. The finest aspects of the poem, most readers have agreed, are Arnold's description of the

Oxfordshire environs which had supposedly become the scholar–gypsy's haunt and the elegiac tone with which he evokes a vanished life, "with its sick hurry, its divided aims," where he can roam freely in the countryside nourishing his "project in unclouded joy,/And every doubt long blown by time away," and is seen "Still nursing the unconquerable hope,/Still clutching the inviolable shade." To the admiring narrator of the poem, the scholar–gypsy's decision to flee "the feverish contact" of his contemporaries and to continue to seek a life of calm and solitude while becoming an absent presence is particularly exemplary. The scholar–gypsy might have decided to elude them physically, but from his haunt in Oxford he will offer them, from time to time, the fruits of his experience. The "dark Iberians" with whom he has chosen to deal in his retirement are "shy traffickers" and this is why for them "on the beach [he still] undid his corded bales."

Viewed now and in the overall context of Nirad Chaudhuri's life, it is easy to see how he has *become* the scholar–gypsy and how the poem has become an allegory of his life. Of the many reasons he has chosen to have his house in Oxford, surely the most cogent, even if the most allusively stated one, is this: forced to seek refuge in Oxford after being disappointed and exhausted by his experience in his native land, he can still nurture his favorite project—to remind Bengalis of the success they once had because of their enlightenment—without coming into direct and debilitating contact with them. Like the "grave Tyrian trader" of Arnold's concluding simile, he can use his elusive position to deposit his wares for his Bengali readers, without having to see them anymore!

References

Abrams, M. H. *A Glossary of Literary Terms*. 6th ed. New York: Harcourt Brace & Co., 1993.

Abrioux, Cynthia. "A Slow Alienation: Nirad Chaudhuri's Bengali Childhood in *The Autobiography of an Unknown Indian*." *Commonwealth: Essays and Studies* 15 (1992): 20-28.

Chaudhuri, Nirad. *The Autobiography of an Unknown Indian*. 1951. Reprint, New York: Addison–Wesley Publishing Co., Inc., 1989.

———. *A Passage to England*. London: Macmillan & Co. Ltd., 1959.

———. *Thy Hand, Great Anarch! India 1921-1952*. 1987. New York: Addison–Wesley Publishing Company, Inc., 1988.

———. "Why I Am Living in England" (Ami Keno Achi). Pp. 77-110 in *Amar Debotter Shampati*. Calcutta: Anando Publishers Private Ltd., 1994.

Fallowell, Duncan. "Nirad C. Chaudhuri: At Home in Oxford." *The American Scholar* 60 (1991): 242–46.

Naipaul, V. S. *The Enigma of Arrival*. Harmondsworth, England: Viking, 1987.

Sabin, Margery: "The Beast in Nirad Chaudhuri's Garden." *Essays in Criticism* 44 (1994): 26–48.

Suleri, Sara. *The Rhetoric of English India*. Chicago: University of Chicago Press, 1992.

Zaman, Niaz. "*The Enigma of Arrival*: Or, A Place for Mr. Naipaul." Pp. 125–35 in *Other Englishes: Essays on Commonwealth Writing*, edited by Niaz Zaman, et al. Dhaka: University Press Ltd., 1991.

4

THE ENIGMA OF DEPARTURE: THE DYNAMICS OF CULTURAL AMBIGUITY IN ROHINTON MISTRY'S *SWIMMING LESSONS AND OTHER STORIES FROM FIROZSHA BAAG*

Geoffrey Kain

> . . . the further they go,
>
> the more they'll remember.
>
> —"Swimming Lessons"

Rohinton Mistry emigrated from Bombay to Toronto in 1975. Since 1984 we have seen a modest number of his short stories published in various journals, most of these stories subsequently organized as a collection, first published in Canada in 1987, under the title *Tales from Firozsha Baag* (published in the United States as *Swimming Lessons and Other Stories from Firozsha Baag* in 1989). He has also published two novels, *Such a Long Journey* (1991), and *A Fine Balance* (1995). Though he has not been prolific, Mistry's work has earned him several marks of high distinction.[1] The vivid detail, dry humor, and gentle irony that characterize his depictions of a cross section of the Parsi community involve us in a world that is, like most communities, memorable for its own qualities of excellence and peculiar charms, as well as for its own sources of repugnance and absurdity.

Aside from some of the engaging and truly memorable aspects of his characters' lives, one of the necessarily intriguing elements of Mistry's fiction is that while the author himself has resided in Canada for twenty years, the nearly unvarying focus of his writing has been India—specifically, a restricted range of territory within Bombay. Mistry's own cultural ambivalence is disclosed as he professes that he does "not want to forget anything about Bombay" while he remains committed to life in a nation which has shown him what he identifies as "subtle discrimination" (Hancock, 145)—which he claims he would certainly prefer to the "overt racism of the Melting Pot" which he associates with experience in the United States.[2] Despite Mistry's persistent authorial attachment as a writer to Bombay as setting, it is a Bombay he confesses to find "very bleak" (Hancock, 149) and where, significantly, he grew up "outside of Hindu India," being Parsi.

As Mistry draws us into life in the housing complex known as Firozsha Baag, we become most familiar with several young characters who eventually leave the life they (and, ultimately, we) know in Firozsha Baag for the traditional promise of greater opportunity in the United States and Canada. The brief exposure we have to the experience of these characters, especially through the narrative voice of the sensitive and perceptive character Kersi ("Of White Hairs and Cricket," "Lend Me Your Light," and "Swimming Lessons"), provides us with poignant (however limited) insight into the emigrant experience—into what is revealed to be not just the impact of emigration on the émigré himself, nor only the effects of departure on those who are left at a distance, but the complex and slowly changing web of consciousness that, taken together, defines the immigrant experience in Mistry's fiction. In *Stories from Firozsha Baag*, Mistry skillfully and playfully explores the psychological dis/connection among individuals involved in the departure from home, as well as the émigré's own evolving understanding of the dynamics of cultural hyphenation, revealing with grace, humor, and a trace of sadness, the plight of those who, like himself, occupy the interstices between cultures.

Mistry toys with the complex, multi-faceted nature of the theme of self as "other" as he adopts multiple narrative personae in the volume of short stories and invites readers to peer into the experiences of characters who are necessarily "other" for author (despite some suggestively autobiographical elements) as well as reader, and who themselves struggle (variously) with the perplexities of what it means to be "other" in a new culture—a process which also distances as "other" the native culture and its previously hyper-familiar fixtures (family members and all elements of the home environment)—usually counter to the will of the émigré. One therefore emerges from Mistry's collection of stories with a wry sense that he has not only witnessed but has also been personally engaged by the author in the experience of a multilayered distancing or dislocation, an experience which finally establishes itself as the essence of the short story collection.

Stories from Firozsha Baag contains eleven tales; roughly the first half of the volume is consistently given to familiarizing the reader with the tenor of life in the housing complex, and introducing us to some of the more notable and venerable individuals who call the Baag home. "Of White Hairs and Cricket," the sixth story in the collection, examines more closely the home life of the teenage boy Kersi (a character introduced in one of the earlier stories). We find Kersi carefully plucking white hairs from his father's head while his father combs through the want ads in the *Times of India*, searching for employment that will ease the family's difficulties. This week's source of excitement is a listing for a "dynamic young account executive"; as Kersi continues to "uproot the signposts of mortality" on his father's scalp, his father announces, "If I can get [this job], all our troubles will be over":

> Mummy listened to such advertisements week after week: harbingers of hope that ended in disappointment and frustration. But she always allowed the initial wave of optimism to lift her, riding it with Daddy and me, higher and higher, making plans and dreaming, until it crashed and left us stranded, awaiting the next advertisement and the next wave. (112)

Despite his ongoing search for more profitable work, Kersi's father is of course well aware that his efforts are nearly futile. Frustrated but refusing to despair, he invests his hope in his sons. To Kersi he says, ". . . one day you must go . . . to America. No future here. . . . Somehow we'll get the money to send you. I'll find a way" (112).

Signs of near desperation, of frustration in the face of what is depicted as a general and progressive social dilapidation—a dilapidation suggested also through the structure of the very buildings of Firozsha Baag itself—are witnessed throughout the text; this, in fact, is the note that is struck in the first story of the volume, "Auspicious Occasion." The story opens with Rustomji's disgust at the tenement's faulty plumbing; a leaking toilet threatens to absorb his full attention on the sacred day of *Behram roje*. In contrast to his wife Mehroo's traditional preparations for sacred ritual, much narrative attention is given to the rapid decline of the Baag's physical structure. We witness Rustomji's bitter anger toward an indifferent bureaucracy (the Trustees of Firozsha Baag) as its cheaply constructed building steadily crumbles. Rustomji realizes that his anger has tainted the sentiment appropriate for a day marked by purification rites (just as his brilliant white *dugli* is later badly stained by someone spitting *paan* from a bus window), but he confesses he has lost feeling anyway for "customs [that are] dead and meaningless" (7–8). A previously idealistic man who in his younger days had volunteered with the Social

Service League, bringing aid to impoverished rural areas, he had "decided long ago that this was no country for sorrow or compassion or pity—these were worthless and, at best, inappropriate" (8).

Embittered by and hardened against varied aspects of decline, characters in Mistry's imagined housing complex nonetheless repeatedly (and sometimes humorously) resist submission to oppressive forces of degeneration, often in isolated moments of compassion and tenderness (however seemingly "worthless" or "inappropriate"). Amin Malak remarks on the resilient nature of Mistry's characters by noting that "despite their near-tragic circumstances, Mistry's characters survive and cherish hopes for better days" (101). Mistry himself remarks that, despite all the causes for pessimism he has noted in contemporary Indian society, "there are still those amazing moments of hope, those sparks . . .that make me feel despite all the misery and sorrow, that life is still good and must go on" (Hancock, 149). In "Auspicious Occasion," after Mehroo returns home from the fire temple, shocked by the murder in the temple of her most beloved priest, and Rustomji returns home from being spat upon and very nearly beaten by a crowd at a bus stop, Rustomji seems on the verge of surrendering to despair ("What is happening in the world I don't know" [20]). But melancholy and torpor in response to threatening circumstance (with the WC "still leaking") is replaced, just at the conclusion of the story, with a soft touch of personal intimacy, as Rustomji and Mehroo, alone in their flat, come together with "tender satisfaction" for a quiet cup of tea.

This moment of quiet connectedness in the midst of glaring disarray is suggestive of several others like it in the volume, moments which help to under-score Kersi's haunting sense of dislocation and mild bewilderment witnessed later in the volume, once he has left the Baag for life in Toronto. In "Of White Hairs and Cricket," Kersi is happy and excited by the prospect of one day going to Canada or the States, but when he slips away from his flat, wearied of his father and his obsession with white hairs, and goes to visit his cricket-playing friend Viraf, he is stunned to find Viraf's father flat in bed, receiving intravenous treatment, struggling to breathe. The story ends with Kersi's feelings of time lost with his own father, with a sense of helplessness before the inexorable advance of time, with the intense urge to hold on to what he knows he values.

The thematic tension between the need to hold on and the need to break free is developed gradually through the accumulation of the individual stories in the volume. In "Condolence Visit," for example, we encounter Daulat who has just been widowed. She continues to burn the oil lamp next to her husband's bed well beyond the prescribed four days:

"Didn't *dustoorji* tell you? . . . For the first four days the soul comes to visit here. The lamp is there to welcome the soul. But after four days prayers are all complete, you know, and the soul must go quickly–quickly to the Next World. So you must put it out, you are confusing the soul." (64)

But Daulat has "no such intention," despite the advice of her well–meaning neighbor. Eventually, however, we witness her going to refill the oil in the lamp once more, but then changing her mind:

From under one of the cups in the living room she retrieved a saucer and re-turned to his room. She stood before the lamp for a moment, looking deep into the flame, then slid the saucer over the glass. She covered it up completely, the way his face had been covered with a white sheet. . . . (76)

The poignant description of Daulat's urge to hold on to her deceased husband, then her resigned letting go, serves as emotive vehicle to help establish the central tension of the volume as a whole which culminates in Kersi's conflicting feelings of attachment and resistance as he separates from family and friends in Firozsha Baag and settles in Toronto. In "Lend Me Your Light," we are drawn into Kersi's experience of departure. Prior to his own emigration, his brother's friend Jamshed is approved by U.S. Immigration:

Jamshed did manage to leave. One day, he came to say goodbye. . . . Jamshed spoke to those of us who were home, and we all agreed that he was doing the right thing. There just weren't any prospects in this country; nothing could stop its downhill race towards despair and ruin. (178)

As Kersi prepares to depart for Toronto, his parents downplay their pangs of separation by insisting on the tremendous opportunities opening for him, especially considering his "education, and . . . westernized background, and . . . fluency in the English language" (178). But as Kersi looks back on his preparation for departure, he recognizes that "in the clichés of our speech was reflected the cliché which the idea of emigration had turned into for so many" (178).

The idea of emigration—that the land of glittering efficiency and tidy promise will deliver the deserving individual emerging from a nation struggling with poverty and mired in corruption—Kersi discovers in his experience to be out of keeping with the much more complex reality. Jamshed, who had railed against India's inadequacies before leaving for New York, continues to rail against India though he is now distanced from it. Jamshed's experience seems to justify the cliché of emigration: even though he came from a privileged background in Bombay, his time in New York has brought him increasing wealth and expanding economic opportunity. Still, Kersi is disturbed when, after a year in Toronto, he receives his first letter from Jamshed, "a very neat missive, with an elegant little label showing his name and address." Jamshed had recently visited Bombay and found it "horrible. Seems dirtier than ever, and the whole trip just made me sick. I had my fill of it in two weeks and was happy to leave" (181). Kersi finds Jamshed's attitude both "irritating" and perplexing:

> It was puzzling that he could express so much disdain and discontentment even when he was no longer living under those conditions. Was it himself he was angry with . . . ? Was it because of the powerlessness that all of us experience who, mistaking weakness for strength, walk away from one thing or another? (181)

Kersi struggles to clarify his feelings toward the place of his birth and toward his present home. He answers Jamshed's letter by inviting him to Toronto where, he says, they can visit Little India and eat various dishes as "authentic as any in Bombay," go to see a Hindi movie, and browse in shops selling imported spices and Hindi records. Kersi writes that he often goes to Little India, a wonderful place, . . . but

> the truth is I have been there just once. And on that occasion I fled the place in a very short time, feeling extremely ill at ease and ashamed, wondering why all this did not make me feel homesick or at least a little nostalgic. But Jamshed did not have to know any of it. My letter must have told him that whatever he suffered from, I did not share it. For a long time afterwards, I did not hear from him. (182)

While Kersi is not the loyal patron of Little India he describes himself to be, he is also not—like Jamshed—the man determined to deny his cultural affiliation, either. He has joined the Zoroastrian Society of Ontario, "hoping to meet people from Bombay." He discovers that his time spent among these people, however, is given to listening to endless conversations about bargains discovered on shopping trips to Bombay, the best airlines to fly to India, etc. Kersi feels no more attached to these people than he does to Jamshed. When he receives a letter from his brother Percy, who has dedicated himself to social and political reform in Maharashtrian villages, Kersi reflects guiltily,

> There you were, my brother, waging battles against corruption and evil, while I was watching sitcoms on my rented Granada TV. Or attending dinner parties at Parsi homes to listen to chit-chat about airlines and trinkets. (184)

When Kersi travels to Bombay for a visit, after two years in Canada, he feels his time away will have allowed him to develop "a lucidity of thought which

[he] would carry back . . . and bring to bear on all of India's problems" (186). What he encounters is a Bombay which "seemed dirtier than ever," and he senses that perhaps Jamshed was right.

Feeling no longer at home in Bombay, yet wanting to keep alive his attachment to his home and all that that implies, Kersi thus embodies and gives expression to the tension between the emotional poles of indigenousness or cultural immersion/attachment (manifest in Percy) and cultural rejection or the quest for full assimilation (manifest in Jamshed), and is left unsure of his place or even of the strength of his conflicting inclinations; by virtue of choices he has made, he now faces the prospect that, as Edward Said has described it, "just beyond the frontier of 'us' and the 'outsiders' is the perilous territory of not belonging . . . where in the modern era immense aggregates of humanity loiter as . . . displaced persons" (359). Kersi has been vaguely disturbed for some time, but after his blighted return to Bombay he brings into sharper focus his evolving nature. As Ajay Heble remarks, Mistry illustrates

> the impossibility of defining immigrant identity exclusively in terms of one's ancestral past or in terms of one's ability to assimilate into the new culture. Identity, as Kersi discovers, is more a matter of process than a fixed condition. (58)

As Mistry explores through Kersi the uncertain and often surprising evolution of émigré identity, this process is lampooned in "Squatter" through the narrative offered by Nariman Hansotia, the whimsical teller of tall tales revered by the boys of Firozsha Baag. Nariman relates for the boys the difficulties encountered by Sarosh (a young man Nariman claims to know) when he emigrated to Canada. During his going–away party, Nariman indicates, Sarosh faced a mixed response to his decision to leave India. Sarosh

> was told by some what a smart decision he had made, that his whole life would change for the better. Others said he was making a mistake, emigration was all wrong, but if he wanted to be unhappy, that was his business. . . . (154)

His mother told him that "it is better to live in want among your family and your friends, who love you and care for you, than to be unhappy surrounded by vacuum cleaners and dishwashers and big shiny motor cars" (155). Sarosh countered those opposed to his move, including his mother, by impulsively claiming that if he did not "become completely Canadian" within exactly ten years, he would return to the country of his birth.

Although wholeheartedly committed to absolute assimilation, Sarosh (now Sid) discovers he is incapable of properly using the Western toilet (hence the story's title). He becomes so obsessed with overcoming this challenge to his total assimilation that he seeks professional help to aid him in making the desired change.[3] Sarosh declines the offer of a surgically implanted device to ease his situation (the risks of malfunction being too great), a device developed, Nariman digresses,

> with financial assistance from the Multicultural Department . . . [a Bureau which is] a Canadian invention. It is supposed to ensure that ethnic cultures are able to flourish, so that Canadian society will consist of a mosaic of cultures—that's their favorite word, mosaic—instead of one uniform mix, like the American melting pot. If you ask me, mosaic and melting pot are both nonsense, and ethnic is a polite way of saying bloody foreigner. (160) [4]

Sarosh must finally face his hopeless inability to achieve his publicly professed goal of becoming 100 percent "completely Canadian." His ten frustrating and anxiety-filled years pass, and he returns to India, "desperately searching for his old place in the pattern of life he had vacated ten years ago. . . . The old pattern was never found" (167). Despondent, isolated, Sarosh reflects that "the world can be a bewildering place, and dreams and ambitions are often paths to the most pernicious of traps" (168).

The travails of Sarosh are related to an audience of eager young boys by Nariman Hansotia, who claims to have gotten the details from Sarosh himself. Nariman's own penchant for humor and exaggeration is evident throughout the narrative, and his own assumptions about the emigration experience color the story from start to finish: the quest for total assimilation can become ridiculous while, on the other hand, the subsequent effort to return "home" is often subverted by the original choice to leave. "Home" then becomes a mental construct developed, in part, through the anxieties of absence. The émigré thus finds himself faced with the difficult task of having to redefine home, and to craft a new relationship between a modified self and a revised mis/understanding of location.

The humorous hearsay "adventures" of Sarosh in "Squatter" are partly contrasted, partly paralleled, by the experiences of Kersi as described in the volume's final story, "Swimming Lessons." We encounter Kersi within his Toronto apartment building, suggesting earlier encounters with him inside the block of Firozsha Baag, but the building and its attendant experiences contrast poignantly with those in Bombay. By now, Kersi has certainly come to know what it is, as Amy Ling has described it, to be "an other among others" (98–99). In contrast to his experience in Firozsha Baag, Kersi knows only one of the other tenants in his building by name—Berthe, the Yugoslavian immigrant and building superintendent; there is "PW" (for "Portuguese Woman"), "the old man" in the wheelchair with whom he exchanges passing courtesies, the "two women," "Berthe's son," "Berthe's husband," etc. The dim but lively, congested hallways and noisy environs of Firozsha Baag have been replaced by the empty, almost antiseptic environment of the apartment building in Canada ("The old man's wheelchair is audible today as he creaks by in the hallway: on some days it's just a whirr" [235]).

Kersi enrolls in a ten-week course of swimming lessons, hoping to overcome his fear of water and also to perhaps meet a young woman who will be interested in him—his "swimming lesson fantasy" (235). As he prepares for the lessons, Kersi recalls earlier efforts to learn to swim at Chaupatty Beach in Bombay, and he contemplates the significant "recurrent imagery" of water in his life and its prominent symbolic functions in his native culture. He considers "the universal symbol of life and regeneration," and the "many religious festivals [that] used the sea as repository for their finales" (235). Although most features of his new existence serve as reminders of his former life in Firozsha Baag (PW reminds him of Najamai, the old man reminds him of his grandfather, the old man's daughter is suggestive of his (Kersi's) mother, etc.), he hopes through the swimming lessons to achieve at least a beginning of a new life, one distinct from the old.

Neither of his initial goals is realized. In the shower prior to his first lesson, three young boys target him as an outsider:

> One of them holds his nose. The second begins to hum under his breath: Paki, Paki, smell like curry. The third says to the first two: pretty soon the water's going to taste of curry. They leave. (238)

Kersi stops attending after just two lessons:

> My [new] Surf King [suit] is relegated to an unused drawer. Total loss: one fantasy plus thirty dollars. And no watery rebirth. (240)

His efforts to "connect" with his new home in Canada have thus far failed him, and his communications with his parents in Bombay have become quite hollow. The story is punctuated by scenes of his parents waiting for, receiving, then disappointedly reading his rather unrevealing letters. When they receive a copy of his collection of short stories—a collection that obviously mirrors *Stories From Firozsha Baag*[5]—they are proud but somewhat critical, and certainly a bit disconcerted by the lack of extensive reference to his life in Canada:

> My hope is, Father said, that there will be some story based on his Canadian experience, that way we will know something about our son's life there, if not through his letters then in his stories; so far they are all about Parsis and Bombay and the one with a little about Toronto, where a man perches on top

of the toilet, is shameful and disgusting, although it is funny at times and did make me laugh, I have to admit. . . . Mother said that she would also enjoy some stories about Toronto and the people there; it puzzles me, she said, why he writes nothing about it, especially since you say that writers use their own experience to make stories out of. (246)

As the volume ends, Kersi remains in Canada, and his parents remain at a distance, waiting and hoping for messages, for information that will allow for the already changed tie with their son to perhaps remain strong. The tension between attachment and resistance—witnessed in various ways and through an assortment of characters throughout the text, and finally embodied in the character of Kersi—is ultimately not resolved. Mistry leaves his character (and his reader) in a state of uncomfortable suspension, remaining in the New Land yet continuing to hearken back, to claim, as Kersi does, that "the further they go, the more they'll remember. They can take it from me" (247).

Notes

1. Mistry received the Hart House Prize for fiction in 1983 and 1984; the Governor General's Award and the Commonwealth Writers Prize in 1991; and The *Los Angeles Times* Book Prize in Fiction, the Giller Prize, and the Commonwealth Writers Prize in 1996.

2. Compare this with Bharati Mukherjee's account of the minority experience in Toronto. She maintains that from speaking with many Indians in Canada she has amassed "endless . . . personal litanies of discrimination" and found herself "being taken for a smelly, dark, alien other" (Connell, 12).

3. Sarosh learns that many other immigrants have sought professional help in order, like him, to achieve full assimilation; one man, for example, sought help because he could not eat Canadian Wonder Bread without vomiting, able to digest only Indian bread made with flour milled in the village from which he came. Through extended treatment, that patient "successfully ate his first slice of whole wheat Wonder Bread with no ill effects. The ultimate goal is pure white Wonder Bread" (158).

4. An interesting parallel to Nariman Hansotia's views on multicultural-ism are those expressed by Mistry himself:

Multiculturalism and the Melting Pot. I haven't followed all the arguments for and against Multiculturalism. I used to think Multiculturalism was an invention

of the politicians, to have a new portfolio, find ways to structure their time, win votes and so on. Lately, I understand that the people Multiculturalism is supposed to help are worried about it. It's become counterproductive, as they say in government offices.
Somebody said Multiculturalism creates Multi-Cul-de-Sacs. Dead ends from which the ethnic community cannot participate, or be assimilated more fully into Canadian life. (Hancock, 145)

5. In an interview with Geoff Hancock for the *Canadian Fiction Magazine*, Mistry remarks on speculation regarding possible autobiographical elements in *Firozsha Baag*:

Mistry: In *Tales From Firozsha Baag*, we have Kersi the narrator whose development we witness from childhood to teenager to young man in Canada. People who should know better see this as the author writing a book for his parents. But it's the narrator of the fiction who's speaking, not me. One interviewer even hoped my next book would be about my years working in a Canadian bank! I smiled politely at that, and gave him a "who knows" type of look. . .

Hancock: Is Kersi, the narrator of *Tales From Firozsha Baag*, your alter ego? . . .

Mistry: No, he isn't. (144,150)

References

Connell, Michael, et al. "An Interview With Bharati Mukherjee." *The Iowa Review* (fall 1990): 7–32.

Hancock, Geoff. "An Interview With Rohinton Mistry." *Canadian Fiction Magazine* 65 (1989): 143–50.

Heble, Ajay. "'A Foreign Presence in the Stall': Towards a Poetics of Cultural Hybridity in Rohinton Mistry's Migration Stories." *Canadian Literature* 137 (summer 1993): 51–61.

Ling, Amy. "'Emerging Canons' of Asian American Literature and Art." Pp. 191-98 in *Asian Americans: Comparative and Global Perspectives*, eds. Shirley Hune, et al. Pullman: Washington State University Press, 1991.

Malak, Amin. "Images of India." *Canadian Literature* 119 (winter 1988): 101–3.

Mistry, Rohinton. *Swimming Lessons and Other Stories from Firozsha Baag*. New York: Penguin, 1989.

Said, Edward. "Reflections on Exile." Pp. 357-66 in *Out There: Marginalizations and Contemporary Cultures*, eds. Russell Ferguson, et al. Cambridge, Mass.: MIT Press, 1990.

Tapping, Craig. "South Asia Writes North America." In *Reading the Literatures of Asian America*, eds. Shirley Geok-lin Lim and Amy Ling. Philadelphia: Temple University Press, 1992.

5

OLD PASSIONS IN A NEW LAND: A CRITIQUE OF BHARATI MUKHERJEE'S "THE MANAGEMENT OF GRIEF" AND BAPSI SIDHWA'S "DEFEND YOURSELF AGAINST ME"

Niaz Zaman

Most migrant writing is marked by a sense of nostalgia, a longing for home, and a sense of displacement. V.S. Naipaul, for example, describes people adrift, with nowhere to go. This sense of alienation has been a dominant theme throughout his writings. A recurrent image in *The Mimic Men* and *A House for Mr. Biswas* is that of a boy at dusk, standing outside his hut not knowing where to go. Dayo, in the short story "Tell Me Who To Kill," from the collection *In a Free State*, is lonely, whether he is sitting alone on a park bench or marrying his English fiancée. Santosh, the Indian servant in "One Among Many," another short story from *In a Free State*, wants to marry a black woman so that he can stay back in America, but has a sense of loss: he has become "one among many." In his autobiographical writings, Naipaul describes his own sense of alienation—from the land of his birth, the land of his ancestors, and the land of his adoption. As Paul Theroux has noted, "For the rootless person, every country is a possible temporary home; but for Naipaul, there is no return either to a past or a place" (77). Neither in England nor in India is Naipaul quite at home. In *An Area of Darkness*, Naipaul writes, "London was not the centre of my world. I had been misled, but there was nowhere else to go" (92). In *The Enigma of Arrival*, this impression is to a great extent corrected, but is never quite wiped out; his past is a colonial's past, constructed—as it was for many other colonials—from the books he had to read at school. Moreover, despite his arrival, a sense of loneliness persists; despite the people he meets, the narrator is alone.

Naipaul was the writer that Bharati Mukherjee chose as her model when she first began to write, as she points out in her introduction to *Darkness* (1985). By 1984, however, this stance changed and Mukherjee started thinking of herself not as an expatriate like Naipaul, but as an immigrant. As Fakrul Alam notes, she moved from the aloofness of expatriation to the exuberance of immigration. In an interview Mukherjee explained the difference between herself and Naipaul:

> I don't write from the vantage point of an Indian expatriate like V.S. Naipaul. Naipaul, who was born in Trinidad because his relatives left India involuntarily to settle there, has different attitudes about himself. He writes about living in perpetual exile and about the impossibility of ever having a home. Like Naipaul, I am a writer from the Third World but unlike him I left India by choice to settle in the US. I have adopted this country as my home. I view myself as an American author in the tradition of other American authors whose ancestors arrived at Ellis Island. ("Interview", 650)

What Mukherjee says here, however, is not quite accurate. She did not leave India with the intent of settling in the States. She came to study in Canada and stayed on—because of her marriage to Clark Blaise, a Canadian—and moved to the States because Canadian racism prevented her from ever feeling at home in Canada. Similarly, though Naipaul's grandfather left India involuntarily, Naipaul left Trinidad by choice for the United Kingdom. Mukherjee's description of Naipaul as the perpetual exile is, however, perceptive. While this feeling of being an exile might be ascribed to several factors, one reason that Mukherjee feels an exuberance as an American citizen and Naipaul does not feel that as a British citizen is perhaps occasioned by the American experience that draws in the immigrant as life in Britain does not. "There is, for example, no British equivalent of the American citizenship ceremony" ("Interview", 650).

Mukherjee's explanation of the difference between her and Naipaul and her repeated assertion that she is an American are significant because they underscore the dominant theme in her fiction: the Americanization of people from the Third World. Bapsi Sidhwa, a more recent American resident, in her latest book, *An American Brat*, also turns to Mukherjee's favorite theme as she describes how the sixteen-year-old Feroza Ginwalla becomes what her mother, horrified at the change in her daughter, calls "an American brat" (279). Unlike Bharati Mukherjee, however, who focuses on the immigrant theme in almost all her fiction, Sidhwa intertwines a commentary on Pakistani politics and an exposition of Parsi society and religious rites with the immigrant theme. In addition, as in all her writing, Sidhwa is concerned with the marginalization and the discriminations against women. Thus, even as Sidhwa writes about the Americanization of Feroza, the culture and politics of Pakistan and the joys and sorrows of being a Parsi woman remain Sidhwa's concomitant concerns.

The distinctiveness of Mukherjee and Sidhwa is clearly manifest in all their writings. To demonstrate this distinction, I am selecting two short stories by the two writers: Bharati Mukherjee's "The Management of Grief," from the collection *The Middleman and Other Stories* and Bapsi Sidhwa's "Defend Yourself Against Me," printed in *Colours of A New Day*. One distinct advantage of a short story over a novel is that it can create one clear impression rather than the welter of images created by a novel. For this reason, writers skilled in both genres may often be suitably approached through their short stories. Mukherjee's "The Management of Grief" and Sidhwa's "Defend Yourself Against Me" thus can help give insight into their authors' respective themes in their longer fiction.

Mukherjee is an immigrant and, apart from her pride in her immigrant status, is also proud of the double perspective that her situation gives her. In "Immigrant Writing" she notes how her experience has given her a "doubleness" of experience:

> The new America I know and have been living in for the last seven years is a world, by definition, of doubles. Characters in this world have the density of 19th century presences; like creations out of Balzac or Dickens, they pass before me leaving real footprints. . . . They're bursting with stories, too many to be told. They've lived through centuries of history in a single life time—village-born, colonized, traditionally raised, educated. What they've assimilated in 30 years has taken the West 10 times that number of years to create. Time travel is a reality—I've seen it in my own life. Bionic men and women are living among us.

Sidhwa, at the time she wrote "Defend Yourself Against Me," was not an immigrant but divided her time between her native Pakistan and the United States. Unlike her earlier novels (*The Crow Eaters* [1978][1] *The Bride* [1983], and *Ice-Candy-Man* [1988]), which are all situated in Pakistan, her short story "Defend Yourself Against Me"—like her latest novel, *An American Brat*—is situated in the States. This story gives a vivid picture of an immigrant Indo-Pakistani community while Sidhwa focuses on her Pakistani heritage and her feminist consciousness. While both Sidhwa and Mukherjee are changing their themes with their popularity—Mukherjee in her latest novel, *The Holder of the*

World, incorporating her Indian heritage, and Sidhwa her American experience—these two short stories aptly suggest their divergences and the concerns that inspire the majority of their work.

Bharati Mukherjee's dominant theme is the immigrant—the process of Americanization, of assimilation and acculturation. Her novels *Wife* (1975), *Jasmine* (1989), and her collections of short stories, *Darkness* (1985) and *The Middleman and Other Stories* (1988), all focus on the immigrant experience. Mukherjee sees herself as a prime example of the American immigrant, suggesting her oneness with the immigrants who arrived at Ellis Island. But Bharati Mukherjee is different from the immigrants who arrived at Ellis Island. The experience of these early immigrants was a bitterly painful one. After days of voyaging, they were put through an immigration process that was rough and insensitive, to say the very least. The experience of these early immigrants is brilliantly summed up in Sam Hamod's *Dying with the Wrong Name* in which the immigration official, tired and indifferent, tells the new arrival, "You only need two names in America" and promptly renames the new immigrant, thus beginning the process of Americanization (19). The process of acculturation and assimilation is long and arduous. Coming from a privileged background, Bharati Mukherjee is different from these huddled masses. A Bengali, she is also different from the mainstream, but this difference does not matter today in a climate of multiculturalism. She does not have to change her name or to anglicize it. She can revel in the difference that permits her a double culture. There need be no loss of her Indian heritage. Instead there is the acquisition of American culture. "I have always felt that I possess both cultures and that I can enter both 100 percent" ("Darkening"). As she points out in her introduction to *Darkness*, difference is "a set of fluid identities to be celebrated" (3).

In *The Middleman and Other Stories*, Mukherjee expands her canvas to include immigrants from different ethnic backgrounds. Thus there is Renata, an Italian American woman with her Afghan date, an Indian motel clerk, an Iraqi Jew, and a Sri Lankan—(the latter, however, does not quite make it to the States). The majority of Mukherjee's stories, however, focus on Indians. Although the eponymous heroine in *Jasmine* undergoes a series of transformations, from Jyoti to Jasmine to Jane Ripplemeyer, Mukherjee stresses the double self that the new immigrant is free to possess. Jasmine does not become subsumed in the "Jane Ripplemeyer" self at the end. Like Mukherjee herself, these Indian immigrants possess both cultures. This theme is clearly manifest in Mukherjee's short story "The Management of Grief."

Bapsi Sidhwa, unlike Bharati Mukherjee, was not an American immigrant at the time she wrote "Defend Yourself Against Me." Though now she has settled down permanently in the States, at the time she wrote "Defend Yourself Against Me" she was dividing her time between her native Pakistan and teaching creative writing at a number of universities in the United States. Sidhwa's main body of work—until *An American Brat*—focused on her home country. As a Parsi in an Islamic country that came into being on the basis of religion, she wrote about her community and also questioned religious and ethnic prejudices and taboos. As a woman in a society dominated by purdah and its mores, she recorded her protest at the discriminations and cruelties perpetrated against women.

As she tells interviewers, Sidhwa was inspired to write after learning about an incident in which a runaway bride was killed for adultery (Yasin 4). The resulting book, *The Bride*, was not published, however, until she gained recognition for *The Crow Eaters* (1978). In her third book, *Ice-Candy-Man*—which was renamed *Cracking-India* in the American edition—the focus is on the turmoil that attended the partition of the Indian subcontinent into the independent states of India and Pakistan in 1947. Against this backdrop, however, Sidhwa depicts man's many forms of cruelty toward woman. Gang-rape, prostitution, child marriage, war crimes against women, religious taboos—all come under attack. *The Crow Eaters* is perhaps the only one of Sidhwa's books that does not strive for women's rights. Even in this book, though, Sidhwa's concern for women manifests itself in the figures of Putli and her mother who, in different ways, hold their own against Faredoon Junglewalla—or Freddy—whose life and fortunes form the focus of the book.

While Sidhwa specifically concentrates on politics only in *Ice-Candy-Man*, a little politics invariably enters in almost all of her books. Thus, *The Bride* begins with the confusion of partition and then follows the girl who is the bride of the title as she and her adoptive father settle down in a new land; and *The Crow Eaters*, while it concentrates on the fortune and foibles of Freddy, touches briefly on the political climate of partition—which Freddy foresees as taking place after his death. In other words, all three novels that Sidhwa wrote before her stay in the States focus in some way on the politics of the subcontinent, in particular the politics of the partition. After Sidhwa's spectacular success as a writer, she was invited to the United States to lecture at a number of universities: Rice University, 1984–86; University of Houston, 1985; Columbia University, 1989. Her stay opened up not only new audiences for her fiction, but also new themes. In the short story "Defend Yourself Against Me," Sidhwa's feminist and political concerns blend with the diaspora theme. A comparison of Sidhwa's short story with Bharati Mukherjee's "The Management of Grief" is both informative and interesting, showing how the concerns of the writers enter their stories. In both stories the old world intrudes into the new, as old political and religious passions affect the lives of the new immigrants. Because Sidhwa was not a permanent resident of the United States when she wrote her story (and therefore focused on women's issues in her native country), the major focus of the story is how women cope with violence and memories of violence; in her story Mukherjee stresses how settlers cope with old world problems in order to become new Americans or Canadians.

Like the other stories in Mukherjee's collection *The Middleman and Other Stories*, "The Management of Grief" is about a new immigrant in North America and the process and emotional adjustment that makes a new immigrant a citizen of his/her adopted country. The story was written in the aftermath of the Air India crash of 1985—about which Mukherjee and her husband also wrote a nonfictional account in *The Sorrow and the Terror* (1987). In "The Management of Grief," Mukherjee describes the effect of this crash on the life of Shaila Bhave who loses husband and both sons in the crash. It could have been any accident that killed Shaila's husband and sons, but Mukherjee chooses an incident which links the accident to India, the home the immigrants left behind when they chose to settle in the west. In telling the story of Shaila Bhave, Mukherjee also looks at other immigrants whose lives are affected by this accident. Young, old, middle-aged, able to cope with tragedy or unable to do so, determined to live a new life in a new country or packing up and going home—all the new settlers are touched by the passions of the old country.

The story of "The Management of Grief" begins quietly in a residential area of Canada peopled by Indian immigrants. Most of these immigrants have made it big. They live in "pink split-level" homes and go back to India during holidays. On one such trip Shaila Bhave's husband and two sons are killed in an airplane crash over England. It is a Sikh bomb that destroys the airplane and the narrator, who had believed that the old ethnic and racial prejudices, jealousies, and fears had been left behind in India, realizes how thin a line separates the new from the old world. Despite herself, though she knows that all Sikhs are not terrorists, she shrinks at the sight of beards and turbans. Old fears come surging back. "I remember a time when we all trusted each other in this new country, it was only the new country we worried about" (193). The crash makes her aware that the past is not dead, that the ethnic and religious conflicts of the home left behind have the power to affect her anew in the new world. The problems of adjustment in a new world are rendered complex by the old problems that have followed her.

Shaila Bhave, like the other Indians, travels to the scene of the accident. Bodies are recovered, but her sons and husband are gone forever. The human toll that tragedy takes, the impact that terrorism makes on ordinary lives, is poignantly touched upon by Mukherjee. Mukherjee's main concern in the short story, however, is the process of adjustment in North America, so she follows Shaila Bhave as she adjusts to life on her own.

The efficient Canadians attempt to "manage the grief" of those who have lost their loved ones in the crash. For some time Shaila accompanies the

Canadian Judith Templeton as she visits the bereaved. But the Canadian way is different from the Indian way, and Shaila realizes that the two cultures are too different for anything to come out of Miss Templeton's visits. She stops accompanying the Canadian social worker.

But though Shaila is different from Judith Templeton, she is also different from the Indians left behind in India—a lesson that she learns when she returns to India with the other grieving relatives. Indians have developed their own ways of "managing grief." Marriages are arranged for widowers. Widows are not supposed to need husbands; instead, they are supposed to spend the rest of their lives mourning for them and praying. So their relations take them to holy places. A friend of Shaila's decides to stay back in India, at an *ashram* in the holy city of Hardwar. Shaila Bhave too is taken by her mother to visit a temple where she has a mystic experience; unlike the experience of her friend, however, it does not tell her to renounce the world. Instead, in a vision she sees her husband who tells her to go back to Canada and finish alone what they started together.

Shaila Bhave goes back to Canada, conscious of her double identity. She can never be wholly Indian, but she can never be wholly Canadian either. She is both Indian and Canadian—and the richer for it. This awareness is not a loss but a gain. Shaila Bhave has the "doubleness of vision" granted only to people who possess two cultures: the culture of the home country and the culture of the adopted land. Shaila Bhave will always be Indian, retaining what is essential of her home culture, but she will also be Canadian, but not Canadian like Judith Templeton who lacks this double vision. Like the new Americans in Mukherjee's other stories, Shaila Bhave is a new Canadian with the sensitivity, the persistence, the resilience needed for every successful immigrant. What Mukherjee succeeds in conveying is that modern immigrants need not and cannot leave their country behind but can carry it with them wherever they go. The exceptional new immigrant, such as Bharati Mukherjee herself, possesses both cultures.

Bapsi Sidhwa is a very recent immigrant. Until recently, she called Lahore, Pakistan, her home. Sidhwa's stay in the States, however, opened up a new milieu for her, the milieu of the Indian/Pakistani immigrant. "Defend Yourself Against Me"—written when Sidhwa was still for all purposes a resident of Lahore—tells the story of Pakistani and Indian immigrants in the States and what happens when the mother of one of the immigrants happens to pay a visit to her son.

The story is told through the eyes of Mrs. Jacobs who has migrated to America and happens to be invited to dinner by an acquaintance named Kishen. At dinner Mrs. Jacobs meets Sikander Khan. "Acclimatized. Americanized" (363). Sikander Khan still speaks English with "a broad Pakistani accent" (363). Mrs. Jacobs soon realizes that she had met Sikander

Khan as a child in Lahore. This realization takes her to the past—a past that she thought she had left behind, not unlike Shaila Bhave. "Too enamored of the dazzling shopping malls and technical opulence of the smoothly operating country of my adoption, too frequent a visitor to Pakistan, I have not yet missed it, or given thought to the past" (363). At Kishen's house—full of Indian bric-a-brac—confronted with Sikander Khan, she is forced to recall the past.

> She remembers when she first met him.
> Lahore, Autumn 1948. Pakistan is a little over a year old. The Partition riots, the arson and slaughter, have subsided. The flood of refugees—12 million Muslims, Hindus and Sikhs fleeing across borders that define India and Pakistan—has shrunk to a narrow trickle. (366)

Before the partition changed everything, Lahore was a city of many religious communities. The Jacobs—Protestants—lived next door to Hindus. After partition the Hindu neighbors fled. Mrs. Jacobs recalls how, as a child, she had noticed signs of occupation in the abandoned house after the Hindu neighbors had left. She remembers seeing Sikander as a small boy, "so extremely thin he [looked] like a brittle skeleton" (368). His body was marked with scars and wounds and on the back of his head was "a raw and flaming scar, as if bone and flesh had been callously gouged out" (369). The scar is still there, years later.

As a child Mrs. Jacobs had not realized the full implications of the little boy's wound, had not realized that when the village had been attacked by Sikhs the women, including Sikander's mother—Ammijee—had been raped. As an adult, years and miles away from home, she learns from Sikander's wife the full horror of what had taken place to bring Sikander and his mother next door to her house in Lahore. The women had wanted to commit suicide, had stored kerosene to pour over their bodies and set themselves alight in case of an attack on their village. But they had had no time to do so when the Sikhs attacked. Young and old, Ammijee and her eleven-year-old daughter, all had suffered equally. Years later, the recital of these wrongs moves the audience— all who had been too young to have fully understood the horrors of partition.

The new immigrants understand that, while on this occasion the Muslim village had suffered the vengeance of the Sikhs, on other occasions Hindu and Sikh villages had suffered in similar fashion, with women bearing the brunt. "God knows how many women were lifted . . . but then, everybody carried women off. Sikhs and Hindus Muslim women. Muslims, Sikh and Hindu women" (373).

Halfway through dinner, two Sikhs join the group. Mrs. Jacobs, knowing Ammijee's story, is surprised that Sikander Khan is friendly with them. She senses a little unease when they inquire about the impending arrival of Sikander Khan's mother, but the next moment the Sikhs are relaxed, talking Punjabi with Sikander Khan's wife and sister-in-law. Mrs. Jacobs thinks she must have imagined the unease.

Later Mrs. Jacobs asks Sikander Khan how he can be so friendly with Sikhs. Weren't Sikhs responsible for what happened to him, his mother and sister? But Sikander Khan tells her that his friends were not guilty of the rapes, and if they were guilty so was he. Hadn't Muslims raped Hindu and Sikh women during partition? "Why quarrel with Kushwant and Pratap? They weren't even born. . . .We Muslims are no better . . . we did the same . . Hindu, Muslim, Sikh, we are all evil bastards" (377).

Mrs. Jacobs meets Ammijee. Seeing the old woman, she is surprised that there are no marks of the past on her. "There's no trace of bitterness. No melancholy. Nothing knowing or hard. Just the open, acquiescent, hospitable face of a contented peasant woman who is happy to visit her son. It is difficult to believe this quiet woman was kidnapped, raped, sold" (377). But the past cannot be so easily forgotten as Mrs. Jacobs soon realizes in the dramatic climax of this story.

One night Sikander Khan invites his Hindu and Sikh friends to meet his mother. Mrs. Jacobs is surprised to see "two huge and hirsute Indian fakirs" instead of the two dapper Sikhs she had met earlier. Prostrating themselves before Ammijee, the Sikhs beg her forgiveness. "Maajee, forgive us! Forgive us the wrongs of our fathers" (380). The kind-faced woman has not forgotten—as the Sikhs have not—and Mrs. Jacobs is surprised to see the kindly woman transformed. "It is as if her features have been parodied in a hidden mask. They are all there: the bitterness, the horror, the hate: the incarnation of that tree of ugly possibilities seeded in my mind when Sikander, in a cold fury, imitating the voices of the street vendors his mother had described, said, Zana for sale! Zana for Sale!" (382). But then, in a strange, unpredictable turn, the old woman of Sidhwa's story exorcises the ghosts of the past. She tells the two Sikhs that she has forgiven their fathers. "My sons, I forgave your fathers long ago. How else could I live?" (383).

The memories of the past, Sidhwa suggests, cannot be wiped out. They follow new immigrants half way around the world, to remind them, as in Mukherjee's story, that the old world remains. The happy community of Hindus, Muslims, Sikhs, and Christians in the little U.S. town is racked by past traumas, but perhaps, as Sidhwa suggests, it is only in this new home away from home that the past can be confronted in this manner and finally exorcised. Acutely aware of the past, Pakistanis and Indians can come together in a new way. Away from their home country these subcontinentals can forget their old enmities but, because the past cannot be left behind, they must confront it. The perpetrators must ask forgiveness for their sins and the victims must forgive because, suggests Sidhwa, without this there is no going on.

The stories of both Sidhwa and Mukherjee suggest that the quarrels and emotions of the old world are never too far behind. But the stories also suggest a new beginning in the new world. Mukherjee, less concerned with past traumas than with how immigrants become Americans, shows how Shaila Bhave is both Indian and Canadian. Sidhwa, with her political and feminist concerns, uses her short story to suggest, through Mary Jacobs, the vulnerability of women: "The vulnerability of mothers, daughters, granddaughters and their metamorphosis into possessions; living objects on whose soft bodies victors and losers alike vent their wrath, enact fantasies, celebrate victory" (380). But even as Mary Jacobs realizes women's vulnerability, she also realizes the strength women must have in order to defend themselves against the forces that would destroy them.

Bharati Mukherjee's concern in "The Management of Grief" is with the way in which a new arrival becomes a new immigrant; Sidhwa is concerned with the trauma of partition and the vulnerability of women—concerns that form the themes of Sidhwa's other books as well. Women's vulnerability, Sidhwa suggests, is not limited to the Indian subcontinent but is experienced worldwide. It is not a matter of the past only, but also of the present. Mukherjee concerns herself with the synthesizing experience. Sidhwa looks within the synthesizing experience at the differences, the age–old passions, and at women's continued vulnerability and strength everywhere.

Note

1. Though written after *The Bride, The Crow Eaters* was published earlier.

References

Alam, Fakrul. "From the Aloofness of Expatriation to the Exuberance of Immigration: Bharati Mukherjee's Progress." Pp. 122–33 in *Migrants, Migration, and the United States*, eds. Niaz Zaman and Kamal Uddin Ahmed. Dhaka, Bangladesh: BAAS, 1992.

"The 'Darkening' of America." *Asiaweek*, 27 April 1990, 50.

Hamod, Sam. *Dying with the Wrong Name.* New York: Anthé Publications, 1980.

Mukherjee, Bharati. *Darkness.* New York: Penguin Books, 1985.

————. "Immigrant Writing: Give Us Your Maximalists." *New York Times Book Review*, 28 August 1988, sec. 7, pp. 3, 28-29.

————. "An Interview With Bharati Mukherjee." *The Massachusetts Review*, (winter 1988–89), 645–54.

————. *Jasmine*. New York: Grove Weidenfeld, 1989.

————. *The Middleman and Other Stories*. New York: Grove Press, 1988

————. *Wife*. Boston: Houghton Mifflin, 1975.

Naipaul, V. S. *An Area of Darkness*. New York: Macmillan, 1965.

————. *The Enigma of Arrival*. Harmondsworth, England: Viking. 1987.

————. *In a Free State*. New York: Knopf, 1979.

————. *A House for Mr. Biswas*. Harmondsworth, England: Penguin, 1969.

————. *The Mimic Men*. New York: Macmillan, 1967.

Sidhwa, Bapsi. *An American Brat*. Minneapolis: Milkweed, 1993.

————. *The Bride*. 1987, Karachi: Liberty Books, 1983.

————. *The Crow Eaters*. 1982. Glasgow: Fontana, 1978.

————. *Ice-Candy-Man*. 1989. Harmondsworth: Penguin, 1988.

————. "Defend Yourself Against Me." *Colours of a New Day: Writing for South Africa*, eds. Stephan Haywood and Sarah Le Fanu. New York: Pantheon Books, 1990.

Theroux, Paul. *V. S. Naipaul: An Introduction to His Work*. New York: Africana Publishing Corp., 1972.

Yasin, Mohammad. "Bapsi Sidhwa—from Housewife to Fiction Writer." *Pakistan Times*, 27 April 1990, 4.

Zaman, Niaz. "Alienation in the Writings of V. S. Naipaul." *Dhaka University Studies*, December 1984, part a, 1–7.

————. "Bapsi Sidhwa's American Brat." To be included in proposed volume of essays on Bapsi Sidhwa to be edited by R. K. Dhawan.

————. "From Bradford to Bharati." Pp. 87–98 in *Migrants, Migration, and the United States*, eds. Niaz Zaman and Kamal Uddin Ahmed. Dhaka, Bangladesh: BAAS, 1992.

————. Personal interview with Bapsi Sidhwa.

6

SPLITTING IMAGES: *THE SATANIC VERSES* AND THE INCOMPLETE MAN

Samir Dayal

The saturation coverage of (admittedly important) issues revolving around Khomeini's *fatwa* has tended to obscure the accuracy with which Salman Rushdie's *Satanic Verses* identifies a central problematic in postcolonial subject-formation, which I want to explore here: the theme of incompleteness. The novel's focus on the diasporic postcolonial resituates the correlation between the postmodern subject's fragmentation and the incompleteness of the socially and politically marginalized postcolonial subject. By turning the reader's attention back to this incompleteness of those who are marginalized in the global economy, Rushdie redirects the emphasis from the almost triumphalist rhetoric of postmodernism (where the West is repeatedly figured as the touchstone for global cultural transformation). This relocation of cultural discourse is presumably along the lines of the radical rethinking Homi Bhabha calls for when he argues that the "very language" of the Western metropolitan cultural community needs to be reconceived with reference to postcolonial critique in the way that Western categories of gender, sexuality, and race have been rethought in response to the intervention of feminism, or gay and black studies ("Postcolonial", 437).

If the adjective in Rushdie's title does not refer merely to the key episode concerning Mahound and Lat, Manat, and Uzza, if it refers to something more general than Islamic orthodoxy, then what is the opposite, "angelic"? What is "satanic" here, who is "demonized," why, and how? What is the cultural urgency of these questions and of the novel? Rushdie's epigraph offers an important clue, insofar as it thematizes the devil's condition as rootlessness and exile, as incompleteness. Translated to the postcolonial context, the topos of the devil's punishment is reappropriated not, *pace* Srinivas Aravamudan, simply as the denial of a "unified terrestrial locale" to a subhuman creature, but as the denial of a locus anchoring a whole subjectivity.

But the devil is interesting precisely because he strives to transgress punishment into potentiality and potency. The significance of the devil's nomadism and exile becomes here a figure for the incomplete subject, a figure that speaks to the condition of Farishta and Chamcha, postcolonial diasporics, and by implication to something that in a weak sense humanizes us all: our distance from the "angelic." But he also emerges in this book as a figure for the transgression or at least resistance of the marginalized "other." This is the core of the attraction of the topos of the satanic, for Rushdie.

Rushdie himself has emphasized that here he is "writing for the first time from the whole of myself. The English part, the Indian part" (Marzorati, 100). Even here Rushdie presents the "whole of myself" as split, and I suggest that this ambivalence is critical to the conception of the main characters. The novel not only refers to his own situation as a well-placed writer in the metropolitan West, but resonates with larger social and political concerns of marginal constituencies in the West. They remain incomplete in terms of political and social self-representation, and therefore in terms of psychic self-representation. It is probably no great exaggeration for Yasmin Alibhai-Brown to speak of the British media's "obsessional need to portray the darkish folk who live on these [British] isles as *demonic* and brutish, especially those who resist total assimilation into mainstream cultural and social life" (28; my emphasis). Rushdie's adjective "satanic" can be read as a description of the damage, psychic and otherwise, sustained by the postcolonial subject, not only in the postcolonial Third World context but also, in a transnational. This is the great subject of the novel.

Gayatri Spivak points to what I have already suggested is a particularly important manifestation of the subject; she writes that the novel has "rather an aggressive central theme: the postcolonial divided between two identities: migrant and national" (219). Rushdie declines to choose between approving of "fanatic exile" and endorsing the postcolonial's "attempt to become the metropolitan" (221). Scrupulously refusing to presume to speak for every postcolonial migrant and territorial native (subaltern?), Rushdie thematizes a critique of his own situation as diasporic in the Western metropole, in the first place by recognizing its complexities. Through the negative example of the exilic (Indian?) Imam the text makes clear that exile "must not be confused with . . . all the other words that people throw around: émigré, expatriate, refugee, immigrant, silence, cunning. Exile is a dream of glorious return. . . It is an endless paradox: looking forward by always looking back. . . . Exile is a soulless country. . ." (*SV*, 205, 208).

What Spivak does not stress, however, is that Rushdie seems to see the *condition of diaspora* as pivotal to rethinking postcolonial agency. The translated transnationals of the novel discover diaspora as a double dispersal: not only geographical dispersal and the attendant splitting of one's sense of an imagined community, of national belonging—the postcolonial's predicament—but also the metaphorical, postmodernist dispersal of the subject across a confused referential field, "fragmented" (not "alienated," for that would be a modernist phenomenon) in Fredric Jameson's terms (63). Rushdie's emphasis is on multiplicity, on the imbrication of the materiality and specificity of the local with flows of desire and (cultural) capital; not on the homogeneity of "the Third World" but its hybridity, its necessary fragmentariness; not on the hope of angelic redemption but on the thoroughly secular possibility of turning incompleteness back into agency within community.

A distinction must be made between incompleteness as a theoretical problematic and incompleteness as a periodized sign of postmodernist times and places, as Jameson might insist. There is, however, some convergence between the two approaches, particularly where the latter has been reenergized by debates about the postmodern moment. While Rushdie's fictional universes are ordered by their own principles, they take their significance from the larger social, political, and aesthetic issues with which they intersect. The investigation of the subject's incompleteness is inextricably linked to Rushdie's meditation on the constitution of a pluralist society. Thus the issue is not what will fill the lacunae in the incomplete (postmodern or postcolonial) subject, but what agency means, as articulated at the ambivalent and hybrid sites of enunciation. This is what saves the novel's obsessive question—*"What kind of idea is He? What kind am I?"* (111; my emphases)— from solipsism or narcissism; as a representative of "minor literature," *The Satanic Verses* thematizes what Gilles Deleuze and Felix Guattari identify, in their topology of minor literature, as "the connection of the individual to a political immediacy" (18).

Rushdie stages a tension between the ideal of the subject as "angelic" plenitude versus the reality of the subject as "satanically" incomplete. Incompleteness, however, is to be understood as having both a positive, productive dimension as well as a negative. Incompleteness in its negative sense is clearly a leitmotiv: Farishta and Chamcha experience the most dehumanizing (and, simultaneously, most humanizing) of experiences: an overdetermined self-division to the point of literal schizophrenia; psychological damage; self-hatred; the loss of home, love, family, country, friendship, and even life. The theme could hardly be more memorably put than in the novel's epigraph from Daniel Defoe which describes the devil's lot as rudderless exile from everything that makes one whole.

This is not the only Rushdie novel to present incompleteness as a kind of demonization. Many of his works present the postcolonial subject as emblematic of an unfinished recovery from colonialism. It is also true that his novels' central themes intersect with developments in postmodernism; here it is important to note that Rushdie's consciousness of the friability of the subject, its fictiveness and discontinuity, is coherent with postmodern notions of the subject as a construction within an antiessentialist paradigm. Saleem Sinai, in *Midnight's Children*, suggests that "a human being, inside himself, is anything but a whole, anything but homogeneous" (283). The body may be "indivisible, a one-piece suit, a sacred temple" (283)—but its wholeness is fragile and tenuous, undone by the loss of a finger or even hairs from the head: "Uncork the body, and God knows what you permit to come tumbling out" (283).

The narrator of *The Satanic Verses*, similarly, intervenes on this crucial issue: "the idea of the self as being (ideally) homogeneous, non–hybrid, 'pure,'—an utterly fantastic notion!—cannot, must not, suffice" (427). Chamcha's antiessentialist education unfolds chiefly under Zeeny's tutelage. She has written a book on "the confining myth of authenticity, that folkloristic straitjacket . . . "(52). Refusing that strategy of containment, Zeeny promotes a transnationalism. She seeks to replace the "straitjacket" by "an ethic of historically validated eclecticism, for was not the entire national culture based on the principle of borrowing whatever clothes seemed to fit, Aryan, Mughal, British, take–the–best–and–leave–the–rest?" (52). In her Rushdie presents the ambition of tracing imaginative and *imaginary* ways of resisting the forcible deterritorialized location of desire in a transcendent principle ("God," "Man," the "nation," the axioms of the capitalist cultural economy, and "The Individual"). While it seems inexact to place Rushdie within what Alex Callinicos calls the "antihumanist" paradigm in Deleuze and Guattari, Derrida or Foucault, one could describe his conceptualization of agency as posthumanist. Thus Zeeny's bon mot in her book title: "She had called it *The Only Good Indian*. Meaning, is a dead. . . Why should there be a good, right way of being a wog? That's Hindu fundamentalism. Actually, we're all bad Indians. Some worse than others" (52).

But Rushdie's main interest here is not in rehearsing a theory of antiessentialism. More relevant is the imbrication of the conditions for antiessentialist agency with the possibility of pluralist community. Such agency is founded on a critique of First World modernity and subjectivistic rationality at which, according to some "postmodernist" accounts, the Third World has not yet arrived but with which the First has already become disenchanted. This is why Rushdie's novel is relevant to discussions of the "posts" of postmodernism and postcolonialism.

There is a "need," as S. P. Mohanty writes, "for a basic definition of human agency, and the conception of rationality it implies should be faced directly by political criticism" (2). But what we need is not the credo of individualism, which Joan Scott observes is, in the U.S. context, the "prevailing ideology" undergirding "the conservatives' critique of multiculturalism" (17). Nor do we need some soft liberal notion of cultural diversity—a safe accommodation. We need a critical energization of the *differential* articulations of the basic categories of class, race, nation, and gender. These categories risk, it is true, turning into an overfamiliar litany. But it is important nonetheless to stress their place in a critique of everyday social life, where the double investigation of agency and community (as *negotiations* of the very definitions of class, race, nation, and gender) are ways of marking the shifting balance of power, of relative access to resources without a teleology of closure.

Therefore, there is an analogy between the incompleteness of the subject and that of the community. The positive or productive sense of unfinishedness entails a recognition of the processual and pluralized nature of agency within the discursive space of society. This also means that the demands of minority groups within the society at large are not once-and-for-all demands. Social life is continual negotiation and interaction, not always among a homogeneous group of people but among splinter groups or ethnic factions who may have conflictual demands.

Accordingly, the productive sense of incompleteness of subject and society also involves a recognition of the *coeval* articulation of the subject and the other, so that what we call "society" has meaning only when political subjects acquire agency in social discourse. Political community—within which agency is enunciated—is, as Chantal Mouffe argues, a "discursive surface" and not an empirical referent: "Politics is about the constitution of the political community, and not something that takes place within the political community" (30).

The text of "the individual" or "the social group" then must be read and reread as a text, even if it sometimes opens the door to the satanic or mischievous *perruque*, as described by Michel de Certeau, of rewriting the social or sacralized or scripturally secured text transgressively, as Salman the foreigner does in that apocryphal episode of *Satanic Verses*. Agency then consists in negotiating the discursive spaces of society, be they mutually opaque. But the political community or society in which agency is articulated need not depend on any illusions of access to a unifying Habermasian discourse of modernity. Jean-Francois Lyotard's rejection of this Habermasian hope as a totalizing discourse of normative consensualism is a necessary reminder of the perpetually unfinished nature of those discursive spaces, and indeed of the untotalizable nature of agency. And Jameson adds the analytic of the cultural logic of late capitalism as a corrective against a naive individualism. But, as I have argued, one must go beyond these crucial postmodernist debates to a postcolonial problematization of agency in political community.

The novel, then, points to a conception of agency within community that does not fetishize or totalize the subject as a self-sufficient construct. In so doing it also underscores the plurality of agency, the plurality of sites and positionalities from which agency is articulated, and the endlessness of negotiation (sometimes even conflict) between and among the various constituencies so represented. Achille Mbembe reminds us that the "postcolony is made up not of one coherent 'public space,' nor . . . determined by any single organizing principle" but rather a "plurality of [discrete but connected] 'spheres' and arenas. . ." (5). But a skewed insistence on the divergence of histories and traditions could result in the kind of communalist tensions that are rife in India as well as elsewhere, although the self-obsessed Chamcha becomes fully aware of them late in the novel (518).

On the other hand, in a global cultural economy, the reification of nation, class, race, ethnicity, or gender as authenticating categories could freeze sites of otherness as ethnological confirmation of the dominant cultural ideology and its location "elsewhere," usually in the metropolitan West. Besides, such a reification could also insinuate itself into the marginalized person's psyche as a "justification" for the sense of a deserved inferiority, because of which the "other" subject participates in her own abjection. Rushdie presents this insight through the Manticore, organizer of the uprising of the literally demonized inmates of an almost Foucauldian sanatorium in Britain, who tells Saladin Chamcha—recently metamorphosed, like Gregor Samsa, his near-namesake—that "they have the power of description, and we succumb to the pictures they construct." (168).

The question irrepressibly presents itself: What is an effective response to this demonization of the marginalized? How can the "others" resist succumbing to the "pictures they construct"? Within the Western metropolitan context of Rushdie's novel, Hanif Johnson certainly emerges as the most confident agent against the describers' discursive hegemony. He is in "perfect control of the languages that mattered: sociological, socialistic, black-radical, anti-anti-anti-racist, demagogic, oratorical, sermonic: the languages of power" (281). Rushdie's novel zealously upholds the primacy of language, as theorized in Lacanian analysis, not only in the sense of the discursive constitution of subjectivity *and* society—that "the world of words . . . creates the world of things" and that there is no subjectivity prior to the Symbolic—but in the sense that the unconscious, too, is structured like a language (*Écrits*, 65; *Four Fundamental Concepts*, 203). Farishta and Chamcha, like Hanif, are nothing if not word men.

But Hanif's relatively successful agency and self-representation, because it is based on the mastery of the discourse of mastery, represents an *elite* mode of resistance that may actually widen gaps among ethnic or cultural groups. This mode of resistance redirects the already charged struggle for resources into a sort of ethnographic Social Darwinist paradigm, minority against minority, rather than encouraging productive negotiation among the minority groups and between minority and dominant groups. The "successful" few from among the ranks of the marginalized are tokenized by the powers that be as "good examples" of *assimilated* minorities, further demonizing those who remain unassimilated.

As for the "dominant Identity, " R. Radhakrishnan argues, it suffers from a kind of neurosis because "it refuses to deal with the historical reality of different alterior constituencies." A symptom of that neurotic insularity is a tendency to "expect that the marginal constituencies make mysterious sense within their respective ghettos. This is a ruthless denial of world-historical possibilities of intelligibility [and] an excuse" not to attend seriously to the alien text (12-13). Like Mouffe, Radhakrishnan theorizes a pursuit of common ground as an alternative to the vitiating politics of race. This pursuit, he says, could relieve political debate in the United States from its "pathological preoccupation with 'race'" and move it toward critical appreciation of different cultures and histories (13). Alleluia Cone's father does not understand the meaning of a plural society; Otto, an Anglophile like Chamcha, misrecognizes the fact that "the modern city . . . is the locus classicus of incompatible realities. Lives that have no business mingling with one another sit side by side upon the omnibus" (314). He undertakes to identify with privileged whites in order to become "a pantomime member of the English gentry." In his lust for assimilation, he nurtures prejudices about racial and political otherness, arguing that "the most dangerous of all the lies we are fed in our lives" is "the idea of the continuum" for in his opinion the world does not "add up," that it is not homogeneous but "incompatible . . . gaga" (295). Allie's interpretation of the American melting pot as a kind of soup in which difference is erased (298) is, similarly, dangerously misguided, particularly because it happens to be a popular understanding.

But separatism on the basis of race and class is not the only recourse: as Bhabha suggests, there is also a kind of social addition of adding to without adding up (Seminar). If we are vigilant we will not let enthusiasm for finding "common ground" distort a willingness to tolerate agential performativity or rationality that conflicts with, or even is opaque to our own, in negotiating community. The health of a community, even a global community, may be measured in its capacity for civil debate, negotiation, and the negative capacity to resist the seductive illusion of closure, in every sense of the word. This kind of addition allows for *tactics* that do not add up to an ossified *strategy* of a rule-bound, closed society—it remains true to the principle of the "incomplete" negotiation of the social. Besides, separatism aborts the endless process of true citizenship. The "End of History" is only the obverse of

Imam's "Untime." Bakhtin's dialogic model of community is better, balancing centripetal forces of community and centrifugal enunciations of agency (272–7).

I am certainly not advocating a hopeless Utopianism in which a sort of ecumenical museum of cultures is set up—booths for culture vultures and ethnographic tourists. What I am suggesting is that civil debate should be welcomed as an engine of social transformation, and the undecidable and indeterminate aspects of articulations of agency must be cautionary even in literary and cultural studies.

What must not be missed is Rushdie's abjuration of transcendence or angelic completeness. This crucial ascesis renders the subject's incompleteness as a fundamentally unusable negativity. But unusable negativity is also a register of pain, particularly psychological damage. Like Baal and Salman, whose great disillusionment leads them into depression and atheism (376), Farishta and Chamcha must come to terms with their own splitting, their psychic pain. Farishta's pain is nothing less than a clinically diagnosed schizophrenia: the plenum of full subjectivity recedes and splinters the closer approached—as Farishta the Angel, or as the farishta (film star) who plays the Farishta on screen, or as the flesh-and-blood Mr. Farishta misguidedly imagining a return to his former eminence as the Actor apotheosized in Indian cinema.[1]

The polyvocal significance of "splitting" can hardly be exaggerated here.[2] Splitting obliquely figures the diasporic condition but also the splitting of the divine word of the Recitation (Qu'ran) by the satanic word—the subversion of power by the *perruque*—of the skeptic Salman, identified with what now seems sublime irony as the Foreigner. Splitting is indeed the book's obsessive image. Farishta "characterize[s] his 'possessed,' 'angel' self . . . in the Beckettian formula, *Not I. He.*" He profanely imagines himself Mahound's adversary and homoerotic other: "Mahound wrestles the archangel, hurling him from side to side, and let me tell you he's getting in *everywhere*, his tongue in my ear his fist around my balls . . ." (122). There are jokes about schizophrenia, and there is the image of Farishta as schizophrenic out for a walk in the city—Deleuze's and Guattari's image. But Farishta is not so much a Deleuzian as a postcolonial, Fanonian, flâneur. He fantasizes himself the "great Transformer," strolling in a postmodern Jahilia, London. He boasts he will "bring [the] metropolis of the ungodly . . . back to God" (320, 322). He threatens to "tropicalize" England: "No more British reserve; hot water bottles to be banished forever, replaced in the foetid nights by the making of slow and odorous love. Emergence of new social values . . . " (354). The Fanonian logic seems to describe Chamcha too: "The native is an oppressed person whose permanent dream is to become the persecutor" (qtd. *SV* 353, 354).

The pain of the two central characters—depressives par excellence—is increased by their obvious specularity. Each one's complaint against the universe is internalized as self-hatred and hatred of the other in whom each sees something of himself and with whom each forms a homoerotic bond, and whom therefore each must destroy, absorbing the opposition and simultaneously retaining the loved other. Julia Kristeva points out that "the analysis of depression involves bringing to the fore the realization that the complaint against oneself is a hatred of the other, which is without doubt the substratum of an unsuspected sexual desire" (11). Chamcha blames his alter ego for abandonment—the "Inexcusable Thing" (426) and wants to wound him, though he is also profoundly protective. Gibreel calls Chamcha his "brother" (438) as well as adversary. Kristeva describes this syndrome of wished destruction and possession as "melancholy cannibalism . . . account[ing] for [the] passion for holding within the mouth (but vagina and anus also lend themselves to this control) the intolerable other that I crave to destroy so as to better possess it alive. Better fragmented, torn, cut up, swallowed, digested . . . than lost" (12). Thus Farishta saves his sworn enemy; Chamcha, despite himself and because of his painful Kafkaesque transformation, becomes a figurehead for antiracist struggle (287).

Chamcha is identified as Farishta's adversary (367, 462, 463) who is also his own enemy: "self-hating, constructing a false ego, auto-destructive" (353). Rushdie, again, invokes Fanon as a frame for this postcolonial self-disgust: "'In this way the individual'—the Fanonian *native*—'accepts the disintegration ordained by God, bows down before the settler and his lot, and by a kind of interior restabilization acquires a stony calm'" (Fanon qtd. *SV*, 353). Thus the satanic aspects of Farishta's and Chamcha's lives is a metaphor for their self-loathing, self-doubt, and splitting as well as their confused desire—"the dangerous interstitial, invaginated relation of the 'factual' and the 'fantasmatic,'" to appropriate Homi Bhabha's expression, that each must traverse.

Like Fanon, Ashis Nandy and others have detailed the self-loathing of the postcolonial, even after the historical fact of decolonization, as fundamental to the aetiology of the postcolonial's self-division. Chamcha wants, like Nirad Chaudhuri before him, "though without any of that impish, colonial intelligence's urge to be seen as an enfant terrible—to be worthy of the challenge represented by the phrase *Civis Britannicus sum*" (398). He acquiesces in the most basic of postcolonial self-subjugations: the necessity to define himself not only in the terms but in the image of the former colonial "master." Indeed, he becomes an apologist for Britain against immigrants insisting on their fair share. He wants to Anglicize himself—he even "[finds] himself dreaming of the Queen . . . making tender love to the Monarch" (169). Chamcha seems nominally to have achieved his ignominious ambition to become "British citizen, first class," through marriage; de facto, he remains a marginalized black man in "proper London," as is clear from his humiliation by the British immigration officers in an episode redolent of racist contempt for and sexual fascination with the dark man, demonized here of course literally and figuratively as well-endowed satyr.

That episode is an unforgettable emblem of the hateful exclusion (itself riven by near-erotic fascination with otherness) of marginal groups from First World society as at once terrifyingly same and different. This is the source of tremendous psychic damage on both sides. The "others" are *different* because no matter how close they come to being British, the content of their subjectivity can always be "described" as "different" by the dominant groups, as is clear in one popular representation of Rushdie himself as being an ungrateful foreigner now seeking the protection of the magnanimous Britain he chose to criticize. They are terrifyingly *same* by virtue of their humanity and by virtue of the fact that they fundamentally want access to the resources and quality of life that the majority wishes to take for granted, and unchallenged by the annoyingly endless negotiation with these marginal groups. This sameness confounds the supremacist, fascist rhetoric of racial and ethnic "purity." It frustrates and troubles racist nostrums of those who seek to exclude the other from enjoying precisely those pleasures that they themselves desire.

Farishta's delusions and splitting destroy him. He is attracted to the "terrifying" singularity—pure self-sufficiency—of Mahound: "One one one" (102). He never rises above his preference for clear ("pure") oppositions and definitions over the "greys" of English life, remaining an "untranslated man" (427). But if he remains uninfected by Chamcha's degrading wish to remake himself in the image of the former colonizer, he is more unworldly (living up to his name) and more unfit for the world. He commits suicide with his worldly confidant and other as witness.

Chamcha muses on life as a continuum of melancholy or sadness, bereft of his four loves: "Culture, city, wife," and the secret dream of fatherhood (400, 516–17). These metonyms of the migrant's desire for rootedness, too, are the stigmata of his demonization, his deracination. Chamcha eventually realizes that simple withdrawal from his Indianness is not an ethically affirmative position. Hadn't his father early diagnosed his acquisition of a British passport as possession by the devil of mimicry? Thus, his Anglophilia is a source of heretical self-abjection (47, 48). The narrator comments, "A man who sets out to make himself up is taking on the Creator's role" (49)—a ("satanic") usurpation of the father's role. Farishta and Chamcha struggle to make themselves up to approximate an ego-ideal that does not quite gel. This struggle is intimately linked to an Oedipal struggle with an imago of the father. Farishta's   Oedipal   struggles   are   imaginary   conflicts—and identifications—with the God whose angel or messenger he hallucinates being. Chamcha's is a more directly Oedipal agon. He goes to the former colonizer's country as an escape from a country, father, and family of which he is ashamed. But in that deterritorialization he finds alienation and marginalization, rather than true agency or citizenship. Ultimately he must return to his father's bed, to resolve the old Oedipal struggle and "fall in love" with his father again (523).

It is then that Chamcha, for the first time in twenty years, "un–Englishes" his name back to Salahuddin Chamchawalla (524), finds his lost Urdu speaking through him again, feels his life illuminated by the "strangely radiant" and uncompromisingly secular death of his father. The process by which Saladin Chamcha, évolué mimic man, reassumes his cast-off cultural inheritance, might be called his maturation. But since this is a "cosmopolitan" novel, as Bruce Robbins insists, it does not champion simply a fixed, "authentic" cultural identity. The return "home" is not an unproblematic return to an essential or coherent self or cultural synthesis. Farishta, not content to be imperfect, human, fulfills his suppressed death wish. Chamcha accedes to a hysteria in which he simultaneously accepts and resists his Indianness, remaining "satanic," split: "He would enter into his new self . . . be what he had become: loud, stenchy, hideous, outsize, grotesque, *inhuman, powerful*" (288–89; my emphasis). He comes widdershins to an occult affirmation of the telescoped credos of Hinduism and Islam: "'*I am*,' he accepted, '*that I am*.' Submission" (289).

Rushdie thus raises important questions of interstitial and transnational agency in the increasingly global cultural economy, including an exploration into what rationality can drive a socius that does not deprecate or impede the *desire* of globally marginalized people who want to taste the fruits of development. Hence the constant threnody in the novel for a pluralist conceptualization of agency and community. Rushdie champions a secular, "satanically" incomplete pluralism as opposed to a utopian, angelic Untime: this unifies the critique of dogma and the exploration of incompleteness with the meditation on the possibilities for a postcolonial diasporic agency. If the marginalized can reinscribe their demonization, his novel suggests, they can unlock economies of the imaginary where possibilities for transnational and transgressive agency can emerge.

Notes

1. The filmic in Rushdie is almost a metaphor for the register of the Imaginary, where the chaotic dynamic of desire is alive. In India, as Stanley Kurtz observed recently during his expedition into that Area of Darkness, the relation between "reality" and the Real is not lined up in the same way as it is in the West, so that the movies can become a representation of divine reality, so that "film is not treated as a profane medium" (18).

2. Split images are a central motif in the novel, as they are in Rushdie's other work. The doppelganger motif is pervasive. Consider the geographical and epochal doublings of Mishal, Hind, and Ayesha, the specular doubling of Allie and Al-Lat (459), and Allie and Rekha. And then there is the episode of the doublings, couplings, and "ecstatic" self-forgettings that occur in The Curtain where the twelve whores become so accustomed to impersonating the Prophet's twelve wives that they forget their own names (390). Baal the satirical wit of Jahilia doubles for the writer, and the heretical Salman doubles in name and function for the author himself—presciently, one might add. Baal is also paired provocatively with Mahound as his specular image (391), as is Gibreel of course, and the narrator permits himself the hubris of identifying himself as God, refusing to clear Gibreel's confusion about whether the God who had summoned Gibreel was *Ooparvala* or *Neechayvala*: the man upstairs or the devil below. Here the implied fungibility of each identification is to the discredit of the other. These may seem merely gratuitous games of coincidence and structural complications, but they are not, as nobody now knows better than Rushdie. It seems safe to say that Rushdie's original motive for this dizzying doubling must have been part of a more general attempt to explode the myth of the singularity of self, human or divine.

References

Alibhai-Brown, Yasmin. "Marriages of Minds Not Hearts." *New Statesman & Society* 12 (February 1993): 28–29.

Aravamudan, Srinivas. "'Being God's Postman Is No Fun, Yaar': Salman Rushdie's *The Satanic Verses*." *Diacritics* 19, no. 2 (summer 1989): 3–20.

Bakhtin, M.M. *The Dialogic Imagination: Four Essays*, trans. Caryl Emerson and Michael Holquist. Austin: University of Texas Press, 1981.

Benjamin, Walter. *Illuminations*. New York: Schocken Books, 1969.

Bhabha, Homi. "The Commitment to Theory." Pp. 111–32 in *Third Cinema Reader*, eds. J. Pines and P. Willemin. London: British Film Institute, 1989.

————. "Postcolonial Criticism." Pp. 437–65 in *Redrawing the Boundaries: The Transformation of English and American Literary Studies*, eds. Stephen Greenblatt and Giles Gunn. New York: Modern Language Association, 1992.

————. Seminar "The Interdisciplinary Imperative: Modernity and the Postcolonial Condition." School of Criticism and Theory. Dartmouth College, 1993.

Brennan, Timothy A. "India, Nationalism, and Other Failures." *The South Atlantic Quarterly* 87, no. 1 (winter 1988): 131–46.

Callinicos, Alex. *Against Postmodernism*. New York: St. Martin's Press, 1989.

Coronil, Fernando. "Can Postcoloniality Be Decolonized? Imperial Banality and Postcolonial Power." *Public Culture* 5, no. 1 (fall 1992): 89–108.

De Certeau, Michel. *The Practice of Everyday Life*, trans. Steven F. Rendall. Berkeley: University of California Press, 1984.

Deleuze, Gilles, and Felix Guattari. "Kafka: Towards a Minor Literature." Trans. Dana Polan. Minneapolis: University of Minnesota Press, 1986.

Easterman, Daniel. "The Erection is Eternal." *New Statesman & Society* 12 February 1993, 26–27.

Habermas, Jürgen. *The Philosophical Discourse of Modernity*, trans. Frederick Lawrence. Cambridge, Mass: M I T Press, 1987.

Kristeva, Julia. *Black Sun: Depression and Melancholia*. Trans, Leon S. Roudiez. New York, Columbia University Press, 1989.

Jameson, Fredric. "Postmodernism, or the Cultural Logic of Late Capitalism." *New Left Review* 146 (1984): 53-92.

Kurtz, Stanley N. *All the Mothers Are One: Hindu India and the Cultural Reshaping of Psychoanalysis*. New York: Columbia University Press, 1992.

Lacan, Jacques. *Four Fundamental Concepts of Psychoanalysis*, trans. Alan Sheridan. New York: W.W. Norton and Co., 1977.

————. *Écrits: A Selection*, trans. Alan Sheridan. New York: W.W. Norton and Co., 1977.

Marzorati, Gerald. "Salman Rushdie: Fiction's Embattled Infidel." *New York Times Magazine* 29 January 1989, 24+.

Mbembe, Achille. "The Banality of Power and the Aesthetics of Vulgarity in the Postcolony." *Public Culture* 4, no. 2 (spring 1992): 1–30.

Mohanty, S.P. "Us and Them: On the Philosophical Bases of Political Criticism." *Yale Journal of Criticism* 2 (spring 1989): 1–31.

Mouffe, Chantal. "Citizenship and Political Identity." *October* (1992): 28–32.

Pines, J., and P. Willemin, eds. *Third Cinema Reader*. London: British Film Institute, 1989.

Pipes, Daniel. *The Rushdie Affair: The Novel, The Ayatollah. and the West.* New York: Birch Lane Press, 1990.

Radhakrishnan, R. "Culture as Common Ground: Ethnicity and Beyond." *Melus* 14, no. 2 (summer 1987): 5–19.

Rushdie, Salman. *The Satanic Verses.* New York: Viking Penguin, 1989.

———. *Midnight's Children.* New York: Avon, 1982.

Scott, Joan. "Multiculturalism and the Politics of Identity." *October* 61 (summer 1992): 12–19.

Spivak, Gayatri Chakravorty. "Reading the Satanic Verses." Pp. 217–41 in *Outside in the Teaching Machine.* New York: Routledge, 1993.

Suleri, Sara. "Contraband Histories: Salman Rushdie and the Embodiment of Blasphemy." *The Yale Review* 78, no. 4 (1988): 694–724.

7

EMIGRATION AS A RESISTANT FACTOR IN THE CREATION OF A NATIONAL LITERATURE: REX SHELLEY'S *THE SHRIMP PEOPLE*

Ismail S. Talib

Paul Virilio, in his *L'Insecurité du territoire*, notes that people whose migratory status is the consequence either of decolonization or of demographic and political changes, pose a real alternative to the authority of the nation state (cited by Said, *Culture and Imperialism*, 395). As a corollary, one can say that literary works which deal with such people create an alternative to the creation of a national literature, and thus create a problem for new states that want to form national literature of their own. This is because such works may question the viability and authority of a particular geopolitical entity such as a nation state, with its people leading a settled existence within its borders: these are ideas that a national literature cannot seriously question. In some postcolonial states, persistent emigration and immigration may constantly change their demographic profiles, thus making it difficult for them to establish a viable nation state, let alone the creation of a national literature.

It can be argued that, partly because of the migratory or "nomadic" character of many people in the world today, such conceptions as *nationality* and the *nation state* and, consequently, the idea of a *national literature*, have become irrelevant or outmoded in the postmodern world. But this argument has been criticized by Ien Ang, who notes that it is not true to say "'we' were all in fundamentally similar ways always–already travelers in the *same* postmodern universe" (4; my emphasis). She rightly points out that in spite of the "postmodern flux of nomadic subjectivities," there is still "the continuity and continuous operation of 'fixing' performed by the categories of race and ethnicity, as well as class, gender, geography, etc. on the formation of 'identity' . . . " (5). In this light, the *nation state* can be viewed as an important category which attempts to "fix" subjectivities in the postmodern world. Its attempt to "fix" subjectivities is ironically helped by some intellectuals who ostensibly claim to present a negative picture of the nation state as a concept, but who still appear to view it in favorable terms as an entity whose people are rooted in a location and are culturally homogeneous.[1]

Owing to the familiar situation described above—that a state is not necessarily a nation (and vice versa)—the two words which make up the concept of the nation state are thus frequently incompatible. A postcolonial state like Singapore, however, must somehow come to terms with itself as a *nation*, with a distinct *national identity*: like many other postcolonial states, it tries to avoid viewing itself merely as a motley collection of peoples within an arbitrary geopolitical boundary which has been incoherently put together, almost by accident, after independence (see Chew; Hussin). A natural accompaniment to its coming to terms with itself as a nation is the attempt to look for, or to create, a national literature.[2]

The search for a national literature, in relation to the attempt to free one's country from the continued influence of a foreign colonial power, is of course not peculiar to Singapore. In Canada, for instance, the Reverend Hartley Dewart made the observation in 1864 that a national literature "is the expression of national unity," and "a people firmly united politically" is aided by "the subtle but powerful cement of a patriotic literature" (ix; cited by Gerson, 888). Dewart's view has been voiced by ideologues of the nation state and its literature in other countries as well, especially in relation to the role of literature in the search for a postcolonial national identity or cohesiveness.[3]

The pursuit of a national literature is usually viewed as being more urgent in a historically new multicultural state which does not have a well-developed literary tradition. But such a pursuit is beset with problems.[4] For example, with reference to the recurring debate earlier this century about the possibility of the creation of the "great American novel" in the United States—whose multicultural make up was created by recent history—James Gibbons Huneker proclaimed in 1917 that "the great American novel" may not be realized because "America is a chord of many nations" (cited by Spencer, 23). In addition, the problem with creating a "great" national novel in a multicultural country is in fact compounded by the genre of the novel itself, which in spite of its close connection to the modern nation state in Western European literary history is, as noted by Mary Layoun (citing Lukács, 86-93), "the literary form of a world marked by a metaphoric and literal 'homelessness' and 'exile'" (3, 6).[5]

In a Singaporean work written in English—Rex Shelley's *The Shrimp People*—we see this tension between the desire to create the "great Singapore novel" and a genre and subject matter which are resistant to it. The novel has been described by Koh Buck Song as having gone "the furthest down the road towards being THE definitive Singapore work" (2, Koh's emphasis). Shelley's work is set during a period of decolonization and of major demographic and political shifts, and centers on the Eurasians, who are a people of mixed European and Asian ancestry. Its narrative time span begins with Singapore being under British colonial rule, followed by a period in which it achieved a semi-independent status, and ends in the period in which it was a state in Malaysia.

Playing an important part in the narrative of *The Shrimp People* is what is known as "the Indonesian Confrontation." During the "Confrontation," Indonesia, under the leadership of President Sukarno (who ignored the fact that Indonesia itself was a good example of what Benedict Anderson has described as an "imagined community" [109-12]) claimed that the separation of Malaysia from Indonesia was created by the artificial division based on territories earlier controlled by Britain and the Netherlands. He believed that this division should be rectified by Malaysia becoming a part of Indonesia. To complicate matters, the narrative of *The Shrimp People* can also be viewed as a retrospective account by a group of Eurasian migrants from Singapore and Malaysia in Australia, more than two decades after the "Confrontation" and the separation of Singapore itself from Malaysia.

If the narrative drift of *The Shrimp People* were determined entirely by the sense of crisis in personal identity arising from the transition to post-colonial rule and the concomitant change or shift of geopolitical boundaries, or if the narrative were determined simply by the problems created by emigration, its analysis would have been less problematic. But in its apparent attempt to be a part of the fledgling national literature of Singapore, it appears to do something which runs counter to this narrative drift. A cursory reaction to this apparent attempt is that there are other important factors which may make it difficult, if not impossible, for the novel to be a part of the national literature of Singapore. It may be argued, for instance, that the Eurasians form only a small minority of the population of Singapore, and the narrative is, in a sense, recounted by a group of Eurasians who have decided to leave Singapore for good. Furthermore, the narrative proper ends before Singapore achieves its present status as an independent nation state. But Koh may somehow be right in regarding the novel as having gone the furthest "towards being THE definitive Singapore work." Singapore itself has been known as a nation of migrants,[6] and it is difficult to separate the fact of migration from literature written by Singaporeans about the country and its people, even in a work like *The Shrimp People*, in spite of its apparently deliberate attempt to be part of the country's national literature.

Strengthening the claim that this work should belong to Singapore's national literature is its use of Singaporean English.[7] In my opinion, Shelley's novel contains some of the best examples of the use of Singaporean English in a literary work. As an indigenized dialect of English, Singaporean English is influenced by the once immigrant or "displaced" language of the colonials taking root in an environment which left it exposed to both the languages of the native population and migrants from non-European countries. As a consequence, it became a dialect of English which is closely associated with Singapore, and not treated as something "foreign" to the country.

It is certainly debatable, however, whether a novel written in the English language can be regarded as belonging to the national literature of Singapore. Although English is one of Singapore's four official languages (the others being Mandarin Chinese, Malay, and Tamil), the national language is Malay. The country's national anthem is in Malay, which is also the language used in military commands. But the usage of Malay has declined over the years. In 1990, only 16 percent of the population was literate in Malay (*Census*, 17). In contrast, the use of English has increased. In 1990, 65 percent of the population was literate in English (17). From its position as a marginalized, culturally displaced language—a relic of colonialism—English has moved into the center and become a language which is used even for such cultural expression as the writing of novels.

The increasing use of English has resulted in the belief, most prominently expressed by Edwin Thumboo, that it is the language which "is likely to be the first to produce a national literature."[8] The view that the language of the former colonial power can be used as the language for the country's national literature is bound to be met with controversy, as on Thumboo's view the experience in other postcolonial countries has shown,[9] and there has been some debate by scholars of Singaporean literature.[10] But what is clear is that it is now possible to think of Singapore's national literature as being written in English, a fact that was not seriously considered, or was even regarded as unthinkable, during the pre-independence and immediate postindependence periods.

In order for a work written in the English language to be regarded as an example of Singapore's national literature, it cannot simply be a case of language use that is borrowed wholesale from Britain.[11] In *The Shrimp People*, Shelley makes a conscious attempt to use the variety of English actually spoken in Singapore and Malaysia. In his preface to the work, entitled "Fiction, Fact and Foreign Words," he indicates that he has used "the variety of English known as 'Singlish'" in the novel (5). The term "Singlish" is a portmanteau created from the first syllable of "Singapore" and the last syllable of "English," and is often treated by scholars of Singaporean English as a low variety of the dialect (Talib, 166–67). When *Singlish* is used, there is a greater inclination toward what linguists call *code mixing*, where words or phrases from another language—in this case, one of the local languages, such as Malay or one of the Chinese dialects—are incorporated.

In *The Shrimp People*, despite the fact that the Eurasians in Australia have emigrated from Singapore, they continue to use Singlish or resort to *code mixing*. Thus, although they have physically emigrated from Singapore, they remain, at least from a linguistic perspective, Singaporeans at heart. Here is an example of *code mixing* from one of the migrants in Australia, Joseph Coombes, who is recalling a riot that occurred while he was a sergeant in the colonial police force:

> *Suma Stop*! *Nanti*! Ray, I must say that was the day way back in 1954 when the Chinese High School students clashed with the police. It was one of the first of many clashes. OK, *tuan, boleh jalan*. (68)[12]

With regards to the view that the novel cannot be considered as part of Singapore's national literature because the Eurasians form only a small minority of the population, one must note that some of the Eurasians in the novel have decided to remain in the country; this factor actually strengthens, in an oblique but effective way, the novel's attempt to be an example of a work belonging to Singapore's national literature. As a people whose European ancestry was not only a source of pride for some of them, but was also given some kind of recognition by the colonial power, the Eurasians in the postcolonial environment of independent Singapore have to find their own identities and sense of belonging in the new country. The formerly colonized races are now the masters. The Eurasians' European blood does not, in practical terms, count for much. This is indeed a good test of how much the Eurasians who remain want to belong to Singapore, as they could have emigrated to other countries if they had wanted to, just like the group of Eurasian immigrants in Australia with whom the novel proper begins.

One way that emigrants, or those who choose to stay in a particular region or geopolitical entity, can psychologically legitimize their belonging to a place is by narrating an ordinary myth of some kind. The ordinary myth of the Eurasians in *The Shrimp People* is narrated in the prologue to the novel, which fictionally traces the origins of the first Eurasians to the relationship of a Malay woman, Bedah, with a Portuguese man who was found on the shores of Malacca, almost 500 years ago. The Portuguese man is a representative figure here, as the Portuguese, together with the Spaniards in the Philippines, were the earliest European colonial powers in the region. From an ideological perspective, Shelley's fictional account appears to underemphasize the colonial connections of the Eurasians: the Portuguese character in the prologue is a lost man on the shore, and not—as the representative of an invading army—an out-and-out colonial. The fictional account also appears to implicitly assert that the Eurasians have a strong claim to being regarded as a native race, as they can trace their ancestry to the native Malays; in addition, it makes the further implicit assumption that as Eurasians, they have been in the region far longer than most of the Chinese, who in spite of being more recent arrivals, are now the politically, economically, and demographically dominant race in Singapore.

The first chapter of the novel proper (which follows the prologue), is an abrupt shift to the future, almost 500 years later. We are no longer in Malaysia or Singapore—which the Eurasians in the novel virtually regard as their native land—but in Perth, Western Australia, where we meet the group of Eurasian migrants in what is a new country for them. They are now examples of what Salman Rushdie has described as "radically new types of human beings; people who root themselves in ideas rather than in places; people who have been obliged to define themselves—because they are so defined by others—by their otherness" (124; also quoted by Ang, 5). As immigrants, they cannot, as yet, comfortably root themselves physically in Australia.

The narrative juxtaposition of the prologue with the first chapter in Australia suggests that the myth of a lost origin—of which Shelley's fictional tale of Bedah and the stranded Portuguese soldier is an example—is embedded in the consciousness of the Eurasian immigrants. The ordinary myth in the minds of migrants, as explained by Ien Ang, who is herself a member of a similar diasporic community in Australia, "is the myth of the (lost or idealized) homeland, the object of both collective memory and of desire and attachment, which is constitutive to diasporas, and which ultimately confines and constrains the nomadism of the diasporic subject" (6). Thus, although the Eurasian immigrants in Australia are physical "nomads," they do not desire to be psychological "nomads": they are at home in their "invisible" or "imaginary homelands" in their minds (Rushdie, 10). Their continued use of facets of Singaporean English can in fact be viewed as a further illustration of their desire to belong to this purely psychological "imaginary homeland."

The Eurasian immigrants' wish for a settled ordinary identity, even if it is purely psychological and mythic, is an antidote to their sense of "otherness" in Australia, their adopted country. From the narrative perspective of the novel, however, the abrupt proleptic 500 year shift to the future in Australia somehow rudely undercuts this ordinary myth: the Eurasian migrants have decided not to continue to live in the country or countries that they have regarded in their minds as the place where they came from and belong. There is thus a disjunction between imagination and reality.

As a reverse reaction to their sense of "otherness" in their adopted country, the Eurasian immigrants in Australia are significantly not fond of tracing their origin to the European countries where their Caucasian forebears came from, but prefer to trace it to their Asian ancestors and the lands associated with them. Paradoxically, the assertion of their European ancestry would have been stronger—as much of the rest of the novel about Bertha Rodrigues and her friends, relatives, and workmates illustrates—had they remained in Singapore or Malaysia. In this regard, we can say that the myth of origin, which contributes to one's sense of identity, is actuated by what makes one *different* from the dominant population which regards one as a member of an *other* race; or, in Rushdie's terms, one is obliged—or virtually forced—to define oneself by one's *otherness*.

Although one's sense of *difference* from the dominant population in a particular location may give one one's sense of *identity*, it may not contribute to one's sense of belonging to the place. In this respect, the Eurasians in Singapore may not be different from those in Australia. As the flashbacks to the story of Bertha Rodrigues illustrate, the Eurasians in Singapore and Malaysia do not feel that they totally belong there. Although many of them descended from the Malays, they are not accepted as such by the Malays in Malaysia and Singapore. As Sylvia, one of the Eurasian immigrants in Australia, recalls, "The half-castes were rejected by the Malays. They could not be reabsorbed by a half-caste marrying a Malay" (214). But this rejection somehow gives them their sense of group identity; they "clung together" due to the rejection by the majority.

As if rejection is not enough, they are called *geragau* (spelled *geragok* by Shelley). *Geragau* is a derogatory Malay word which actually refers to a tiny species of shrimp—hence the title of the book, *The Shrimp People*. The Eurasians were called *geragau* simply because some of the Portuguese Eurasians in Malacca used to earn their living by catching this species of shrimp. In the "Prologue," Shelley pokes ironic fun at this linkage when Pak Khamis suggests to Bedah that she and her future Portuguese husband should earn their living by catching *geragau* but Bedah does not even know what the word means. Pak Khamis explains that they are "a very small shrimp. The tiniest thing we catch for food," and when dried in the sun and mashed into a paste, "they hold the taste of the sun and salt and the sea" (16). From Shelley's incarnation of the Eurasians' ordinary myth, it does seem that in the mind of the migrant, time and distance imbue an essentially derogatory and racialistic term with a tinge of affection!

To be fair, the Eurasians were a privileged class during colonial times, and placed themselves apart from the local population. Sylvia notes this:

> Two generations ago [the Eurasians in Singapore] were the privileged class. The palace slaves. They held the good jobs in the police, on the ships, in the schools. They were far better educated than the others. Now they are one of the poorer groups . . . generally. (219; Shelley's ellipsis)

The Eurasians at that time were not only proud of their European ancestry, but resented associating with anyone who did not actually have European blood in their veins. There is an incident in the novel when some Eurasians show their resentment toward the fact that one Angella Jasper, who plays for the Malacca Eurasians hockey team, is not actually a Eurasian, in spite of her European-sounding surname: her surname is actually derived from "Jaspal Singh."

As if to illustrate the postcolonial Eurasians' lack of a sense of belonging and their allegorical search for a home through the metaphor of movement (cf. Bhabha, "Dissemination", 293), we have the wanderings of Bertha Rodrigues for a good half of the novel through what is now regarded as three separate geopolitical entities: Singapore, Malaysia, and Indonesia. Bertha's movements also seem to be a further illustration of Layoun's view cited earlier that the novel as a genre is "the literary form of a world marked by a metaphoric and literal 'homelessness' and 'exile'" (3, 6): if the Eurasians in Perth are literal examples, Bertha is a metaphoric example of "homelessness" and "exile."

After her failed marriage to a Chinese man, she flees Singapore, and finds herself in a rural part of mainland Malaya (called West Malaysia today), where she works, unwittingly at first, as an Indonesian agent. From there, she goes on to Indonesia, where she is taught some communist ideas and is trained as a guerrilla insurgent. She then returns to Singapore, and is involved in an exchange of gunfire in which she kills a man. After this incident, she goes to Indonesia again, and on her next trip to Malaysia, she changes sides, and is eventually back in Singapore. The novel ends artificially by emphasizing the Singaporean affiliations of the protagonist: "Bertha, woman, Serani [i.e. Eurasian], Singaporean caught in the currents of the conflicts and her past, clinging to her family, her people, her home" (475).

Bertha's peregrinations as an Indonesian agent, and her final change of sides at the end of the novel, are quite implausible. The implausibility stems partly from what Bhabha has said in relation to such metaphoric movements: that they require "a kind of 'doubleness' in writing; a temporality in representation that moves between cultural formations and social processes without a 'centred' causal logic" ("Dissemination", 293). Although her movement between the countries in the region may be partially governed by the genre of the novel, which usually depicts "a world marked by a metaphoric and literal 'homelessness' and 'exile,'" her cross-national movement has "a centered causal logic" about it which makes her final decision to stay in Singapore an unconvincing one.

The implausibility can also be seen in terms of the failure to reconcile the two conflicting pulls in the novel: the theme of migration, and the desire to make the novel belong to Singapore's national literature. These conflicting pulls result in the failure to present a credible or consistent ideological standpoint in the novel. The novel actually has a first-person narrator, Robert Machado, who is, like the other Eurasians immigrants in Perth, a naturalized Australian. But Robert and the group of Eurasian immigrants are abandoned in the text shortly after Bertha starts her wandering. One type of migration is apparently forsaken for another, metaphorical one. But the metaphorical type of migration does conveniently allow one the option to return, whereas this option does not seem to be open to the Australian immigrants: hence the novel's abandonment of the latter for the former.

Although I believe that *The Shrimp People* is one of the best novels in English to have emerged from Singapore, its major fault is its "centered causal logic" which somehow fails to reconcile the opposing thematic pulls between the migratory and the national. It is a novel which makes us wonder whether one can still write a "great national novel" today, despite the reality of emigration and immigration in the postmodern world. Perhaps the lesson to be learned from its failure is that the postmodern nomad, in spite of the inclination of others to "fix" him or her, must eventually abandon the physical nation, and be content with the nation in the mind: the option open to Bertha Rodrigues in Singapore is unfortunately not open to Robert Machado and his Eurasian cronies in Australia, who can only have the psychological nation in their minds. This purely psychological nation (unless academically revived) will eventually die off, as it will cease to exist in the minds of the immigrants' descendants. Emigration, after all, may be a one-way journey without recourse to an actual and permanent return.

Notes

1. In this regard, Benita Parry is right in pointing out that Raymond Williams, in spite of his criticism of what he calls "the alienated superficialities of 'the nation'" in his book *Towards 2000* (193), "does associate culture with fixed location and comes close to naturalizing a conception of the nation as equivalent to the physical and cultural continuities of autochthonous peoples" (Parry, 21–22).

2. Despite the problem of the viability of the concept *national literature* in the contemporary world (see the discussions in Clüver; Mouralis; Ricard; Rushdie, 66–69), the concept does seem to be persistent.

3. For example, it was stated by the Nigerian minister of information and culture, Prince Tony Momoh, in 1987 that literature "is a potent weapon for the development, and organizational sophistication, of the mores, history, cultures, and emotions of a people which at once constitute the fertile soil, upon which the seed of national consciousness can truly and sensibly germinate" (xiv; see also Ricard, 297).

4. For a review of the situation in Australia, see Gunew.

5. See also During for a discussion on the tension not only between the concept of a national literature and the genre of the novel, but between national literature and literature itself.

6. For a brief discussion of immigration to Singapore between the years 1819 and 1978, see Saw, 219–26.

7. Making a related claim, Loreto Todd has argued that in the multilingual community of the Cameroon, Cameroon Pidgin English is the best candidate for the language of the country's national literature.

8. "Writer and Society," 29. See also Thumboo's "Singapore Writers in English," 22; the studies by de Souza, 21–22; and Singh.

9. Good examples of this can be found in the postcolonial countries of sub-Saharan Africa; for a bibliographical survey, see Westley. For more specific instances of the controversy in sub-Saharan Africa on whether a colonial language can be the language of a postcolonial state's national literature (which are also pertinent to the situation in Southeast Asia), see *Special Issue: The Language Question* in *Research in African Literatures* 23, no. 1 (spring 1992).

10. Among scholars who question Thumboo's view are Gordon, 57; Jit, 221; T. Koh, 304; and Kwan-Terry, 115–18, 128.

In this regard, it has been pointed out by some that Thumboo's view that it is likely that a national literature will be written in English arose from his vested interest in the language, as he was a professor of English and wrote poetry in the language.

11. For a survey on Singaporean writers' use of English in literary works, and writers' and readers' attitudes toward it, see Talib, 155–67.

12. The non-English words are all in the Malay language. "*Suma [semua] stop!*": "all stop!"; "*Nanti!*": "wait!"; "*tuan, boleh jalan*": "Sir, you can move on."

References

Anderson, Benedict. *Imagined Communities: Reflections on the Origin and Spread of Nationalism.* London: Verso, 1983.

Ang, Ien. "Migration of Chineseness." *SPAN* 34–35 (October 1992–May 1993): 3–15.

Bhabha, Homi. "DissemiNation: Time, Narrative, and the Margins of the Modern Nation." 291–322.

———. ed. *Nation and Narration.* London: Routledge, 1990.

Census of Population 1990: Advance Data Release. Singapore: SNP Publishers, 1991.

Clüver, Claus. "The Difference of Eight Decades: World Literature and the Demise of National Literature." *Yearbook of Comparative and General Literature* 35 (1986): 14–24.

Chew, Ernest C. T. "The Singapore National Identity: Its Historical Evolution and Emergence." Pp. 357–68 in *A History of Singapore*, ed. Ernest C. T. Chew and Edwin Lee. Singapore: Oxford University Press, 1991.

de Souza, Dudley. "The Role of Literature in the Secondary Schools in Singapore." *The Singapore Journal of Education* 3, no.1 (1980): 18–25.

Dewart, Edward Hartley. *Selections from Canadian Poets.* 1864. Reprint, Toronto: University of Toronto Press, 1973.

During, Simon. "Literature—Nationalism's Other? The Case for Revision." Bhabha 138–53.

Gerson, Carole. "The Changing Contours of a National Literature." *College English* 50 (1988): 888–95.

Gordon, Jan B. "The 'Second Tongue' Myth: English Poetry in Polylingual Singapore." *ARIEL* 15, no. 4 (1984): 41–65.

Gunew, Sneja. "Denaturalizing Cultural Nationalisms: Multicultural Readings of 'Australia'." Bhabha 99–120.

Hussin, Mutalib. "Singapore's Quest for a National Identity: The Triumphs and Trials of Government Policies." Pp. 69–96 in *Imagining Singapore*, ed. Ban Kah Choon, Anne Pakir and Tong Chee Kiong. Singapore: Times Academic, 1992.

Jit, Krishen. "Modern Theatre in Singapore: A Preliminary Survey." *Tenggara* 23 (1989): 210–26.

Koh, Buck Song. "Singapore Literature: Taking Stock." *Arts on Campus* 1, no. 4 (March 1992): 1–2, 14.

Koh, Tai Ann. "The Singapore Experience: Cultural Development in the Global Village." *Southeast Asian Affairs 7* (1980): 292–307.

Kwan-Terry, John. "Ulysses Circling the Merlion: The Invention of Identity in Singapore Poetry in English and Chinese." Pp. 115–38 in *Perceiving Other Worlds*, ed. Edwin Thumboo. Singapore: Times Academic, 1991.

Layoun, Mary N. *Travels of a Genre: The Modern Novel.* Princeton, N.J.: Princeton University Press, 1990.

Lukács, Georg. *The Theory of the Novel.* 1920, trans. Ann Bostock. Reprint, Cambridge, Mass.: MIT Press, 1971.

Momoh, Prince Tony. "Keynote Address." Pp. xiii–xix in *Literature and National Consciousness*, ed. Ernest N. Emenyonu. Ibadan: Heinemann Educational Books, Nigeria, 1989.

Mouralis, Bernard. "L'Évolution du concept de litterature nationale en Afrique." *Research in African Literatures* 18 (1987): 272–79.

Parry, Benita. "Overlapping Territories and Intertwined Histories: Edward Said's Postcolonial Cosmopolitanism." 1947. Pp. 19–47 in *Edward Said: A Critical Reader*, ed. Michael Sprinker. Oxford: Blackwell, 1992.

Ricard, Alain. "Museum, Mausoleum, or Market: The Concept of National Literature." *Research in African Literatures* 18 (1987): 293–303.

Rushdie, Salman. *Imaginary Homelands: Essays and Criticism 1981-1991.* London: Granta, 1991.

Said, Edward W. *Culture and Imperialism.* London: Chatto, 1993.

Saw, Swee Hock. "Population Growth and Control." Pp. 219–41 in *A History of Singapore*, ed Ernest C. T. Chew and Edwin Lee. Singapore: Oxford University Press, 1991.

Shelley, Rex. *The Shrimp People*. Singapore: Times Books International, 1991.

Singh, Kirpal. "Towards a Singapore Classic: Edwin Thumboo's 'Ulysses by the Merlion.'" *Literary Criterion* 15, no. 2 (1980): 74–87.

Special Issue: The Language Question. Edited by Richard Bjornson. *Research in African Literatures* 23, no. 1 (spring 1992).

Spencer, Benjamin T. *Patterns of Nationality: Twentieth Century Literary Versions of America*. New York: Burt Franklin, 1981.

Talib, Ismail S. "Responses to the Language of Singaporean Literature in English." Pp. 153–74 in *Language, Society and Education in Singapore: Issues and Trends*, ed. S. Gopinathan, Anne Pakir, Ho Wah Kam and Vanithamani Saravanan. Singapore: Times Academic, 1994.

Thumboo, Edwin. "Singapore Writers in English: A Need for Commitment." *Commentary* (Singapore) 2, no. 4 (May 1978): 20–25.

———. "The Writer and Society: Some Third World Reminders." *Solidarity* 99 (1984): 24–32.

Todd, Loreto. "E Pluribus Unum? The Language for a National Literature in a Multilingual Community." *ARIEL* 15, no. 4 (Oct. 1984): 69–82.

Virilio, Paul. *L'Insecurité du territoire*. Paris: Stock, 1976.

Westley, David. "Choice of Language and African Literature: A Bibliographic Essay." *Research in African Literatures* 23, no. 1 (spring 1992): 159–71.

Williams, Raymond. *Towards 2000*. 1983. Reprint, Harmondsworth, England: Penguin Books, 1985.

8

NINOTCHKA ROSCA'S
STATE OF WAR AND JESSICA
HAGEDORN'S *DOGEATERS*:
REVISIONING THE PHILIPPINES

Rocio G. Davis

Salman Rushdie's 1982 essay "Imaginary Homelands" may be read as a paradigm of the discourse of writers in the between-world condition. In this piece, he describes and defines the situation of those writers who are, in the words of Michael Ondaatje's English patient, "born in one place and choosing to live elsewhere. Fighting to get back to or get away from our homelands all our lives" (176). More specifically, Rushdie analyzes the theme of the homeland in the works of this type of writer, pointing out that the attempt to portray one's land of origin is inevitably coupled with the failure to be faithful to any objective reality. Although he refers principally to Anglo-Indian writers, his observation and analysis of the situation clearly applies to most writers who share the transnational experience:

> It may be that writers in my position, exiles or emigrants or expatriates, are haunted by some sense of loss, some urge to reclaim, to look back, even at the risk of being mutated into pillars of salt. But if we do look back, we must also do so in the knowledge—which gives rise to profound uncertainties—that our physical alienation from India almost inevitably means that we will not be capable of reclaiming precisely the thing that was lost; that we will, in short, create fictions, not actual cities or villages, but invisible ones, imaginary homelands, Indias of the mind. (10)

Taking as his point of departure the writing of *Midnight's Children*, Rushdie dwells on the complexity of fictionally re-creating the land he had left more than twenty years before into the saga of a child and of a nation. Recognizing that the distances of time and space distort facts, he revisioned his novel in order not to fall into the trap of having to validate his remembered experiences with objective realities. He centered his efforts on making the novel "as imaginatively true as I could," knowing that "what I was actually doing was a novel of memory and about memory, so that my India was just that: 'my' India, a version and no more than just one of all the hundreds of millions of possible versions" (10). Any writer who writes about his homeland from the outside, Rushdie claims, must necessarily "deal in broken mirrors, some of whose fragments have been irretrievably lost" (11). Nonetheless, it is precisely the fragmentary nature of these memories, the incomplete truths they contain, the partial explanations they offer, that make them particularly evocative for the "transplanted" writer. For Rushdie, these "shards of memory acquired greater status, greater resonance, because they were *remains;* fragmentation made trivial things seem like symbols, and the mundane acquired numinous qualities" (12).

The attempt to build a novel about one's homeland on the basis of memory has been shown to be both an irresistible challenge and a compelling necessity for many exiled or immigrant writers. There is a palpable obsession to set down, with or without the help of fiction, the collection of memories that form the writer's idea of his homeland, perhaps in an attempt to reconcile himself to both past and present. This is the case with a great number of ethnic minority writers in the United States, Canada, and England. In his first two novels, for instance, Anglo–Japanese writer Kazuo Ishiguro deliberately sets out to write the Japan he had not seen since the age of six, "because I wished to re-create this Japan–put together all those memories and all those imaginary ideas I had about this landscape I called Japan. I wanted to make it safe, preserve it in a book before it faded away from memory altogether" (76). Once set down, the narrative may serve as a touchstone, that needed point of reference for identity and meaning, perhaps in an attempt to find comfort by denying Rushdie's assertion, and one's nagging sensation that somehow, inescapably, "it's my present that is foreign, and that the past is home, albeit a lost home in a lost city in the mists of lost time" (9).

Rushdie's essay may also serve as the framework for a study of two novels by Philippine women immigrants to the United States, Ninotchka Rosca's *State of War* (1988) and Jessica Hagedorn's *Dogeaters* (1990). The novels recreate the multifariousness of Philippine culture by looking back at both the country's history and more recent events in Philippine political life. Interestingly enough, although the primary focus of both writers is on the political upheavals that took place during the Marcos dictatorship, they do not fail to include the two colonial experiences undergone by the Filipinos and the lasting effects these have left behind. Philippine history therefore becomes a resource for constructing a discourse of nationalism. In this manner, through their literary revision of a homeland and that country's history, Rosca and Hagedorn ultimately present a portrait of the creation of the Filipino.

The position of both Rosca and Hagedorn as immigrant writers in the United States provides them with a privileged vantage point from which to view their country's culture and past. The authenticity of their narratives springs from the validity of their voices, those of the expatriates, the exiled voices that are both marginal and central, divided in their loyalties, but committed in their struggle with competing identities. Rosca's and Hagedorn's perceptions of the Philippines are thus made profound and complex because they are formed by examining the past with what Rushdie has designated "stereoscopic vision...a kind of double perspective: because they, we, are at one and the same time insiders and outsiders in this society" (19). The narrative will therefore also spring from the consciousness of an "at once plural and partial" identity: the feeling that sometimes "we straddle two cultures; at other times, we fall between two stools" (Rushdie, 15). But once again, as Rushdie has pointed out, "however ambiguous and shifting this ground may be, it is not an infertile territory for a writer to occupy. If literature is in part the business of finding new angles at which to enter reality, then once again our distance, our long geographical perspective, may provide us with such angles" (15).

This "double perspective" simultaneously provides an epiphany for Filipino American writers in general. E. San Juan, Jr. has pointed to the problem and the need to reinvent the Filipino in the United States, articulating the long-suffered silence and invisibility for creative artists: the master narrative of the migrant worker's odyssey used by Carlos Bulosan and the interior monologues of Bienvenido Santos' expatriates marooned in the megapolis can no longer serve as generic models (123). San Juan believes that a beginning must be made from the realities of immigrants in the eighties and from the experience of Filipino Americans born in the sixties and seventies. In this regard, Oscar Campomanes argues for a literature of exile and emergence rather than a literature of immigration and settlement whereby life in the United States serves as the space for displacement, suspension, and perspective. Exile becomes a necessary, if inescapable, state for Filipinos in the United States—at once susceptible to the vagaries of the (neo)colonial U.S.-Philippine relationship and redeemable only by its radical restructuring (51). Nonetheless, San Juan claims,

> this cannot be done without evoking the primal scene coeval with the present: the neocolonial situation of the Philippines and its antecedent stages, the conflicted terrain of ideological struggle which abolishes the distinction/distance between

Filipinos in the Philippines and Filipinos in the U.S. Continuities no less than ruptures have to be articulated for an oppositional practice to emerge. The terrain is less geographical than cultural—culture defined as the complex network of social practices signifying our dominant or subordinate position in a given social formation. (123)

The subject of both *State of War* and *Dogeaters* is the formation of the Filipinos' elusive, problematic, palimpsestic identity as a people and as a nation and, ultimately, Rosca's and Hagedorn's positions as women and artists, caught in a world of binary oppositions: Filipino/American, home/exile, past/present, real/fantasy. In an essay entitled "Myth, Identity and the Colonial Experience," Rosca explores the creation of the Filipino self in literature. She feels that the way the fictional self has turned out to be a collective one as far as Filipino writers are concerned is part of the historical evolution, not only of writing in the country, but also of the country itself. Like most writers of the Third World, Filipino writers have a well-developed sense of the national self, of national life, and of the contradictions that make it problematical to even have a "self" in this context at all. The attempt to resolve, for instance, the conflict between the orientation of the bedrock culture and the fragmenting effect of colonialism is a dominant theme in Philippine writing and, in particular, in the writing by Filipinos outside the Philippines (Rosca 1990, 240).

> This is then what one finds in Filipino fiction: a self that shares in all of the contradictoriness of the national self. It is difficult for a Filipino writer to conceive of judging events solely from a personal, individual point of view . . . what he or she attempts to do, consistently throughout the years, is to locate himself or herself within the collective self and to look at the world with the eyes of his or her people and his or her history. . . . By representing this self in fiction, the writer assumes part of the responsibility for defining it even as he or she reflects it - as he or she defines it, so it becomes more his or her definition. . . . We do not have objective manifestations of the self that have been evolving since prehistory. . . . Our materials are perishable: language and memory—uncertain, imperfect. But they fit well the volatile nature of this, our self, for they can change as fast as we can, as we flicker through myths and identities, unravel the impact of colonialism on our selves, and go through our metamorphosis. Memory, most of all, anchors us, for, though it is fragile, it is also the longest umbilical cord. (Rosca, 242)

In this regard, irony as the predominant tone of both novels becomes one mode of self-defining discourse. Much of Philippine life and culture is itself intrinsically doubled and therefore at least structurally ripe for irony. Its history offers many binary oppositions: native/colonizer, East/West, indigenous superstitions/Roman Catholicism, Filipino/Spanish. The binary oppositions were made more complex when the arrival of the Americans added a third pole to the conflict. Furthermore, the Philippines is a country that is characterized by both immigration (where, at least for a time, all the nonnative inhabitants have felt dual allegiances), and expatriation (which, brought on by successive histories of colonization, is itself a form and an inseparable part of Filipino identity) (Lim, 68). Doubleness—of identity, of culture, of loyalties, often of language—is the basis of the experience of immigration. The very doubleness inherent in irony—the need to keep literal and ironic meanings afloat together—disrupts any notions of meaning as single, stable, or complete. Linda Hutcheon suggests that irony is one way of coming to terms with that duplicity, for it is the trope that incarnates doubleness, and it does so in ways that are particularly useful to the "other": irony allows "the other" to address the dominant culture from within that culture's own set of values and modes of understanding, without being co-opted by it and without sacrificing the right to dissent, contradict, and resist, opening up new space, literally between opposing meanings, where new things can happen (49).

Irony is evident in the way that both *State of War* and *Dogeaters* fall into the category of roman a clef. Through the use of metaphors and allusive names, the writers demand a second-level reading of the works as both historical and political statements and cultural analysis. As Rosca has stated, "The problem was how to tell a story that was not anybody's story and yet was everybody's story?" (Mestrovic, 90). *State of War* is ambitious in its attempt to update whole centuries of Philippine history through the lives of a few interbreeding families. Rosca's basic strategy in this novel is to use history to suggest the chronic intrusion of foreign powers into the life and culture of the Filipino people as she revisions the whole stretch of colonial history in the context of the period of the Marcos dictatorship through a melange of dreamy sequences, historical vignettes, and hyperrealized characters and events. In this manner, she implies that Filipinos have been locked in a continuous state of war against military, economic, and cultural invasions ever since Magellan intervened in Lapulapu's tribal affairs and lost his life at Mactan. Her timeframe moves from the late stages of the dictatorship of Marcos (here called the Commander), during the Festival (Ati–Atihan) celebrated annually on the Visayan island of K–; to a narrative reprise of centuries of putative colonial influence on Philippine bloodlines, apparent in such families as the Banyagas, Villaverdes, and Batoyans; with a final return to the Festival as it deteriorates into a wild, frustrated assassination attempt. Leonard Casper believes that the intent of this strategy is to provide an indirect, but dramatic, appeal for a truly independent nationalism (1990, 203).

Rosca balances allegory with personal history in the triadic relationship of her main characters, Anna Villaverde, Adrian Banyaga, and Eliza Hansen, whose genealogies and symbolic stories intertwine in a series of historical wars and developments that are symbolized by a twenty four hour period of festivity and political conspiracies. The interrelated merrymaking and political conflict are emphasized by narrative pattern and design, as exemplified by the three–"book" structure of the novel. The first and the last, "Acts" and "Revelations," follow the movements of the three central characters during the Festival. The middle section, "Numbers," traces the genealogy of these characters and thus the history of the Spanish occupation to the present day. Oscar Campomanes has pointed out that the novel is an obvious footnote to the triangulated characteristic of Linda Ty–Casper's *Awaiting Trespass* as articulated in the preface: "A small book of hours about those waiting for their lives to begin. . .a book of numbers about those who stand up to be counted. . .a book of revelations about what tyranny forces people to become; and what, by resisting, they can insist on being"(71).

The book focuses on three minor players in the Philippine conflict: Adrian, the wealthy heir; Anna; the vengeful widow of a revolutionary; and Eliza, the frivolous and independent mistress of a millionaire. Their genealogies provide the most complex maze in the novel, and point to the direction the novel will take in charting identities. Old Andy, grandfather of Adrian Banyaga, is the grandson of a Capuchin monk who is also the father of Carlos Lucas de Villaverde, husband of Mayang Batoyan. She later has an illegitimate child, Luis Carlos, with the German chemist Hans Zangroniz. Luis Carlos is to be the father of Anna Villaverde who marries Manolo Monreal, whose father Jake betrays Luis Carlos during the Japanese Occupation and is eventually killed by Luis Carlos. Hans Zangroniz, meanwhile, has changed his name to Chris Hansen, gone to the southern part of the archipelago, and become the grandfather of Eliza Hansen. No one seems to realize that this complicated web of relationships exists, and that the three main characters are actually related. In the present, Adrian and Anna are lovers while Eliza and Anna are inseparable friends who appear to share a sort of sentimental sisterhood, but never quite the recognition that they are cousins.

Emphasis is constantly placed on the view of the Philippines as a land of beginnings, and on the importance of knowing about a historical past in order to go forward in time. The diverse biological and cultural influences that formed the Filipino are of concern to the writer: "But where Eliza was of that rare fortuitous sienna skin, accidentally bred by a mingling of Caucasian and Malay blood, Anna was fair, of a gold tint that testified to an indefinable mixing of Chinese, Malay and other strange bloods. A true child of the Philippine archipelago" (12). Anna Villaverde's first solemn declaration as a child, "everything in this country happens in the morning. . .Because it is a country of beginnings"(328) is an echo of the Chinese guerrilla's declaration to Mayang that "this country—it has no continuity. It is only a country of beginnings. No one remembers" (292). The need to preserve and know history is obsessive, just as its corollary, not to know the past, is a condemnation. After the war against the Japanese, Luis Carlos and the soldiers who surrendered to the Americans realized that "in the newness to come, it was important. . . that a little of history remain" (307). The manipulation of history is another danger, seen through the eyes of Anna, named thus in her father's hope that she would be "the start of better things" (326): "'They monkeyed around with the language, Eliza, while we were growing up. Monkeyed around with names. Of people, of places. With dates. And now, I can't remember. No one remembers. And even this'—she waved a hand toward the Festival—'even this will be forgotten. They will hide it under another name. No one will remember'" (149).

Rosca seems to imply that because most of the persons involved are not aware of their history or their bloodlines, they are condemned to repeat the errors of the past: illegitimacy breeds illegitimacy; Manolo Monreal will betray the guerrillas, as his father Jake did before him, and die for this at the hands of his wife, daughter of the man who killed his father in revenge. The author's cyclical and deterministic view of history is expressed in metaphors of time looping in and in lyrical descriptions of characters hurled into a sort of time warp of the past and "young minds already twisted by the histories to be learned" (338). The characters, their ancestors, and their descendants are destined to meet again and again in a series of extraordinary coincidences. Anna Villaverde laughs at this "fractured history," marked by "war treading on the heels of a just–concluded war in a country of beginnings" (339). In a surreal scene toward the end of the novel, she mentally revisions the events from the time Magellan's boats sailed to Mactan, where he met his death, to the time Dewey steamed into Manila Bay and sank the Spanish fleet. "So it began, the country's confusion over language and memory, so that in this Festival of commemoration, there remained no more than this mangled song. . ." (338).

The novel ends tragically, with shattered dreams and death. Eliza is murdered and her body is washed ashore four days after the Festival; Adrian is crippled, his mind hurled into a "time warp, fixing him forever in a maze of words, a verbal account of four hundred years, tortured and tormenting" (376). Only Anna survives and goes to teach children in a small village in the mountains. Pregnant with Adrian's child, she awaits the birth of her son, "who would be nurtured as much by her milk as by the archipelago's legends . . . and he would be the first of the Capuchin monk's descendants to be born innocent, without fate . . . her son would be a great storyteller, in the tradition of children of priestesses. He would remember, his name being a history unto itself, for he would be known as Ismael Villaverde Banyaga"

(382). Rosca's preoccupation with the transmitting of history, and the creation of the Filipino identity through it, once again comes to the fore. Only when one has a history, and can recount it, she implies, can one, and one's country, be made whole.

Hagedorn's *Dogeaters* is written as a scrapbook of memories and precise images of life in Manila from about 1956 to 1985. The chapters of this discontinuous narrative are like fractals, those mathematical forms that present a series of overlapping shapes, endlessly repeated. Hagedorn uses a flashy, disconcerting, rapidly moving technique to approach the elaborately complex riddle that is Philippine culture. Characterized by postwar popular culture, the novel offers a picture of ruin in Philippine society, in which the characters perceive the world through a screen of movie memories and radio soap operas and try to act in tune with song lyrics and poignant cinematic poses. *Dogeaters* thus has the coherence and flow of gossip, and presents a world that lacks the steadiness of the truth as an anchor.

The book is a bildungsroman, and its center is the education of youth—in this instance a girl belonging to the privileged class in any society in the throes of change. The two main characters, who speak in first person, are displaced, and their voices are powerless and uncritical. Rio is the teenage daughter of the rich Gonzaga family. Hers is a world of luxury, gossip, extravagant meals, and travel: the reader witnesses her progress from a soap opera fan to an observer–commentator of events and episodes of a troubled nation. Joey Sands is a young male junkie–prostitute, son of a black Navy serviceman who abandoned the woman who bore his son and eventually killed herself. After witnessing Senator Avila's assassination, he goes to fight with the guerrillas in the mountains

Leonard Casper has commented that the novel's title, "dogeaters," might well be a pejorative term applied generically to all Filipinos, although anthropologists using it could allude with some accuracy only to certain mountain tribes of the north. Clearly it is an ethnic slur, originating among non–Filipinos. What Hagedorn appears to be portraying is a sort of cultural cannibalism: Filipinos devouring one another, by careless accident or by deliberate design, and in varying degrees. The violence of Colonel Pepe Carreon and General Ledesma is an extension, only, of the mindless self-satisfaction of the Gonzaga family. The novel's covert purpose is to present variations on the theme of greed; to portray normal appetites out of control, bodies in the service not of spiritual vision but of voids so desperate for gratification verging on gluttony that they incite, in the ruling class, extreme forms of avarice (1990b, 153).

As in Rosca's novel, space and time spiral deceitfully to stay the same, and the unwitting intermingling of the characters' lives reflects the nostalgic the nostalgia mode colonizes the present by having the pastiche of the stereotypical past endow the present reality and the openness of the present history with the spell and distance of an image. A historical novel such as *Dogeaters* does not set out to represent the historical past, for it can only represent our ideas and stereotypes about that past, and it is aware of this. We see in Hagedorn's text the deliberate proliferation of brand names, whether real (as in historical) or fictive soft drinks, perfumes, fashion, nail polish, cars—which not only contribute to the reality effect of the text but also serve as the self-present modes by which the absent past is refracted as always and forever out of reach. (117)

Soap operas and movies are clearly portrayed as integral parts of Filipino life, suggesting the importance of fantasizing for the Filipinos. The underlying idea of the obsession with the radio serial *Love Letters* is that the world is unendurable without some kind of fantasy, and the society provides its people with many possible outlets for this need. In the novel, Lola Narcisa and the house servants weep unashamedly listening to the radio serial, Baby Alacran finds escape watching her TV show, Romeo Rosales dreams of success at the movies. The First Lady echoes public sentiment when she explains: "What would life be like without the movies? Unendurable, *di ba*? We Filipinos, we know how to endure, and we embrace the movies. With movies, everything is okay *lang*. It is one of our few earthly rewards . . ." (224). There is also the popular phenomenon of the beauty and talent contests, in which unknowns can literally become stars overnight. The American Dream is translated into Filipino life in the form of Hollywood success.

The need to dream becomes for too many not a transcendence toward a higher reality, but escape from reality, just as Freddie Gonzaga likes to consider himself a Spaniard, though he is Filipino born; and Rio keeps referring to her "Rita Hayworth" mother; and Romeo's real name is Orlando. The use of dreams is also very interesting and very pointed. Hagedorn recounts several dream sequences that reverberate with irony as when the First Lady dreams of partying at the Waldorf Astoria, suddenly noticing she has no shoes on and later rushing into an elevator run by George Hamilton. Rio's dreams, as an immigrant, are a reflection of her displacement: "In dream after dream (my brother and I) are drawn to the same silent tableau: a mysterious light glowing from the window of a deserted, ramshackle house. . . The meaning is simple and clear, I think. Raul and I embrace our destiny: we fly around in circles, we swoop and dive in effortless arcs against a barren sky, we flap and beat our wings in our futile attempts to reach what must surely be heaven" (247). In this sense, the metaphors of dreams and fantasies acquire greater resonance as they come to reflect not just personal escape from unwanted reality, but a collective refusal to admit to the way things have become. The book is firmly anchored in martial law Manila, when the government was most busily engaged in providing the trappings of a free, democratic, and rich capitalist society. Military power came with a gentle veneer but could be brutal: Daisy is tortured by a general who talks to her like a daughter. Hagedorn focuses on the Manila Film Festival and a beauty contest, presumably the Manila Miss Universe Contest, as symptomatic signs of the times, with the emphasis on show and pretense—blocking out the tourist's view of squatter locations with board fences (Evangelista, 51).

The Filipino's colonial mentality—the unflinching belief that everything made in the USA is automatically better than anything made at home—becomes a major trope in the novel. Rio's and her cousin Pucha's tastes are dictated by the stereotype: they admire Gloria Talbott for her casual arrogance that "seems inherently American, modern, and enviable" (4); Pucha loves pork and beans "because they're gooey with molasses, but most of all because they're expensive and imported" (62). Only Senator Avila is pragmatic about this particular postcolonial malady and declares that "our torrid world is threatened by its legacy of colonialism and the desire for revenge. . . We Pinoys suffer collectively from a cultural inferiority complex. We are doomed by our need for assimilation into the West and our own curious fatalism . . . (We are) a complex nation of cynics, descendants of warring tribes which were baptized and colonized to death by Spaniards and Americans . . . a nation betrayed and then united only by our hunger for glamour and our Hollywood dreams" (100–1).

The revelation of the complex nature of the Filipino, as a cultural amalgamate of East and West, is essential to Hagedorn's discourse. "The chamber orchestra was playing *merienda* music—a little Strauss waltz mixed in with the Jealousy tango, maybe some *kundiman* mixed in with the cha–cha—*alam mo na*, real *halo–halo* stuff" (57). A patent consciousness of the Filipino as a species of "created" identity comes through in some of the characters. Isabel Alacran is outstanding as a model of what colonial admiration impulses one to achieve. In her youth, she was a nightclub hostess, a beauty contest winner (Miss Postwar Manila, Miss Congeniality), and a movie starlet. After marrying one of the country's richest men, "she takes a lot of airplanes, perfects her English. . . . She develops a Spanish accent, and learns to roll her r's. She concentrates on being thin, sophisticated, icy. Her role models include Dietrich, Vicomtesse Jacqueline de Ribes, Nefertiti, and Grace Kelly. She is an asset to her husband at any social function. She is manicured and oiled, massaged and exercised, pampered like some high–strung, inbred animal. She has reconstructed her life and past, to suit her taste" (20). Severo Alacran's flippant judgement concerning one of his paintings may thus be applied to his wife: "I can no longer tell what's authentic from what's fake" (21). Identity seems therefore to be principally something one constructs, rather than thing one is. And this definition does not preclude double identities, as in Rio's father, who "believes in dual citizenships, dual passports, as many allegiances to as many countries as possible at any one given time" (7).

It is Rio who ultimately must come to terms with what being Filipino is and means. She tells her friends that when she grows up she will make movies, not act in them. When the story ends, she has immigrated to the United States, but lives "anxious and restless, at home only in airports" (247). And the movies she makes as an expatriate may well be in and of the mind only: the history that she is forced to invent for herself. On a return trip to the Philippines, as she tries to recapture her childhood, her father warns her not to visit their old house, saying, "You'll be disappointed. Memories are better" (245). But memories, as Rushdie has pointed out, are characterized by their elusiveness and their unreliability. In *Dogeaters* the subversion of the referentiality of fiction is deliberate. The events that Rio later narrates are called into question in the penultimate chapter, in which Pucha's version of the same events is so radically different that there is no possibility of reconciling the two threads or of choosing the more reliable narrative. As Caroline Hua contends, the novel "underlines in its ironic way the realization that any reading of the text consists not in the study of mimetic mirroring or subjective projecting but in an exploration of how we see ourselves (or are seen by others), and how we construct our notions of self in the present and the past" (121). The past as representation is therefore no more "accurate" than any fiction.

Latin American writer Isabel Allende, whose themes mirror those of Rosca and Hagedorn, has said that "in a novel we can give an illusory order to chaos. We can find the key to the labyrinth of history. We can make excursions into the past, to try to understand the present and dream the future. In a novel we can use everything: testimony, chronicle, essay, fantasy, legend, poetry and other devices that might help us to decode the mysteries of our world and discover our true identity" (45). Rosca's and Hagedorn's novels, as reflections of Filipinos' views of the Philippines from America, are powerful articulations of the discourse of the discovery and construction of the Filipino identity. The interaction of historical facts and memory are the tools that construct the immigrant's elusive story as the need to see beyond superficial accounts and tell their own versions, albeit fictionally constructed—to create, ultimately, a mythos rendered official in the telling.

Note

I would like to thank the Spanish Ministry of Education and Culture for funding that helped in the research for this chapter, part of the research project on "Historical and Fictional Worlds," of which this article is a result.

References

Allende, Isabel. "Writing as an Act of Hope." Pp. 41–63 in *Paths of Resistance: The Art and Craft of the Political Novel*, ed. William Zinsser. Boston: Houghton Mifflin, Co., 1989.

Campomanes, Oscar V. "Filipinos in the United States and their Literature of Exile." Pp. 49–78 in *Reading the Literatures of Asian America*, ed. Shirley Geok-lin Lim and Amy Ling. Philadelphia: Temple University Press, 1992.

Casper, Leonard. "Minoring in History: Rosca as Ninotchka." *Amerasia* 16, no. 2 (1990a): 201–10.

———. "Bangungot and the Philippine Dream in Hagedorn" *Solidarity* 127 (July–September 1990b): 152–57.

Evangelista, Susan. "Jessica Hagedorn and Manila Magic" *MELUS* 18, no. 4 (winter 1993): 41–52.

Hua, Caroline S. "*Dogeaters*, Postmodernism and the 'Worlding' of the Philippines." Pp. 113–27 in *Philippine Post-Colonial Studies: Essays on Language and Literature*, ed. Cristina Pantoja Hidalgo and Priscelina Patajo-Legasto. Quezon City: University of the Philippines Press, 1993.

Hutcheon, Linda. *Splitting Images: Contemporary Canadian Ironies.* Toronto: Oxford University Press, 1991.

Shirley Geok-lin Lim. *Nationalism and Literature: English–Language Writing from the Philippines and Singapore.* Quezon City: New Day Publishers, 1993.

Mestrovic, Marta. "Ninotchka Rosca" *Publisher's Weekly*, 6 May 1988, 90–91.

Rosca, Ninotchka. "Myth, Identity and the Colonial Experience" *World Englishes* 9, no. 2 (1990): 237–43.

Rosca, Ninotchka. *State of War.* New York: Norton, 1988.

San-Juan, E., Jr. "Mapping the Boundaries: The Filipino Writer in the U.S.A." *The Journal of Ethnic Studies* 19, no. 1 (spring 1991): 117–31.

9

POSTCOLONIAL FEMINIZING OF AMERICA IN CARLOS BULOSAN

Sheng-Mei Ma

> There is a beautiful lady
> surrounded with swords.[1]
> —Tagalog riddle

Ronald Takaki in *Strangers from a Different Shore* (1989) cites this Tagalog riddle to exemplify how *manongs*—first-generation Filipinos—cautioned their fellow countrymen newly arrived in the United States.[2] This riddle splits America into two halves and genders them as the beautiful lady (with the spontaneous association of the Statue of Liberty), for whom male immigrants yearn,[3] and as the masculine phallic symbols which forbid any communion with the "essence" of America—its femininity. The attraction for the "imagined community"[4] of a feminized America manifests itself as the persistent theme of postcolonial interracial romance for writers such as Carlos Bulosan, only to be repeatedly repulsed by a racist, largely "masculine" America. This erotic desire stemming from, in Frantz Fanon's term, the colonial complex,[5] intriguingly intersects with Bulosan's socialist activism against the masculine America. These two seemingly contradictory dimensions, in fact, complement each other in a postcolonial consciousness such as Bulosan's: the harsher the persecution by American men in the form of factory and farm owners or members of the police force along the West Coast, the more desperately the victims would embrace the escapist icon of Caucasian women. Eroticizing America appears to offer Filipinos a minimum sense of masculinity—through, ironically, enslaving themselves to idealized white women—in a land where they have been all but emasculated.

This complementariness of social formation and sexual fantasy has been explored, among other works, by *Nationalisms and Sexualities* (1992).[6] The blurring of "lines of national affiliation and sexual attachment" (Introduction, 2) observed by the editors of the collection exists in the minds of Bulosan's Pinoys longing to merge into America as well as in the minds of Pinoy-haters—American males who justify their discrimination against Filipinos in the name of national, racial, and sexual integrity. Indeed, the anti-Filipino sentiment in the United States during the depression years often exhibits itself as racism characterized by sexual anxieties. For instance, white Californian males' indignation over miscegenation focuses on what is regarded as aberrant Filipino sexuality, evident from the string of virulent statements quoted in Takaki: "The Filipinos are hot little rabbits, and many of these white women like them for this reason," a union greatly feared for it would allegedly propagate a "new type of mulatto," an "American Mestizo" (328-29). But this qualm over racial purity veils the economic cause of the persecution and the individual's desire for control. An avowed public concern arises, in fact, from private neurosis. Bulosan suggests such a hidden motive when he casts the castrated Leroy in "Life and Death of a Filipino in the USA" as none other than a union activist. Both the Californian men who made the racist remarks and Leroy's murderers in the story rationalize their actions on the basis of sexual mores (hence, Leroy's severed genitals) rather than economic and social reality. This enables them to account for their heinous crimes as preserving the integrity of the white race, thus masking their personal failure to compete in the labor market and in the social hierarchy.

The link Bulosan tacitly establishes between Leroy's mutilation and profession reflects the writer's own traumatized life and pro-union career in the United States. He devoted a major portion of his short life to social activism, writing for and editing union publications to fight for the exploited workers. His socialist leaning can be traced to his background. He grew up in an impoverished peasant family in the Philippines, a childhood meticulously recorded in his magnum opus, *America is in the Heart* (1943, 1973). This autobiographical fiction subsequently expands from his individual to the collective Filipino experience from the island-nation to the New World. Bulosan's dispossessed background sets the stage for his later conversion to union activism, as he relates easily to the plight of workers in a capitalist country in terms of his own origin. This transformation from a common laborer to an activist is chronicled in *America*; moreover, Bulosan makes outright assertions about his socialist conviction: "What I am trying to do . . . is to utilize our [Filipino] common folklore, tradition and history in line with my socialist thinking" (qtd. by E. San Juan, Jr. in *Bulosan: An Introduction with Selections*, 18). The exact contour of Bulosan's political affiliation, however, remains elusive. While clearly harboring Communist sympathy and Marxist ideology, he never once admits to them in his own writing. The word he constantly resorts to in characterizing his literary enterprise, as shown above, is "socialist." This might be an act of self-preservation in the anti-Communist atmosphere permeating the United States throughout his stay here—from the depression to World War II to the McCarthy era. Granted that these three terms—Marxist, Communist, socialist—have drastically different meanings, a non-theoretician operating in tight censorship as Bulosan did might have sensed some overlapping in their definitions and sought to exploit that accordingly. This paper will nevertheless respect his self-description and use henceforth the word "socialism."

Statements such as the one on his "socialist thinking" notwithstanding, Bulosan was, as P.C. Morantte testifies in *Remembering Carlos Bulosan: His Heart Affair with America* (1984),

> a bit too sentimental to be a bigoted Marxian doctrinaire and he always kept open his heart to the entry of noble souls high in the political and social ladder even though they happened to be of a different ideological persuasion from what he himself professed. (22)

It may be the biographer's own bias to stereotype Marxists as "bigoted . . . doctrinaire[s]," but Bulosan's political stance is correctly diagnosed as ambiguous. His ambivalence comes through most vividly in terms of the fusion of body politic and white bodies, of the interlocking of his faith in socialism and his obsession with Caucasian women. Long before socialism enters the consciousness of the teenage Filipino protagonist struggling with poverty in *America*, the pattern of entanglement of social commitment to the downtrodden and of sexual fantasy for white women has materialized: amidst the protagonist's misery, Mary Strandon from Spencer, Iowa, descends like a guardian angel to deliver him. The deifying and fetishizing of white women are strengthened by Strandon's story of Abraham Lincoln who liberated the slaves. Her physical presence supposedly foretells the narrator's own emancipation; a woman's corporeality meshes with the histories of the colonizer and the colonized on both sides of the Pacific Ocean. As *America* proceeds to reconstruct a Pinoy's brutalized life in the underworld on the West Coast in the 1930s and 1940s, the protagonist's socialist awakening converges unrelentingly with Caucasian female savior, whose clone-like duplications are variously named Mary Strandon, Judith, Marion, the sisters Lily and Rosaline, Dora Travers, Harriet Monroe, Alice and Eileen Odell, and so forth. (The only exception in *America* is Helen, a strike-breaker sabotaging union leaders' effort.) The politicized and the eroticized strands eventually become inseparable, since women are portrayed as, among other roles, mentors introducing him to a wide range of readings to raise his consciousness. This model of union activities interwoven with colonial romance continues unabated throughout the book. A number of critics, such as Elaine Kim and Susan Evangelista, have pointed out that white women offer some kind of saving grace in the hostile land of *America*, but this "redemption" is premised on the "purgatory" or even "hell" associated with the male side of America, which triggers Bulosan's socialist reaction.

The source of the gendering of two Americas and the resultant attraction/repulsion lies in the postcolonial condition. The ethos of iconizing white women was indeed widespread amongst Filipinos of Bulosan's time.[7] In his introduction to Bienvenido N. Santos's *Scent of Apples* (1979), Leonard Casper writes that Filipino immigrants used to be dubbed "blonde chasers" (x), which did not come entirely from white racist paranoia. Filipinos themselves admit to as much; Morantte explicates this mentality:

> Carlos felt insecurity, tinged with indignity, in his relationship with white girls. Like his countrymen Carlos liked white women. Filipinos tend to like white women insofar as they represent a type of feminine beauty of Hellenic standards: stately form, fair skin, light or blonde or brown hair, shapely nose, limpid blue or brown eyes, sensual lips. (18)

Quite tellingly, the verb tense shifts from the past with regard to Bulosan's specific case to the present as Morantte universalizes one Filipino's sexual preference, a move indicative not so much of Morantte's personal views of Bulosan but of a sentiment shared by many of the expatriates. The physical description of the ideal "Hellenic" femininity illustrates the extent to which postcolonialism pervades people's lives, including that of a union activist grappling with the hegemony which legitimizes the dominance of a particular ethnic group, along with its aesthetics. Such a colonial complex of inferiority surfaces unremittingly in Morantte's memories of Bulosan:

> Carlos loved America. However, it was a kind of idealistic love, with a tinge of romanticism, as one would love a beautiful girl above one's station in life—a rich girl, endowed with fame and power and glory, seemingly beyond the reach of ordinary mortals like him. . . . He was inwardly excited at the sight of Lady America holding a torch in one hand and a book of freedom and justice in the other. The symbol portended not the hopelessness of the situation but the promise of fulfillment of the dreams of all those coming to her shores. (95)

Rather than be taken in by such luring romanticism (which, at any rate, deconstructs itself subliminally—"the hopelessness of the situation"), one might see that the infatuation with Caucasian women comes from the fact that they symbolize America—its affluence and power, euphemized as enlightenment ("torch"), "freedom and justice." Put another way, even sexual preferences, guarded as the core of the private self, are not immune from the intervention and regulation of public discourse, such as the racial and cultural ideology of imperialism. Similar to the drive for domination underneath white racists' rage over miscegenation, Filipinos' fascination with white women is likewise rooted in political economy, which disguises itself as interracial eroticism.

Interracial eroticism is indisputably Bulosan's lifelong obsession and one of his paramount literary motifs. He writes about it extensively but still faults himself for not capturing it in the texts. This sense of inadequacy recurs in his correspondence. In a letter dated 2 November 1949, Bulosan digresses from a contemplation of his future masterpiece, "a series of four novels covering 100 years of Philippine history," to dwell on his favorite topic of "a novel covering the ideal friendship, courtship and marriage of a Pinoy and an American white woman" (San Juan, 152). The proximity of the two projects compels one to wonder which weighs more heavily in the author's mind. In another letter dated 24 September 1945, Bulosan claims that "[m]y recent poetry reflects the agonies of a Filipino lover loving a white woman in America, using the racial conflicts in California as a background" (San Juan 146). Whether "recent" in 1945 or at any given moment in his career, this theme of interracial romance proliferates with amazing frequency and intensity.

While these women in *America* function as deux ex machina to rescue the protagonist, Bulosan's short stories exhibit an identical yearning for and frustration over these female icons. "As Long As the Grass Shall Grow" revolves around an American woman, closely resembling Mary Strandon in *America,* who volunteers to teach Filipino children how to read and write—in English, needless to say. The idolization of Caucasian women commences early in childhood due to their alleged kindness.[8] "The Soldier" deals with the romance between a Filipino soldier and a Caucasian woman in the midst of a racist climate. In the quasi-autobiographical story "The Time of Our Lives," one of the characters, Morantte (Bulosan's biographer), asks a Caucasian woman bluntly: "Would you marry a Filipino?" (San Juan, 49). The story ends on an ominous note as "the small Filipino with the tall blonde" (San Juan, 52) whom the narrator and Morantte met in the bar is murdered. "Sometimes It's Not Funny" delineates the bankruptcy of the interracial dream as several Filipinos perfunctorily take turns proposing to Margaret, an American woman, who accepts every advance as perfunctorily. This trivialization of human emotion constitutes the initiation into this culture for the innocent narrator ready to propose to Margaret himself. Margaret and other women like her, by virtue of their seductress image, begin to complicate the stereotype of the Virgin Mary (Strandon). These two contrasting images form the opposite ends of a spectrum of women deployed to chart Filipino's desires in Bulosan. Finally, the image of heartless temptress is best represented in "The Romance of Magno Rubio" by a white "Goddess," Clarabelle, worshipped by Rubio, *"Four-foot six inches tall. Dark as a coconut. Head small on a body like a turtle's"* (San Juan, 59). This woman swindles the hard-earned savings of the Filipino laborer who, burdened by his subhuman self-image, bears no grudge against his idol.

On the contrary, whenever Bulosan portrays females in the Philippines (seldom in the States, for there were few Filipino women here during and after the Depression), they usually live in squalor. The lengthy depiction in *America* of the narrator's mother and sisters marks Filipino femininity with hunger and pain, as opposed to Caucasian women associated with emancipation and well-being. Despite their resourcefulness, these Filipino women could not overcome the social forces in the Philippines eroding their lives, from which the protagonist only wishes to flee. Indeed, the protagonist leaves for the New World in *America* and, in "Homecoming," takes his leave yet again after returning from the United States an ailing man. Even in *The Laughter of My Father* (1942), where America and its legendary females are noticeably absent, Filipino femininity epitomized by, once again, the young narrator's mother and sisters, is already fated to endure misery. In addition to all the instruments of feudalistic oppression in the island-nation from the husband who occasionally exhibits at times magical power in outwitting the rich yet who, alas, is frequently unemployed, irresponsible, and drunk. Filipino women are portrayed as the ultimate victims, occasionally at the hands of their peasant husbands.

The varying representations of Filipino and Caucasian womanhood grow out of the power structure inherent in postcoloniality. That the momentary respites in the narrator's dreadful vagrancy in Bulosan's corpus are almost always blessed with the company of angelic women is symptomatic of postcolonial desires. At first glance, *The Power of the People* (1977, 1986), his last work and published posthumously,[9] seems to be an exception to Bulosan's consistent erotic imaginings, with the text's unmistakably Communist ideology and its focus on a group of underground insurgents. In other words, its overt political scheme rather contests the claim of inextricability of the public and the private. The story follows seven "Huk"— Communist guerrillas in the Philippines, a term never mentioned in the text perhaps due to the McCarthy era and similar paranoia in his home country— fighters trekking across the island to the city of Manila to rendezvous with Felix Rivas, a courier from the United States bringing them money for the

Communist cause. This journey proves to be a prolonged homecoming for the guerilla members, as each of them visits his or her hometown to see what is left of the family and village and to convert the peasants to the Communist cause. More significantly, this book is Bulosan's own wish-fulfillment of homecoming and of a successful proletarian uprising in his homeland, two thwarted dreams which remain unrealized until his death in 1956.

Jingoistic and didactic at times, cinematic and suspense-filled elsewhere, this novel, unique in Bulosan's corpus, thrives on military action—assassinations, ambushes, sabotages, getaways. Its plot of an indigenous struggle leads one to assume it has little to do with America and *manong*'s psyche. But America remains the subtext of this novel on the Communist rebellion in the Philippines. Dante, a member of the group, used to befriend Felix while in the States and hence is the only person who can identify the courier. Not only are Dante's experiences intimately entwined with America but both Dante and Felix are spinoffs of the narrator in *America*. Both migrated to the New World in a similar way that was as to the narrator; both suffered immense hardships and were hospitalized; Felix's testicles were crushed by racists and were nursed back to health by Caucasian women who brought him books and new horizons of consciousness—episodes based closely on the plot of *America* and on what appears to be the "master narrative" of Bulosan's literary imagination.

Undoubtedly, he harbors an intensified bitterness against America, where men and women "destroyed my humanity" (201). The American dream conceived in *America* via the perfect bodies of angelic females turns nightmarish more than a decade later as Dante makes love—for the sake of the mission, which is never adequately explained—with the disfigured virgin, Mameng, a fighter who symbolizes the beloved nation pristine in spirit yet long defiled. Bulosan's disillusionment with America, however, is rendered in a highly problematic manner: Dante dies toward the end without identifying Felix and the mission grinds to a halt. Because the success of their assignment relies on, yet again, a promise of delivery/deliverance from America, America continues to, like its females, frustrate just as it entices. This may or may not be the end intended by Bulosan (who died just months after the text's alleged completion in 1955), since no sense of closure informs the concluding chapters except Dante's foreboding demise. But as a narrative of a political revolt in the Philippines as well as a sexual one against the romanticized white femininity, it is significant that both occur in Bulosan's fantasy. The latter, in particular, represents not so much a total refutation of his lifelong obsession with the feminized America; rather, it reaffirms the pattern of desire for and disenchantment over America, the ensuing melancholy bound to accompany any excessive romantic longing.

The apparent lack of Caucasian female characters in *Power* does not keep Bulosan from utilizing one of his favorite tropes—feminizing the land, the "mother earth," part of the cultural and linguistic legacy of patriarchy. This metaphor in fact foreshadows the consummation of Dante and Mameng:

> There was a rise on the hillside below them. . . . the rise became a woman in repose, undinal and containing the orgiastic truth of life . . . ululant now and vibrant with life . . . The femaleness of it, the fecundity of it all. (100-1)

Long preceding this textual strategy of eroticizing local landscape through male gaze, Bulosan has deified American women by merging them with the promised land. For instance, the object of desire in "Five Poems for Josephine" readily coalesces with America, in accordance with the notion of "motherland." That the land does not consider the narrator a native son ironically intensifies his urge to possess it by possessing its woman:

> Now I contemplate this our land, flowing
> With her full breasts into hamlets and villages,
> Full of life and strength, with her arteries
>   Running along the Mississippi;
>   With her blue eyes in the Great Lakes,
> And her fertility in corn and wheat and grapes
> . . .
> And my new country! And my new paradise!
> O Josephine! O Josephine! O Josephine!
> (Evangelista 98-99)

The central metaphor rather befits the poem's expansive, romantic impulse. Yet even during the bleakest moments prior to *Power*—moments antithetical to the verse's utopian vein, the dual gendering of America as a literary deployment serves to compartmentalize Bulosan's experience, thus safeguarding the mother earth's innocence and impunity: "And this land . . . is not yet denuded by the rapacity of *men*. Rolling like a beautiful woman with an overflowing abundance of fecundity and murmurous with her eternal mystery, there she lies before us like a great mother" ("Be American," San Juan, 37 emphasis mine). The dark hours of the writer's experience are attributed to "the rapacity of [American] men," whereas femininity harbors both seduction and security.

The pliant myth of a feminine America is, in some cases, obliquely embraced by Bulosan's critics. In addition to chapters and passages rightfully assigned to examine Bulosan's relationship with white women in their respective works, a number of Filipino/Filipino American/American writers appear to compose in terms and metaphors akin to Bulosan's postcolonial romance. P.C. Morantte casts his biography of Bulosan in the trope of the writer's "affair with America" (part of the sub-title.) Postcolonial aspiration continues to be treated as an unadulterated romance between a Pinoy and "a beautiful girl above one's station in life," whereas the material conditions formulating the private drive go uninterrogated. The colonial complex created by the infrastructure of power seems to plague Bulosan's critics as much as it does Bulosan himself. The Marxist critic E. San Juan, Jr., on the other hand, opens his *Bulosan: An Introduction with Selections* (1983) with a photograph of Bulosan and a white woman. No explanation is offered as to who that woman is and in what manner she is important enough to merit the limelight. But perhaps that is exactly the point: her personal identity does not matter. The fact that she is white and slightly taller valorizes her as the symbol of Caucasian females adored not only by Bulosan but by the collective postcolonial psyche.

Notes

1. Originally *"Isana magandang señora libot na libot ng espada,"* this Tagalog riddle is taken from Ronald Takaki's *Strangers From a Different Shore.* Takaki asserts that this riddle serves to "warn[ed] the newcomers" to America (316).

2. This article uses "America" to indicate the idealized image of the United States, which immigrants long to attain. "The United States" becomes more of a geopolitical term signifying the nation.

3. Based on the historical fact that most Filipinos in the United States around the time Bulosan composed his works were males, this article concentrates solely on the male psyche of *manongs.*

4. Benedict Anderson defines "nations" as "imagined communities" in his pioneering work, *Imagined Communities.* While he seeks to reconfigure nationalism from within each state and its tradition, I borrow his concept to describe how it is done from without, how "aliens" such as Bulosan conceive "America."

5. See "The So-Called Dependency Complex of Colonized Peoples" in Fanon's *Black Skin, White Masks.*

6. Most case studies in *Nationalisms and Sexualities* (Parker, et al.) investigate how nationhood is conceived and crafted from within, by that nation's own members. It does not focus on the subject of this article—the fact that "aliens" such as Bulosan in a host country similarly labor to conceptualize the nation-ness of that state. In this particular instance, Bulosan deliberately feminizes America to embolden the alien protagonist's masculinity.

7. This sexual preference is common in literature. The kind of interracial eroticism involving Caucasian woman and Asian man is created by male immigrant writers not only from the Philippines but from elsewhere. Moreover, this obsession with the idealized bodies of white women is continued by second- or third-generation ethnic male American writers as well. See my "Interracial Eroticism in Asian American Literature: Male Subjectivity and White Bodies," *Journal of American Culture* (Forthcoming).

8. "As Long As the Grass Shall Grow" was analyzed by Lina B. Diaz de Rivera who utilized feminist theories, but de Rivera's high praise for the story was refuted by L.M. Grow.

9. Originally titled *The Cry and the Dedication, The Power of the People* was written circa. 1955 and was initially published in Canada in 1977. The 1986 edition came out in the Philippines.

References

Anderson, Benedict. *Imagined Communities: Reflections on the Origin and Spread of Nationalism.* London: Verso, 1983.

Bulosan, Carlos. *America Is in the Heart.* 1943. Reprint, Seattle: University of Washington Press, 1973.

———. *The Laughter of My Father.* New York: Harcourt, Brace and Co., 1942.

———. *The Power of the People* 1977. Manila: National Book Store, 1986.

Casper, Leonard. Introduction. Pp. ix-xvi in *Scent of Apples: A Collection of Stories,* by Bienvenido N. Santos. Seattle: University of Washington Press, 1979.

De Rivera, Lina B. Diaz. "The Female Principle and Woman Reading in Carlos Bulosan Story." *Diliman Review* 37, no. 3 (1989): 11-14.

Evangelista, Susan. *Carlos Bulosan and His Poetry: A Biography and Anthology.* Seattle: University of Washington Press, 1985.

Fanon, Frantz. *Black Skin, White Masks.* New York: Grove, 1967.

Grow, L.M. "Carlos Bulosan: a Quagmire for Critics." *Pilipinas* 18 (spring 1992): 19-37.

Kim, Elaine H. *Asian American Literature: An Introduction to the Writings and Their Social Context.* Philadelphia: Temple University Press, 1982.

Ma, Sheng-mei. "Interracial Eroticism in Asian American Literature: Male Subjectivity and White Bodies." *Journal of American Culture.* (Forthcoming.)

Morantte, P.C. *Remembering Carlos Bulosan: His Heart Affair with America.* Quezon City, Philippines: New Day Publishers, 1984.

Parker, Andrew, Mary Russo, Doris Aommer, and Patricia Yaeger, eds. *Nationalisms and Sexualities.* New York: Routledge, 1992.

San Juan, Epifanio, Jr. *Bulosan: An Introduction with Selections.* Manila: National Book Store, 1983.

Takaki, Ronald. *Strangers from a Different Shore: A History of Asian Americans.* New York: Penguin, 1989.

10

MAXINE HONG KINGSTON AND THE DIALOGIC DILEMMA OF ASIAN AMERICAN WRITERS

Amy Ling

In June 1993, at Cornell University, during the tenth national conference of the Association for Asian American Studies, Robert Ku, a lecturer at Hunter College, delivered a provocative paper lamenting that Asian American writers themselves use the language of anthropological ethnography and thereby partake of the hierarchical binaries of Same and Other, Normal and Exotic, Advanced and Backward, Superior and Inferior. As "native informants," they naturally fall within the second half of these categories. To demonstrate the similarity of their language, Ku read five brief unidentified passages, two by noted social scientists and three by noted Asian American writers. He later identified the authors of these passages as Bronislaw Malinowski, Carlos Bulosan, Younghill Kang, Maxine Hong Kingston and Sigmund Freud.

What these passages had in common, it seemed to me, was not so much their language as their subject matter. Each passage described an event or ritual, either a marriage or punishment for a violation of a prohibition, that entailed customs specific to a culture outside of the dominant Anglo-European culture, such as the peasant wedding in the Philippines in the first chapter of *America is in the Heart*, in which the bride is discovered not to be a virgin and therefore stoned by the villagers, and the similarly brutal treatment of the No Name Woman in Kingston's opening chapter of *The Woman Warrior*. Ku was disturbed and distressed by the "uneasy relationship

Reprinted by permission of *Bucknell Review* where it originally appeared in Vol. 39:1.

between literature, ethnography, [and] psychoanalysis"[1] which Asian American writers, by their very position within a dominant society, cannot escape. He was puzzled and paralyzed because he wants to write his own story, presumably a Korean American bildungsroman, but cannot figure out how to do it without sounding like an ethnographic "insider informant." Moved by his predicament, I tried to console him by remarking that his role and that of all minority writers in this society, if we wish to be understood by a majority audience, cannot help but be cultural explainers until such time as everyone is informed on the myriad cultures that make up the United States. Given the size of the task and the inertia or chauvinism of most people, this universal enlightenment is not likely to happen in the near future. We have no choice, except of course, if we choose to speak only to others exactly like ourselves. If Ku wishes to address exclusively a Korean American audience, then, he can feel relieved of what he considers an onerous duty. But he will also be relieved of a great many readers. Moreover, I thought, in my self-righteous missionary mode, as teachers, it is our mission and our privilege to educate.

I suggested also that it is not so much the specificities of what is being conveyed as the tone and manner in which they are conveyed that sets apart the outsider standing aloof and above from the insider standing beside. The outsider creates the sense of otherness; the insider relates the norm.

At the same time, of course, we are all doubly conscious, in the Du Boisian sense, constantly aware of how we are being perceived while we are in the act of perceiving. Readers from outside the Asian American perspective, readers who may be reluctant in the first place, such as students taking a course in Asian American literature because they must satisfy an ethnic studies requirement for graduation, will complain that the material is so foreign and strange that they cannot possibly relate to it. (One would think they'd been asked to read stories written by baboons.) When confronted with several such responses this semester, I finally replied, "What about relating to this material as a human being?" (My sense of mission and privilege as an educator was growing faint.) The other response I found totally exasperating was the "Is-this-characteristic-of-Asian-Americans?" response. For example, "The narration in this text is fragmented. Is this a characteristic of Asian Americans?" Or "These novels devote a lot of time and space to food and family—are these characteristically Asian American concerns?" Where does such lack of comprehension come from? Is it so impossible for such students to think of Asian Americans as part of the human species? Teaching Asian American literature to white students in the midwest can be at times comparable to handling nitroglycerin; the material, the students and I are all, for different reasons, volatile.

Kingston herself has published an essay about the cultural misreadings by two thirds of the reviewers of *The Woman Warrior*, who measured "the book and me against the stereotype of the exotic, inscrutable, mysterious oriental":

> I thought the reality and humanity of my characters would bust through any stereotypes of them. Simple-mindedly, I wore a sweatshirt for the dust-jacket photo, to deny the exotic. I had not calculated how blinding stereotyping is, how stupefying. The critics who said how the book was good because it was, or was not, like the oriental fantasy in their heads might as well have said how weak it was, since it in fact did not break through the fantasy. . . "How amazing," they may as well be saying. "That she writes like a human being. How unoriental." [2]

It is not just reviewers from other cultures that "misread" an author's intent. Readers from within that very culture feel particularly free to use their own authors for target practice. Perhaps the author has objected to a cultural practice close to the heart of the reader, but such an objection is an author's right. It is bold and courageous, for example, for Kingston to counteract the erasure of her transgressive paternal aunt by writing about her, as it is bold and courageous of Alice Walker to depict the act and the consequences of clitorectomy. It is good and right of Bulosan to sympathize with the bride who did not pass the virginity test and to call her stoning a "cruel" and "backward" custom.

But these bold and courageous stands are also provocative acts which place the multicultural writer in a visible and vulnerable position, susceptible to attack from all sides. All too often the most vociferous slings and arrows are flung from those within the minority culture itself, with such barbs as these: "This writer is a traitor to the community and to the cause; she's not telling the story right or she's telling the wrong one; he's hanging out dirty laundry for other people's eyes; she's falling into stereotypes and catering to base appetites for the exotic and the barbaric." Amy Tan, David Henry Hwang, and particularly Maxine Hong Kingston—the best known Asian American writers—have all been attacked along these lines by Asian American critics.

Sau-ling Wong, a Hong Kong-born scholar, takes American-born Amy Tan to task for mistranslating the Chinese words "tang jieh" as "sugar sister" instead of "older female cousin on the father's side," but this translation may also be seen as poetic license and further, as affirmation of what it is to be Chinese American. Tan's mistake in homonyms confirms the distance between Chinese and Chinese American, a distinction most Asian Americans are vocal and insistent about maintaining. William Chang has complained that there are no positive images of Asian males for him to identify with in David Henry Hwang's "M. Butterfly." Since the only Asian male in the play is a transvestite, he berates Hwang for not presenting the Asian male in a favorable light. But I haven't heard any French men complaining that they are being portrayed as idiots who after twenty years do not know the sex of their own lovers. The problem is clear: despite the recent efflorescence in Asian American literature, we still do not have enough writers to allow each one the right to write according to his or her own lights.

But most vociferous and persistent among Asian American critics is Frank Chin, who stands out for being uncompromisingly hostile. He has publicly called Kingston a "yellow agent of stereotype" who "falsifies Chinese history" and thereby "vilifies Chinese manhood." [3] When I protested during my only conversation with Frank Chin last fall that Amy Tan and Maxine Hong Kingston were not racists, as he has been asserting, but feminists, his retort—a scream—was "Feminists are racists!" In the "Afterword" to his collection of short stories, *The Chinaman Pacific & Frisco R. R. Co.* (1988), Chin writes a scathing parody of Kingston's *The Woman Warrior*, which he calls "The Unmanly Warrior." As a counter move to Chinese American feminism, and to the effeminization of Chinese American men, Chin offers the Chinese heroic tradition found in *Romance of the Three Kingdoms* and *The Water Margin*, certain of whose heroes he incorporates into his latest novel, *Donald Duk*. But critic King-Kok Cheung has rightly pointed out that "the refutation of effeminate stereotypes through the glorification of machismo merely perpetuates patriarchal terms and assumptions," and she asks plaintively, "Is it not possible for Chinese American men to recover a cultural space without denigrating or erasing the feminine?" [4]

As means of putting Chin in his place, though she publicly denies that this was her intent, Kingston has captured Chin's voice and character in her protagonist, Wittman Ah Sing, in her novel *Tripmaster Monkey*. Instead of placing Chin in the tradition of Gwang Gung, the God of Literature and War, one of the one hundred and eight heroes of *Romance of the Three Kingdoms*, which Chin claims for himself, Kingston finds his counterpart in the mischievous and irrepressible Monkey King, a trickster figure, from the picaresque Chinese folk novel *Journey to the West*. [Shawn Wong, novelist and colleague of Chin's, told me that he was amazed at how accurately Maxine had caught Frank's voice; he phoned Frank to say, "She must have been a fly on the wall when you were talking!"] [5] Kingston, however, claims that the narrative voice in this novel belongs to Gwan Yin, the Goddess of Mercy, and it is her power that disarms the militant Wittman, transforming him into a pacifist, and her voice that has the last word, "Dear American monkey, don't be afraid. Here, let us tweak your ear, and kiss your other ear." Her tone is slightly mocking and yet loving, like that of an indulgent mother with a naughty but beloved son.

Other Chinese and Chinese American readers have complained that Kingston has mixed up Cantonese and Mandarin romanizations of Chinese words, that she has combined the legends of Fa Mu Lan and Yueh Fei—*he's* the general who had words carved into his back—that she shouldn't have written about the monkey brain feast, that she mustn't emphasize footbinding and misogynist Chinese sayings because these are only a small part of Chinese culture and tradition. But these complaints seem petty and in no way diminish the considerable achievement of *The Woman Warrior*, which in my opinion stands as the supreme Chinese American feminist text. To read this text as insider informant, as exotic orientalism or as community historian is to miss the forest for some mosses under certain trees. It is to deny the text its complexity and richness as the embodiment of a multiplicity of perspectives, of reflexivity, dialogism, and heteroglossia. Let us now focus on these aspects of this text.

In the indeterminacy of its narrative style, we find what anthropologists like Barbara Myerhoff are calling reflexivity, the visible sign in the text of the writer's awareness of the act of writing, the writer in dialogue with herself. In "No Name Woman," for example, Kingston tells the aunt's story many times, first giving her mother's brief version, the bare-bone facts, then imagining all the possible narratives behind these bare-bones, freely employing the word "perhaps" and the conditional present perfect tense "A bun could have been contrived" to indicate the tentativeness of these versions. Later, in the story of Moon Orchid's meeting with her long-lost husband, Kingston gives us a detailed version of the encounter in her chapter "At the Western Palace" and in the next chapter undercuts the entire narration by stating, "What my brother actually said was. . . " and correcting herself and becoming even more specific, "In fact, it wasn't me my brother told about going to Los Angeles; one of my sisters told me what he'd told her." In other words, narratives are all created and creative acts; "reality" is created through words, and words are ripe with possibility. In providing her reader with so many possible narratives, Kingston demonstrates her awareness of the act of writing as a reflection of multiple and multiplying images. Where the "truth" lies is not her concern; her delight is in the richness of possibilities and in her own creativity in imagining them.

In applying Bakhtin to *The Woman Warrior*, one may read the entire text as an extended exploration of the internal dialogism of three words: *Chinese, American,* and *female.* Each term carries a multitude of meanings in dialogue, if not open warfare, with each other. To be specific, what does the word Chinese mean from the inside, that is, to the people so designated? What does it mean to the first-generation immigrant, to the second-generation American born, to the fourth or fifth generation? At what point does an immigrant Chinese become an American? What does the term mean from the outside, to the designators, to the stereotypers, to whites who feel that their places have been usurped? What are the word's historical, political, and social ramifications, underpinnings, and overlays? How does it differ from other related terms, such as *Japanese* or *Korean*? Similar questions may be applied to the other two terms: *American* and *female*. The entire book is devoted to an exploration of these words in an attempt at a self-definition that, finally, is never definitive in the sense of complete, conclusive, static. Paradox, flux, a "surplus of humanness," a defiance of fixation and categories characterize *The Woman Warrior*, as they characterize life. *The Woman Warrior* has gone further than any other text in exploring the complexities of these terms.

We find dialogism and polyphony most apparent in the fissures or fault lines in the narrative, in the places where Kingston's language shifts abruptly and the disrupture is visible. It is these fissures between and overlappings of linguistic plates which are the most revealing. One obvious example occurs in the first chapter. Between describing the lengths that women and girls endured to be Chinese beautiful, Kingston interjects this sentence: "I hope that the man my aunt loved appreciated a smooth brow, that he wasn't just a tits-and-ass man."[6] The abruptness of this male-locker room or fraternity-house lingo in the midst of rather detailed even poetic, if painful, descriptions of Chinese female beauty secrets brings the reader up short. In Bakhtin's terms, Kingston here "exhibits" these American male words as a "unique speech thing," [7] language that is totally alien and unassimilable in the context, and yet it is a voice, one of thousands, in Kingston's head. That Kingston places this particular sentence in this particular setting is not only a linguistic act with stylistic ramifications but a culturally significant statement as well; for form, style and content, as Bakhtin noted, are all inextricably linked. The context, the sentences surrounding our "tits and ass man," show the excruciating pain that Chinese women endure in the removal of eyebrow and forehead hairs, and facial freckles in order to win favor from the male gaze, but their attention to such Lilliputian detail is wasted in the United States where the Brobdingnagian male gaze is ostensibly only concerned with gross anatomical parts. The linguistic shift, the insertion of this sentence, emphasizes the contrast between the Chinese women's attention to fine detail and the jock expression's reductionism and objectification.

But Kingston's own position between the two is ambiguous. Is she proud of the "needles of pain" which her mother forced her to endure for the Chinese ideal of beauty or relieved that, in America, a woman is free from these "Chinese tortures"? Does she interject the slang expression to parody its reductionist view or does she appropriate this language to counteract the "demure" and silent Chinese girl stereotype that she hates?

I would argue that Kingston does both and that the ambiguity of her tone in this small episode reflects her tone throughout the entire text. Let us look at another example.

In the "White Tigers" chapter, when the young girl, let's call her Maxine, first meets the old couple who will be her teachers on the mountain, we find this dialogue:

> "Have you eaten rice today, little girl?" they greeted me.
> "Yes, I have, " I said out of politeness. "Thank you."
> ("No, I haven't," I would have said in real life, mad at the Chinese for lying so much. "I'm starved. Do you have any cookies? I like chocolate chip cookies.")
> (*WW*, 25)

The first exchange of question and response is pure Chinese convention, valuing politeness, displaying modesty and consideration of the other, saving face. It is, in fact, so conventional a question that it has become a salutation rather than a request for information—much as Americans ask "How are you?" but don't really expect an answer other than "Fine, thanks." The parenthetical addition—what she would have said "in real life"—is of course, the assimilated American response, valuing honesty and directness, frankly looking out for number one, and tinged with humor. Kingston's words denote impatience with the Chinese way; nonetheless, by the very act of presenting the two opposing ways of greeting strangers, she allows readers to judge for themselves the preferable social code. The expressed fondness for chocolate chip cookies seems a playful and somewhat greedy response, which I'm sure Kingston intended. Can it then be that Kingston is advocating Chinese politeness at the same time that she is complaining about it? Is she subverting American directness while seeming to embrace it? Is she, consciously or unconsciously, displaying the linguistic habit that her mother finally revealed, "That's what the Chinese say, We like to say the opposite" (*WW*, 203). The answer would seem to be yes to all the above, for as Kingston explains, "I learned to make my mind large, as the universe is large, so that there is room for paradoxes" (*WW*, 29). And in her text, paradoxes abound, and dialogues are continuous.

A third shift in gears, a major one, which certainly every reader of *The Woman Warrior* cannot help but notice, occurs in "The White Tigers" chapter. After twenty-six pages embroidering on the 62-line Chinese narrative poem, "Magnolia Lay," after recounting the young girl's rigorous fifteen-year training in physical, spiritual and mental self-control in lush, mystical, fantastic language, Kingston concludes the story of this paragon of virtue: "From the words on my back, and how they were fulfilled, the villagers would make a legend about my perfect filiality." We are given a brief intermission of a narrow-blank space and then the prosaic line, "My American life has been such a disappointment." From the rich, colorful heights of Chinese imaginative wish-fulfillment, we are suddenly dropped to the depths of mundane American life. Though elsewhere in the text Kingston complains that Chinese is "the language of impossible stories" (*WW*, 87) in "White Tigers" she clearly indulges herself in embellishing the Chinese story, in making it overwhelmingly beautiful, seductive, desirable because filled with power and valuation for the usually degraded Chinese girl. The Chinese woman warrior could do it all: excel in the "masculine" sphere of warfare and still return home to take up the "feminine" roles of mother, wife, daughter-in-law.

In fiction, everything is possible. Furthermore, as creator of the fiction, the author has control; she can make the rabbit jump into the fire to provide nourishment; she can have her characters live happily ever after. But "real life" is neither perfect nor controllable. American glories cannot compete with the Chinese glories of Fa Mulan; Maxine's straight A's cannot save her family's laundry, put food on the family table, or eliminate racism. Paradoxically, what Maxine calls "my American life" includes the "binds that China wraps around my feet," which include the misogynist sayings her parents and the other emigrant villagers imported to America: "Feeding girls is feeding cowbirds." "There's no profit in raising girls." "When you raise girls, you're raising children for strangers." "There is a Chinese word for the female I— which is 'slave.' Break the women with their own tongues!" (*WW*, 46-7). Another paradox: the same culture that inspired her with the heroic model of Fa Mulan also oppressed her with hateful sayings that caused her, as a child, to throw tantrums in protest. Words have power. These misogynist sayings of her parents and the racism of her American employers, "Order more of that nigger yellow, willya?" (*WW*, 48), are the demons that Maxine, the Chinese American woman warrior, must fight. They are what make her American life such a disappointment, for as demons, they lack the poetry of swords fighting in midair without hands.

Even in the first portion of the chapter "White Tigers" Kingston has not simply retold a Chinese myth, but has given her readers "one transformed by America, a sort of kung fu movie parody" ("CM", 57). The story of Fa Mulan may be a glorious model for a girl to dream about, serving as an antidote to the *No Name Woman*, but "White Tigers" is also a gross exaggeration, a wish fulfillment which the author indulges in with a smile on her face. The humor and irony are subtle and infrequent, but visible, as in this paragraph:

> So the hut became my home, and I found out that the old woman did not arrange the pine needles by hand. She opened the roof; an autumn wind would come up, and the needles fell in braids—brown strands, green strands, yellow strands. The old woman waved her arms in conducting motions; she blew softly with her mouth. I thought, nature certainly works differently on mountains than in valleys. (*WW*, 23)

In the last sentence, of course, we find the dialogic imagination of Kingston at work. She shifts gears and changes tone, moving from serious-poetic to ironic-parodic, interjecting another perspective on the narrative as she progresses, allowing another voice within her head to comment on the one that has up-to-now held the floor.

That Kingston's perspective fluctuates between Chinese and American is clearly visible in her shifting choice of personal pronouns; sometimes she identifies with the Chinese, using the first person plural "we"; at other times, she is distanced, referring to the Chinese as "they." Near the end of chapter one, for example, we find these sentences:

> In an attempt to make the Chinese care for people outside the family, Chairman Mao encourages us now to give our paper replicas to the spirits of outstanding soldiers and workers, no matter whose ancestors they may be. My aunt remains forever hungry. Goods are not distributed evenly among the dead. (*WW*, 16)

Not only is Kingston here assuming the perspective of her father's extended family in China, but, against her frequent assertions of her Americanness, she here identifies with the Chinese living in the People's Republic: "Chairman Mao encourages us." In chapter two, in the voice of the woman warrior general nearing the end of her glorious career, Kingston writes:

> I stood on top of the last hill before Peiping and saw the roads below me flow like living rivers. Between roads the woods and plains moved too; the land was peopled—the Han people, the People of One Hundred Surnames, marching with one heart, *our* tatters flying. The depth and width of Joy were exactly known to me: the Chinese population. (*WW*, 42, emphasis added)

Here again, we find the narrator's expression of pride in the land and unity with the people of China; she is the general and though her army has suffered, their tatters are hers.

At the other end of the spectrum, however, are many passages in which the narrator distances herself from the Chinese, speaking of them in the third person: "Chinese people are very weird" (*WW*, 158), Maxine and her brothers and sisters tell each other, rejecting their connection with their mother's incomprehensible sister, Moon Orchid, and asserting their difference. In another significant passage, Maxine clearly situates herself between Chinese and American, attributing an identity to herself through the modulation of voice:

> Normal Chinese women's voices are strong and bossy. We American-Chinese girls had to whisper to make ourselves American-feminine. Apparently we whispered even more softly than the Americans. (*WW*, 172).

Volume here is a trope for confidence and power. In the social hierarchy of Maxine's world, Chinese mothers have the loudest voices, the most power; American girls are next, with voices softer and more feminine. Chinese American girls have the softest voices of all, the least power. From Maxine's perspective, Chinese mothers are tyrannical forces to be struggled against; American girls are the enviable models to emulate; and Chinese American girls, straining to reject one model and to imitate the other, have no confident sense of self, for to whisper is to have no voice, and to have no voice is to be powerless. "Most of us eventually found some voice, however faltering. We invented an American-feminine speaking personality, except for that one girl who could not speak up even in Chinese school" (*WW*, 172). "If you don't talk, you can't have a personality" (*WW*, 180), Maxine screams at this totally silent Chinese girl whom she shockingly and unsuccessfully bullies. Maxine lashes out at this girl in a fury of self-hatred and also of rage against the powerless position of all Chinese American girls. As she punishes the silent girl for not conforming to the American norm, Maxine simultaneously uses her as a scapegoat for her own rage over her necessity to "invent an American-feminine speaking personality." Caught in a double bind, Maxine has been simultaneously silenced by a misogynist Chinese society, including a loud-voiced, domineering mother who may have cut her frenum, and also forced by American social pressures to assume an "invented" personality and voice.

In still another passage, the narrator spurns Chinese ways and seeks refuge in an American identity:

> To make my waking life American-normal, I turn on the lights before anything untoward makes an appearance. I push the deformed into my dreams, which are in Chinese, the language of impossible stories. Before we can leave our

parents, they stuff our heads like the suitcases which they jam-pack with homemade underwear. (*WW*, 87)

"Homemade underwear" is itself a multivalent trope, bursting with an internal dialogism encompassing both humiliation at these ill-fitting economy measures and, at the same time, pride in the determined parental love that defies poverty and hardship. On the one hand, one senses that the child leaving home is embarrassed by the homemade underwear packed into her suitcase; on the other hand, she knows that the parents who "jammed-packed" and "stuffed" the suitcases were motivated by a surplus of love. As far as the parent is concerned, the beloved child leaving home to brave the world alone cannot be over-protected, cannot have too much to cushion her from the cold she is certain to encounter. One cannot help but be touched by this concern. But who wants awkward, ill fitting homemade underwear? On still another hand, isn't it good to be loved so well, and who sees one's underwear anyway? The words "jam-packed" and "stuffed" also carry countervailing forces. These are parents who overwhelm with their undesired shows of love. It is no matter that their grown children will not wear this home made underwear; these parental offerings cannot be refused. (Amy Tan calls parental gifts of food "stern offerings of love.")

Just before this passage, Kingston had been retelling her mother's monster stories: the ape-man that attacked her, the baby born without an anus. In reaction to these frightening tales that haunt her nightmares, she clings to what seems "American normal"—the illuminated, the rational, and logical, plastics, neon, and periodic tables. A few pages later, "I would live on plastic" (*WW*, 92), Kingston says in disgust over the objects her mother has placed on her dinner plate. But again here is a dialogic passage. As plastic does not nourish the body, so periodic tables do not nourish the imagination. Although her mother's stories may have frightened her as a child, these stories, now that she is adult and a writer, are her mother's legacy, for they provide the color, texture and substance of the daughter's text. Although the daughter/narrator states a preference for the clean, the illuminated, and the plastic, she weaves her actual text from the monstrous, the frightening, the powerful—her mother's stories. The words say one thing; the text does another.

In fact, though the working out of a whole range of meanings around both ethnicity and gender is located in the Chinese/American dichotomy, it is most particularly situated in the mother-daughter relationship. Much of *The Woman Warrior* deals with the oppression of silencing and the liberation of speaking out. [8] And this theme is embodied in the problematic, dialogic mother-daughter relationship which informs the entire book. The mother's voice is so overpowering, the daughter cannot speak, even believing that her mother has cut her frenum and, by extension, her vocal cords. Maxine's reaction to this act, imagined or real, is again ambivalent and overtly expressed: "Sometimes I felt very proud that my mother committed such a powerful act upon me. At other times, I was terrified—the first thing my mother did when she saw me was to cut my tongue" (*WW*, 164). Identifying with her mother, she is proud of such strength and power; considering herself, however, the recipient of the operation, she is terrified. Is it an act of tyranny and silencing, as she fears, or an act of love, as her mother claims? "I cut it so you would not be tongue-tied. Your tongue would be able to move in any language. . . . You'll be able to pronounce anything," her mother explains (*WW*, 164). Later, Kingston writes, "I shut my teeth together, vocal cords cut, they hurt so. I would not speak words to give her pain. All her children gnash their teeth" (*WW*, 101). The daughter is both the pained and angry victim of her mother's powerful act of mutilation, or freeing, as well as the considerate daughter who will not speak words to give her mother pain. [Writing them, however, is another matter, because "the reporting is the revenge" (*WW*, 53).]

Describing the trip to Los Angeles to regain Moon Orchid's straying husband, Kingston writes, "Brave Orchid gave her sister last-minute advice for five hundred miles" (*WW*, 143). Note the dialogue within this sentence between the earnestness of the mother—"last minute advice" and the ironic context supplied by the daughter/author "for five hundred miles." Throughout *The Woman Warrior* we find the dialogue between anger/bitterness and love/tenderness as the daughter seeks self-definition apart from the mother. Since the struggle is defined as one of words and voice between one who is a powerful talker with many stories and one who has yet to find her voice, so the resolution of this struggle, and of the book, is a verbal and narrative one in that the final story of T'sai Yen is a collaborative effort between mother and daughter: "Here is a story my mother told me, not when I was young, but recently, when I told her I also am a storytalker. The beginning is hers, the ending, mine." It is, however, impossible to tell in this story where the beginning ends and the ending begins; which part of T'sai Yen's story is the mother's, which part the daughter's. Thus, the daughter's journey for her own voice is a struggle in which the mother-tongue" must be both refused and embraced, both preserved and modified, both acknowledged and gone beyond.

In the critical scene when Maxine finally "confesses" to her mother the two hundred plus items that had been weighing on her conscience "that I had to tell my mother so that she would know the true things about me and to stop the pain in my throat" (*WW*, 197), when her voice, so long repressed finally erupts before the person in whom she had invested all power and authority, she finds "No higher listener. No listener but myself." This scene is critical because in it, Maxine comes into her own voice at the expense of her mother's voice, her mother's authority. She makes an existential discovery—that she must be her own voice, her own listener, her own authority. This discovery is both frightening and liberating, both humiliating and exhilarating. And the voice that she reveals in this book is a composite of many voices: her mother's, her own physical voice, her imaginative voice, the Chinese culture's, American males', American females'. The tonal range is broad, encompassing complaint, confusion, anger, bitterness, pride, resignation, poetry, resolution.

Kingston eventually sees the similarities between herself and her mother, "a dragoness ('my totem, your totem')" (*WW*, 67). "At last I saw that I too had been in the presence of great power, my mother talking-story" (*WW*, 20). The Chinese customs that had been oppressive and incomprehensible for the child Maxine, the Chinese stories that had frightened and haunted her waking and sleeping are now seen by the adult Maxine, the writer Kingston, to be a rich source of inspiration, unique materials for her pen, a legacy to show off at the same time as one complains about it.

In her last chapter, "A Song for a Barbarian Reed Pipe," Kingston writes of the Chinese rituals her mother followed without bothering to explain, leaving a confused Maxine to hypothesize about the Chinese in the alienated third person plural:

> I don't see how they kept up a continuous culture for five thousand years. Maybe they didn't; maybe everyone makes it up as they go along. (*WW*, 185)

This sentence sums up the dialogic style of Kingston's book; both impulses—the pride of inheritance and a revisionist compulsion—are in dialogue. Her surface tone is complaining and disparaging, but there is an underlying pride in the inclusion of "five thousand years"—this length of time cannot help but be impressive. "Maybe everyone makes it up as they go along" seems to belittle Chinese culture, but for the daughter of a story-talker who is herself a masterful story-talker, as testified to throughout this text, what could be more wonderful than making up stories as one goes along?

In asserting racial and cultural difference, we Asian Americans run the risk of being dismissed as irretrievably and irrevocably Other. We also run the risk of falling into the stereotypes of difference created by the dominant culture. The obverse, however, is that if we assert our similarity to others, our humanness above our cultural specificities, we would seem to be eliminating the reason for multicultural studies in the first place. That Asian Americans are seen as irrevocably Other was forcibly brought home to me again last fall when our Wisconsin Senator Scott Klug was campaigning on the campus of the University of Wisconsin; he handed fliers to all students except those with Asian faces. His reasoning apparently went like this: these fliers cost money; Asian students are foreigners who cannot vote; therefore, why waste money on foreigners? As Elaine Kim wrote in the recent issue of *A Magazine,* "While we don't generally ask European Americans how come they speak such fluent English, how long they've been here, and when they are going back, these are common questions for Asian Americans." [9] These are what novelist Joy Kogawa has called "ice breaker questions that create an awareness of ice." [10] They are so frequently asked that we've come up with our own answers for them. When I'm complimented on how good my English is, I usually retort, "It should be, I teach it." Maxine Hong Kingston's standard response is kinder and wittier: "Thanks. So's yours."

In *Woman, Native, Other,* Trinh T. Minh-ha expresses the "Third World" writer's dilemma thus:

> Every path I/i take is edged with thorns. On the one hand, i play into the Savior's hands by concentrating on authenticity, for my attention is numbered by it and diverted from other, important issues; on the other hand, I do feel the necessity to return to my so-called roots, since they are the fount of my strength, the guiding arrow to which i constantly refer before heading for a new direction. [11]

This passage vividly delineates the dialogic dilemma of a person of color: we are identified anthropologically by the outside world according to external physical characteristics and expected by virtue of these characteristics to be "authentic," "the real thing." I note Trinh Minh-ha's expression, "i play into the Savior's hands"—by being singled out for attention from the First World, we are being lifted up and saved from the Third World status into which we were born. Should we be grateful or angry? Are we being rescued or insulted? To be rebellious and subversive, we could, as some of us do, reveal the deceptiveness of exterior signs by asserting our ignorance of that which we are thought to have inside knowledge of and to demonstrate how much we belong to the First World by showing off our ability to employ its "discursive" jargon and by displaying our "inside" knowledge of its canonical texts. On the other hand, are we not then also demonstrating how thoroughly we have been colonized, how disadvantaged and depleted we've grown in being so cut off from our "roots"? Further complication is added when those "roots," as in the case of Chinese American women, are not nurturing but devaluing. As a small example, my father said to me years ago,

"Why do you need to go to college, you're only a girl; you'll only get married." What sustenance can we get from such traditions; how can they be "the fount of . . . [our] strength"? These are questions that Maxine Hong Kingston wrestled with in *The Woman Warrior* and she answered them as well as anyone can, I believe, in her line: "I learned to make my mind large, as the universe is large so that it can contain paradoxes."

I conclude with another quote: "I write to show myself showing people who show me my own showing" (*WNO*, 22), writes Trinh Minh-ha to emphasize the multiple reflexivity, the many-mirrored images bouncing back and forth in dialogue with one another when an Asian American speaks and when she writes.

Notes

1. Robert Ji-Song Ku, "Can the Native Informant Write?: The Ethnographic Gaze and Asian American Literature." Paper delivered at the Association for Asian American Studies Conference, June 3, 1993. Typed manuscript Ku faxed to me on 25 November 1993.

2. Maxine Hong Kingston, "Cultural Mis-readings by American Reviewers," *Asian and Western Writers in Dialogue: New Cultural Identities*, ed. Guy Amirthanayagam (New York: Macmillan, 1982), 55–57. Hereafter "CM," cited in the text.

3. Frank Chin, Lecture, Oakland, Calif., 15 September 1989, quoted by Elaine H. Kim in "'Such Opposite Creatures': Men and Women in Asian American Literature" *Michigan Quarterly* (winter 1990): 76.

4. King-Kok Cheung, "The Woman Warrior Versus The Chinaman Pacific: Must a Chinese American Critic Choose between Feminism and Heroism?" in *Conflicts in Feminism*, ed. Mariane Hirsch and Evelyn Fox Keller. (New York: Routledge, 1991), 242.

5. Conversation with Shawn Wong. Madison, Wisconsin, October 1991.

6. Maxine Hong Kingston, *The Woman Warrior: Memoir of a Girlhood Among Ghosts*. (New York: Alfred A. Knopf, 1976), 9. Hereafter *WW*, cited in the text.

7. M. M. Bakhtin, *The Dialogic Imagination: Four Essays*, translated by Michael Holquist. (Austin: University of Texas Press, 1981) 255. Hereafter *DI*, cited in the text.

8. See King-kok Cheung, "Don't Tell: Imposed Silences in *The Color Purple* and *The Woman Warrior*," *PMLA* 103 (1988): 162-74 and her recent book *Articulate Silences: Hisaye Yamamoto, Maxine Hong Kingston, Joy Kogawa* (Ithaca: Cornell University Press, 1993).

9. Elaine H. Kim, "Business: The Color of Money," *A Magazine* 2, no. 1 (spring 1993): 30.

10. See Joy Kogawa, *Obasan*, 1981 (New York: Anchor, Doubleday, 1993), 271.

11. Trinh T. Minh-ha, *Woman Native, Other: Writing Postcoloniality and Feminism* (Bloomington: Indiana University Press, 1989), 89. Hereafter *WNO*, cited in the text.

11

The Semiotics of "China Narrative" in the Con/Texts of Kingston and Tan

Yuan Yuan

1. China and "China Narrative" in Con/Texts

"How 'Chinese' is *The Woman Warrior*?" Sau-ling Cynthia Wong asks in her essay "Kingston's Handling of Traditional Chinese Sources" (27). I believe this complex issue concerning nativity of ethnic literature deserves our serious consideration and intelligent discussion. At the same time, I notice, what has escaped our critical attention so far is not so much the nativity of ethnic narratives as the narrative complicity of nativity in literary representation. That is to say, the whole issue of nativeness requires our careful examination in the con/text of cultural differences and in relation to subject positions. The present essay attempts to explore the theoretical implication of this "native" issue by inquiring into the semiotics of "China experiences" in terms of "China Narrative" within the contexts of Maxine Hong Kingston's *The Woman Warrior* and *China Men*, and Amy Tan's *The Joy Luck Club* and *The Kitchen God's Wife*.

I observe that "China experiences," represented by Kingston and Tan, have unanimously emerged as a displaced narrative within "other" contexts. Which means, various narratives of China experiences have always been constructed against the background of American society and within the context of American culture. Hence, "China Narrative" in their novels informs a complex process of translation, translocation and transfiguration of

Printed with permission of *Critique*, published by Heldref Publications, 1319 Eighteenth Street, NW Washington, DC 20036 con/text, related to other locations, other times, other people and other histories. All kinds of "China Narratives," I argue, inevitably assume a specific form of representation—recollection. Actually, China experiences are transfigured into a "China Narrative" only after they have lost their reference to China, related more to the present American situation than the original context of Chinese society. Instead, it is the present American context that provides meaning and determines the content of "China Narrative." In short, only under such circumstances of loss of origin can China experiences emerge as a China Narrative—a text within different contexts. Eventually, China as a geographical location is transliterated into a semiotic space of recollection; China as personal experiences is translated into a cultural repository for reproduction; and, as a text, China is reconfigured into a variety of discourses: myth, legend, history, fantasy, films and talk-stories.

In the novels by both Kingston and Tan, "China Narrative" serves as an undercurrent but central text that structures the present relationship between mothers and daughters because of the specific position it occupies in their lives. Therefore, the cross-cultural hermeneutics of China is conducted within this domestic space, between two generations generally and between the Chinese mothers and their American-born daughters specifically.

As products of different cultures and histories, mothers and daughters abide by different cultural values and possess different modes of interpretation. In fact, they speak entirely different languages whenever they talk about China. "My mother and I spoke two different languages, which we did," Jing-Mei Woo says in *The Joy Luck Club*, "I talked to her in English, she answered back in Chinese" (23). The bilingual conversion turns into a game of translation, and in this translation, meaning is transfigured, displaced, and occasionally, lost. As Jing-Mei Woo says, "We translated each other's meanings and I seemed to hear less than what was said, while mother heard more" (27).

Constantly, both mothers and daughters have to reevaluate their "China Narratives" that are grounded in entirely different cultural contexts, with different historical references and subject positions. For the mothers, China Narrative informs a process of recollection (history or loss of it) while for the daughters, having never been there, China Narrative becomes a text of culture. In other words, China experiences as a semiotic text emerge in two different modes of discourse: History and Culture. This dichotomy is dramatized essentially through the dialogic position between mothers' historical recollection and daughters' cultural reproduction. Hence, the reconstitution of China experiences is achieved through choice of different discourses.

China, eventually, becomes a semiotic site where culture and identity are fought over, negotiated, displaced and transformed. Instead of a static ontological presence of a unitary category, China becomes a hermeneutic space for articulating identity and difference, a process that governs the cultural and historical reconstitution of the subjects. Within the context of the novels by Kingston and Tan, China becomes a fiction and functions as a signifier, and paradoxically, it is exactly this fiction that divides mothers and daughters and it is exactly this signifier that splits their identities and generates their tensions.

II. Mother's Loss Narrative: Recollecting and Repositioning

"China Narrative" emerges in the process of recollection in Tan's *The Joy Luck Club* and *The Kitchen God's Wife*. Recollection, viewed from a postmodern perspective, always implicates loss or forgetting. In Tan's novels, even though mothers and daughters interpret China with different codes and from different positions, they are all overshadowed by a prevalent sense of loss. To quote Ying-Ying St. Clair in *The Joy Luck Club*, "We are lost" (64). The daughters seem to have lost between cultures while the mothers appear to have lost everything. Later in the same novel, Jing-Mei Woo says of her mother, "She had come here in 1949 after losing everything in China: her mother and her father, her family home, her first husband, and two daughters, twin baby girls" (141).

Loss/lost functions as the central metaphor for mother's recollection and the central code to decipher her existence. Each mother's narrative of China eventually develops into a semiotics of loss. Hence, translocating into America means to her loss of identity and the reality of existence. The mothers become simply the "ghosts" without a past in an alien territory.

In *The Kitchen God' Wife*, "China Narrative" is based on Winnie's painful experiences in China. In fact, pain and suffering are central to Winnie's recollection that invites more repression than remembrance. In this case, China Narrative discloses itself as the unspeakable experience and repressed memory. As Winnie says, "Now I can forget my tragedies, put all my secrets behind a door that will never be opened, never seen by American eyes" (81). For Winnie, memory embodies loss or pain so that China Narrative essentially requires concealing instead of unfolding. Remembering inevitably entails pain and, eventually, desires for repression transform into a necessity of repression. Winnie's experience of China is transfigured into a discourse of repression and her recollection of China experiences is translated into a narrative of loss.

Within the American context, mother's recollection of China experiences demonstrates more loss of memory rather than recalling of the past. Forgetting, paradoxically, becomes the key to memory. That is why Winnie keeps repeating to herself, "Now I no longer know which story is the truth, what was the real reason why she left. They are all the same, all true, all false. So much pain in everyone. I tried to tell myself. The past is gone, nothing to be done, just forget it. That's what I tried to believe" (130). Because of loss of memory, there is simply no prior text present for translation to occur in the first place. Hence, recollection radically alters itself in a creative process. "Loss narrative" becomes the unconscious motif for mother's recollection. In short, China lies at the absolute distance from the present remembrance, irretrievably lost beyond recall, made present only through a narrative that invites forgetting instead of remembering. Mother's reflection of China signifies nothing more than the lost memories of vanished reality.

Ironically, China, lost or otherwise, functions as the locus that defines mother's sense of reality. American experience, on the other hand, only characterizes her marginal existence and alien position. Mothers tend to have their home and identity centered elsewhere—in China. In *The Woman Warrior*, Kingston writes, "Whenever my parents said 'home,' they suspended America" (99). Life in America, for her mother, is too disappointing to be real. China experience, at least, can be transliterated into a body of ideas and vocabulary that gives her a unique sense of reality and presence. Hence, China Narrative, that is both defining and defined by the mothers, becomes an imaginary text of China with a displaced mentality and exile consciousness, conditioned by both repression and nostalgia.

Therefore, recollection reveals a process of negotiation with the past, constantly translating and revising the past into a narrative that grants reality to present situations. In a displaced context, the mothers have constructed China Narrative for oneself and for each other. One of the mother figures in *The Kitchen God's Wife*, Helen, comments on the question of the past with Winnie: "She and I have changed the past many times, for many reasons. And sometimes she changes it for me and does not even know what she has done" (69). It is indeed ironic that at the end of the novel both of them are compelled to tell the truth that they no longer remember, and tell them only after they have lost memory. That is why Pearl, Winnie's daughter, complains, "I laughed, confused, caught in endless circles of lies" (524). The past, paradoxically, is lost in the process of recollection.

China is, so to speak, a "mother land," a repository of history with haunting memories and extraordinary experiences—a repository for reproduction. The mothers constantly revise their "China Narrative" in terms of their present conscious needs and unconscious desires, related to American experiences and culture.

China experiences, or the past in general, even though forgotten to a certain extent, have always been recomposed by mothers to carry out a special mission: to control the fate of their "American-made" daughters. Thus, the loss narrative is transformed into an authoritative discourse. In *The Kitchen God's Wife*, Winnie says to her daughter, "In China back then, you were always responsible to somebody else. It's not like here in the United States— freedom, independence, individual thinking, do what you want, disobey your mother. No such thing" (162). In this case, she has transformed an absent text into a powerful narrative for the purpose of domination. She is using China Narrative to establish and reinforce her present authoritative position in America.

Lacking ontological stability and lost in constant recollection, China Narrative is fabricated and manipulated in various forms. Ironically, the power of China Narrative resides precisely in its "loss of reality." In *The Joy Luck Club*, the mothers, assuming the absolute authority on China, turn China into a semiotic space wherein they can exercise their power that they have lost in the other context—the Chinese society. Thus, collectively, they have constructed another cultural territory, actually an extra-territory within American society. Eventually, China experiences in mothers' narratives are translated into a mode of discourse, a style of domineering, a tongue for control, and a gesture for having authority over the daughters' life and molding their subjectivity. In this case, China becomes less a geographical location than a cultural extra-territory that the mothers have created in order to construct the subjectivity of their "American-made" daughters.

Thus, "China experiences" become a repository from which the mothers reproduce excessive narratives to generate their power and exercise their control. Sometimes, they turn their China experiences into a disciplinary lesson that reinforces the restrictive cultural value; sometimes they translate their personal memory into a fantastic tale with powerful seduction; and sometimes they transliterate China into a secret text where daughters are excluded, and to which only the mothers themselves have direct access. As Lena St. Clair in *The Joy Luck Club* says, "When we were alone, my mother would speak in Chinese, saying things my father could not possibly imagine. I could understand the words perfectly, but not the meaning" (109). That is, only the mother possesses the key to decode the meaning of China narrative. Hence, Chinese, a secondary language to the daughters, becomes mothers' primary discourse strategy to manipulate their daughters. Like *The Book of the Twenty-Six Malignant Gates* described in *The Joy Luck Club*, because it "is written in Chinese," as the mother reminds the daughter, "You cannot understand it. That is why you must listen to me" (87).

In *The Joy Luck Club*, Jing-Mei Woo says of her mother, "Over the years, she told me the same story, except for the ending, which grew darker, casting long shadows into her life, and eventually into mine" (7). Apparently, the mothers are using their narrative power to construct their daughter's identity, as if to continue the "remarkable" China experiences, and to extend Chinese history and culture through their daughters' existence.

Although transfigured into an authoritative discourse that dominates the daughters, China Narrative is in effect grounded on the semiotics of loss. It is inevitable that China narrative subverts its own authority in this self-undermining process since its very formation informs the process of forgetting and absence. Actually, China Narrative plays the role of a ghost narrative: an absence residing at the center of the text and determining its ultimate signification.

III. Daughter's Translation: Father's Silence and Mother's Talk-Stories

In Kingston's *The Woman Warrior* and *China Men*, the daughter's experience of "China" as a semiotic space is always structured in a polarized position between mother's complicated talk-stories on the one hand and father's impenetrable silence on the other. It is this intertextual relationship between presence and absence that determines the semiotic function of China Narrative for Kingston. She has to decode her father's silence and her mother's speech. This decoding of the "other" tongue informs the operation of the second order linguistic system. Kingston is not simply locating her mother in *The Woman Warrior* or seeking her father in *China Men*. In both novels, Kingston finds herself by negotiating her relation to her parents, to a semiotic space defined as China Narrative, and to the Chinese culture.

Kingston's *China Men* is composed against the background of her father's silence. To her father, Kingston writes, "You say with the few words and the silences: No Stories. No past. No China" (14). For Kingston, China is a country she made up within the American context. Equally, she makes up her history, her family mythology in *China Men*. She dramatizes her ancestor's memory in a grand style by transliterating the "oral history" into a cultural epic.

As a daughter, Kingston feels both compelled and obligated to speak on her father's behalf, to decipher his silence of the past, to hear his narrative of China. She attempts to write into American history the contributions of the Chinese laborers by reconstructing a legendary text for the "people without history." Kingston writes, "I'll tell you what I suppose from your silences and few words, and you can tell me that I'm mistaken. You just have to speak up with the real stories if I've got you wrong" (15). She wants to know "the Chinese stories"; she wants to go back to China to see her "ancestral village"; and she wants to meet "the people with fabulous imaginations." Kingston writes, "I want to discern what it is that makes people go West and turn into Americans. I want to compare China, a country I made up, with what country is really out there" (87).

Thus, father land, or China in Kingston's *China Men*, is formulated in an imaginary space wherein Kingston offered various versions of her father's origin. However, root-seeking always ends up elsewhere. She has to speak truth by creating legends, making a legendary history of her father, reconstructing a China narrative for him in his absence. In short, she translates the silent other into a mythical narrative.

In *The Woman Warrior*, Kingston is asking, "Chinese-American, when you try to understand what things in you are Chinese, how do you separate what is peculiar to childhood, to poverty, insanities, one family, your mother who marked your growing with stories, from what is Chinese? What is Chinese tradition and what is the movies?" (5-6). Kingston confronts the perplexing issue of China Narrative within the context of her mother's talk-stories and her.own fantasy, forbidden tales and her own dreams. In regard to her mother's talk-stories, Kingston observes: "I couldn't tell where the stories left off and the dreams began, her voice and the voices of the heroines in my sleep" (19). It seems that "real" China lies at the distance of the inevitable loss.

China Narrative in *The Woman Warrior* is, first of all, translated from the realm of the real into that of the imaginary. Her mother's China Narrative is based on the recollection of her direct experience of China, thereby transfiguring the body of experience into a "historical" text. This "historical" text is further translated into a symbolic inter-text which consists of daughter's recapitulation of the reflective narratives her mother passed down to her. Evidently, Kingston's experience of China is based on the experience of her (m)other's narratives and, eventually, her China Narrative becomes a translation of a translation—in fact, a cultural reconstruction. In this case, historical and cultural reconstructs of China are divided along bicultural views and bifocal perspectives.

Daughter's China Narrative, based on the primary text of mother's recollection, via myths, legends, talk-stories, informs the operation of a second order linguistic system. That is to say, the daughter's cognition of China seems to be always already structured, mediated and overdetermined by the semiotics of the (m)other tongue that serves as the first order symbolic signification. Therefore, the daughter's reconstruction of China Narrative is based on the signifier of the first linguistic order (mother's narrative) which assumes a historical reference to China. Mother's narrative functions as the ultimate interpretative frame of the daughter's reconceptualization of China, actually, the absolute horizon of the daughter's cognition of China.

Put more precisely, China Narrative itself constitutes the absolute horizon of the daughter's recognition of China experiences. Hence, China Narrative informs a process of displacement, transformation, and absence. Displaced by (m)other's tales that made China absent from presence, this China Narrative is inevitably a translation, a transformation of the past for the present usage.

China in her mother's talk-stories resides in a domain of memory based on personal experience of social reality in China. China for Kingston indicates a territory of dream and fantasy. In her dreams, Kingston has revenged her family, fantasizing her China experiences as compensation for "disappointing American life," and these "China experiences" in her dreams are entirely based on the tales of and from China via the talk-stories of her mother that have already been translated in a new cultural context and with reference to their American experiences.

In *Boundaries of the Self: Gender, Culture, Fiction*, Roberta Rubenstein points out, "Their offspring born in America inherit this split between cultures without ever having seen their ancestral land, except imaginatively, through their elders' eyes" (166). Exactly, Kingston's vision is filtered through her mother's eyes and her mother's tongue. Her mother's stories radically shape her vision of China and Chinese—the place of her ancestral origin. From this displaced context and removed memory, she invents a China in a space of fantasy. Growing up in America, she has to distinguish what is supernatural and what is real, what is ghost and what is people.

IV. Individuation from the (M)other: Ghost or Otherwise

In Kingston's *The Woman Warrior*, the boundaries between the self and the other are not clearly defined until past; the China experience is confronted and reinscribed by the daughter. The daughter is forced to negotiate her position between conflicting sets of discourses: of family, ethnicity, culture, history and nationality. In order to reach a reconciliation, Kingston has to come to terms with herself in relation to the historical situation she inherits from her mother and chooses her own subject position.

Both mother and daughter develop multiple discourses to encode their existences. Both attempt to carve out a personal space in an alien culture that has limited and marginalized their lives, their heritage and their language. Kingston, however, living on the edges of two communities, has to choose between her mother's home culture and the alien culture. *The Woman Warrior* represents how Kingston grows up among contradictions and confusions between cultures and languages. Wendy Ho remarks, "Like her mother, the daughter negotiates the preservation and the subversion of aspects of traditional Chinese culture against the pressures of mainstream Western society. However, she is in a precarious position of her own: she is not Chinese enough for her mother, father and ethnic community and not American-feminine enough to find a home among the white 'ghosts'" (227).

Kingston writes, "They would tell us children because we had been born among ghosts, were taught by ghosts and were ourselves ghost-like. They called us a kind of ghosts" (183). Ghost represents tension and problems of language and cultural system. However, Kingston refuses to be reduced to simply a ghost in "an alien culture." Instead, she positively recreates a unique identity separate from the ghost position. Kingston indicates in *The Woman Warrior* that she has to confront all the ghosts from China with which her mother has haunted her childhood: Fa Mu Lan, her mother—Brave Orchid, the dead aunt, Moon Orchid and herself. She has to transcend this ghost terrain into "a ghost-free country."

The ghost in her narrative possesses multiple perspectives. It is a signifier with diverse meanings, especially when configured in a multi-cultural context. In "*The Woman Warrior* as a Search for Ghost," Gayle K. Fujita Sato remarks, "The ghost defines two antithetical worlds that threaten the narrator's sense of a unified self. How is she to articulate her own location, which is 'Chinese American,' when history, tradition, and family have formulated 'China' and 'America' as reciprocally alien territories?" (139).

Kingston refuses to live a hyphenated experience and remain a victim to her mother's China Narrative. She manages to go beyond her mother's talk-stories by subverting the designated position defined by her mother's past experience. Self-production depends upon both preservation and progression. On the one hand, Kingston resists her mother's codification of her identity as a Chinese slave-girl and disrupts the "slave narrative," and on the other hand, she rejects the ex-centric self, discontent with being reduced to an unnameable ghost in an alien culture. In effect, Kingston transcends the boundaries of both cultures by rewriting China Narrative once authorized by mother's talk-stories and rejecting the displaced "China experience" in American society.

In *The Woman Warrior*, Kingston is refuting not simply China, Chinese culture or the (m)other tongue, but the "Chineseness" that is specifically produced under the new historical and cultural circumstances. She resists being victimized by establishing her separate identity from the "Chineseness" forged in America—the artificial construct of Chinese that diminishes her status and delimits her power. Therefore, her separation from the mother signifies the individuation process from both mother's land and mother's tongue, which results in her finding her own reality and space in existence and creating her own language and authority. Kingston is determined that she has to "leave home to see the world logically." She says: "I continue to sort out what's just my childhood, just my imagination, just my family, just the village, just movies, just living. . . . Soon I want to go to China and find out who's lying. . . ." (205).

V. Translating the In-Between Position: Recreation

Each ethnic group constructs a unique self-image that reflects its response to the impact of the dominant culture. Their reactions vary according to their different positions to the social environments and the dominant value systems. The self thus emerged can be defensive, aiming at preserving the original cultural values and keeping its alienation and marginality; the self can be extensive: losing marginality by mediating between two cultures. Thus, the bicultural environments force each ethnic group to balance the duality and negotiate the distance.

In *The Woman Warrior*, Kingston is both part of and apart from the two separate worlds, positioning herself across languages and across cultures. The double perspective of the home culture and the other culture can be both disabling and enabling, delimiting and empowering. Instead of repeating the previous ideas that the deracinated self fails mediation and dangles as a double-alienated outsider, I would argue that the self can succeed in bridging the two cultures and merging the duality.

The in-between situation, I believe, does not necessarily inform a split duality of inherent contradiction, it signifies not so much a fissure as a bridge that both divides and connects. Kingston acknowledges the influence of both cultures which exist not in antithesis that excludes each other but as integration that combines both. She is at home in this duality. She does not want to build a wall that divides, but create a bridge that connects.

For instance, Kingston does not simply question but also incorporates the traditional mythology of China in her writing. Thus part, the useful part, of the mythology is revived instead of repressed. Kingston's appropriation of China Narrative emerges as a paradox: she is using the power of Chinese mythology to reinforce her American identity, thereby transcending the customary ways of defining the self, and defying the village mentality of Chinatown. In this case, ethnicity no longer hampers her ways of thinking but enriches her imagination which is feasting on diverse traditions and cultures.

Instead of "feeling of being between worlds and at home nowhere" (Amy Ling, Between Worlds, 105), I would argue that this in-between position is not inherently a negative one. It can be positively employed. Kingston's novels demonstrate the phenomenon of multi-cultural texts. In *The Woman Warrior*, Kingston says, "I learned to make my mind large, as the universe is large, so that there is room for paradoxes" (29). That is why Kingston is asking her mother, "Does it make sense to you that if we're no longer attached to one piece of land, we belong to the planet?" (107). Evidently, she creates a paradoxical self in *The Woman Warrior* to reflect the diversity of American culture.

I entirely agree with what Amy Ling says in *Between Worlds: Woman Writers of Chinese Ancestry*:

> The very condition [of the between-world] carries both negative and positive charges. On the one hand, being between worlds can be interpreted to mean occupying the space or gulf between two banks; one is thus in a space of suspension, accepted by neither side and therefore truly belonging nowhere. . . . On the other hand, viewed from a different perspective, being between worlds may be considered as having footholds on both banks and therefore belonging to two worlds at once. One does not have less; one has more. . . . the person between worlds is in the indispensable position of being a bridge. (177)

Kingston's use of China Narrative transcends its original contexts. Her translocation of Chinese mythology signifies cultural replacement and reposition which help her form a distinctive identity for her own. She creates her own mythology within the myth of Fa Mu Lan. This paradoxical borrowing emerges as a border issue of bridging instead of separating. She has to separate herself from her ancestral village, the home tradition and enter the complex multicultural reality of her American experiences. Paradoxically, it is her fantasy of China that has saved her from a totally depressing fate in America. The Chinese mythology functions as a semiotic empowerment in the process of her identity formation.

Nevertheless, what is the American identity if not paradoxical? Historically, the American identity has always been defined in relation to the other: other places, other cultures and other times. This double perspective is a uniquely American phenomenon. In fact, her perplexity over identity touches on an issue essential to the American culture. Hence, her search for identity reveals this complex cultural transaction: her American identity is reinforced by Chinese mythology which, even though somewhat relegated to the "other" category, nevertheless functions as the ideological basis of her self construction.

Therefore, she is not simply repeating what has been taught to her, but adapting Chinese mythology to her present situation with an imaginative creation. As Sau-Ling Cynthia Wong says, "Whether her alterations to traditional material constitute creative adaption or willful exploitation, realistic reflection or second-generation cultural disorientation or irresponsible perversion of a previous heritage, is a question teachers must work through with their students" (35).

Robert G. Lee also mentions that "for Kingston, myths, necessarily rebuilt, have a strategic value in helping to analyze contemporary events. She recognizes that the power of myth resides in its capacity to be recontextualized and inscribed with new meanings" (59). Apparently, Kingston has to re-fabricate the mythical texture as required by the new historical circumstances. In her essay "Cultural Mis-Readings by American Reviewers," Kingston argues that the Chinese mythology in *The Woman Warrior* is "but one transformed by America" (57). She reminds us of what many people fail to recognize—that the "Chinese myths have been transmuted by America" (58).

Kingston herself observes in her "Personal Statement" that myths and lives maintain a dialogic interrelation and "the myths transform lives and are themselves changed" (24). "Sinologists have criticized me for not knowing myths and for distorting them. . . . They don't understand that myths have to change, be useful or be forgotten. Like the people who carry them across oceans, the myths become American. The Myths I write are new, American" (24). Instead of being controlled by Chinese mythology, Kingston rewrites it to create her own American myth.

In "'Emerging Canons' of Asian American Literature and Art," Amy Ling asks, "Must the multicultural writer/artist be totally and exclusively answerable to his or her ethnic community, be the spokesperson of that community, tell the community's stories and tell them accurately? Or can she or he claim the right to express an individual vision and personal concerns, and to modify the myths and legends of a group to his or her own artistic purpose?" (195). I believe that this question involves the issue of subject position for both Kingston and Tan. That is, who is writing, Chinese or American?

I argue that writing for Kingston and Tan means a process of confrontation, discovery and creation of their cultural identities. Both assert themselves as American novelists of Chinese descendants, resisting the hyphenated experience embodied by the so called "mestiza consciousness." Accordingly, their novels represent American people and contribute to

American literature. Therefore, their writings mark a transition from the position of separation, alienation to that of accommodation and reposition, initiating a positive self-invention instead of a denial of ethnic origin. Apparently, it goes beyond merely the justification of ethnic identity, but is related to the issue of recreation and replacement. The creative negotiation between self and the other can effectively reinforce the ethnic subject—the assertion of the repressed subject within a multicultural context.

Both Kingston and Tan write to reconstitute the American experience through the strategy of difference, highlighting the importance of difference within American cultures by challenging the status quo of American identity. Both argue for participation of cultural construction instead of remaining in a stereotypical position as the temporary sojourners—the alienated and displaced personalities. I believe this gesture challenges the very constitution of the Americanness of American culture and identity.

In the interview with Paula Rabinowitz, Kingston remarks,

> Actually, I think my books are much more American than they are Chinese. I felt that I was building, creating, myself and these people as American people, to make everyone realize that they are American people. . . .
>
> Also, I am creating part of American literature, and I was very aware of doing that, of adding to American literature. (177-78)

In "Cultural Mis-Readings by American Reviewers," she reasserts her position as an American writer: "I am an American. I am an American writer, who, like other American writers, wants to write the great American novel. *The Woman Warrior* is an American book" (57). Interestingly enough, the issue of China Narrative in the novels by Kingston and Tan ends up somewhere in American literature.

References

Ho, Wendy. "Mother/Daughter Writing and the Politics of Race and Sex in Maxine Hong Kingston's *The Woman Warrior*." Pp. 225-38 in *Asian Americans: Comparative and Global Perspectives*, ed. Shirley Hune, Hyung-Cha Kim, Stephen S. Fugita, Amy Ling. Pullman: Washington State University Press, 1991.

Kingston, Maxine Hong. "Cultural Mis-Readings by American Reviewers." Pp. 55-64 in *Asian and Western Writers in Dialogue: New Cultural Identities*, ed. Guy Amirthanayagam. London: Macmillan, 1982.

————. *The Woman Warrior: Memoirs of a Girlhood among Ghosts*. New York: Random House, 1975.

————. *China Men*. New York: Knopf, 1980.

————. "Interviewing Maxine Hong Kingston with Paula Rabinowitz." *Michigan Quarterly Review* 26, no. 1 (winter 1987): 177-87.

————."Personal Statement." Pp. 23-25 in *Approaches to Teaching Kingston's The Woman Warrior*. Edited by Shirley Geok-Lin Lim. New York: Modern Language Association, 1991.

Lee, Robert G. "*The Woman Warrior* as an Inversion in Asian American Historiography." Pp. 52-63 in *Approaches to Teaching Kingston's The Woman Warrior*. Edited by Shirley Geok-Lin Lim. New York: Modern Language Association, 1991.

Ling, Amy. *Between Worlds: Woman Writers of Chinese Ancestry*. New York: Pergamon Press, 1990.

————. "'Emerging Canons' of Asian American Literature and Art." Pp. 191-98 *Asian Americans: Comparative and Global Perspectives*. Edited by Shirley Hune, Hyung-Cha Kim, Stephen S. Fugita and Amy Ling. Pullman: Washington State University Press, 1991.

Rubenstein, Roberta. *Boundaries of the Self: Gender, Culture, Fiction*. Chicago: University of Illinois Press, 1987.

Sato, Gayle K. Fujita. "*The Woman Warrior* as a Search for Ghosts." Pp. 138-47 in *Approaches to Teaching Kingston's The Woman Warrior*. Edited by Shirley Geok-Lin Kim. New York: Modern Language Association, 1991.

Tan, Amy. *The Joy Luck Club*. New York: Ballantine Books, 1989.

————. *The Kitchen God's Wife*. New York: Ballantine Books, 1991.

Wong, Sau-Ling Cynthia. "Kingston's Handling of Traditional Chinese Sources." Pp. 26-36 in *Approaches to Teaching Kingston's The Woman Warrior*. Edited by Shirley Geok-Lin Lim. New York: Modern Language Association, 1991.

12

NAMING ONE'S PLACE, CLAIMING ONE'S SPACE: LITERATURE ABOUT IMMIGRANT WOMEN

Pushpa N. Parekh

The delineation of Asian diasporic experience, in terms of exile and migration, and female subjectivity as transcultural literary constructs in the new immigrant narratives, is an area of increasing critical debate and discussion. The discourses of coloniality/postcoloniality that characterize a number of the new immigrant narratives and their critical reception, especially in the last twenty years, as well as those of multiculturism, interpreted in many different ways, have intersected in these discussions and debates. In my essay I will explore the culturally embedded articulations of the problematics implied in usage of such terms as "diaspora" and "subjectivity." The term "Asian diaspora" complicates the issues involved because it tends to homogenize and unify and ultimately conflate the unique historical, political, and cultural exigencies that distinguish each of the several diverse cultures and geopolitically defined nationalities. I therefore problematize the term by exploring two diverse representations of Asian immigrant and Asian-American experiences. Ranging from evocations of shared history, which often place the discussion of Asian diasporic experience within the discourses of "colonial dislocations" (Nelson Intro, x) to disavowal of essentializing categories implicit in hyphenated ethnic identities, the voices of Jasmine, in Bharati Mukherjee's *Jasmine*, and Olivia Ann Osaka, in Cynthia Kadohata's *The Floating World*, narrate the experiences of migration, exile, border-crossing, and female subjectivity.

Located at the sites of convergence of multiple places and cultures, my discussion will focus on negotiation and renegotiation of female subject positions and the reworking of female migratory identity across geographical and national boundaries. Carol Boyce Davies in *Black Women, Writing and Identity: Migrations of the Subject* refers to the "Re-Mapping and Re-Naming" of terminologies and categories as signs of resistance to "the narrow terms of the discourses in which we are inscribed." But each of the terms we use to name ourselves, such as "black African, African-American, black British, Minority, Latina/o, West Indian, Caribbean, Hispanic, People of Color, Women of Color, Afro-Caribbean, Third World and so on, carry their strings of echoes and inscriptions. Each represents an original misnaming and the simultaneous constant striving of the dispossessed for full representation" (5). In my analysis, transnational migrations, viewed specifically through literary representations of women of Indian and Japanese ancestry, imply constant arrival at new definitions and new interrogations of these definitions.

Mukherjee's *Jasmine* is about an illegal immigrant woman from a small Punjabi village, Hasnapur, in India, who travels to the United States and encounters both violent and sustaining forms of transforming self and notions about America. Cynthia Kadohata's *The Floating World* is about three generations of a Japanese American family, as viewed and understood by Olivia from the age of twelve to sixteen. As she travels with her family from one town to another across the American landscape in the post-World War II and post-internment period of the 1950s in the United States, she expresses both in humorous and reflective tones the complexity of growing up in two cultures. Articulating the redefinitions of self within the spatial parameters, both literal (geopolitical) and metaphoric (ideological), Mukherjee and Kadohata through their works address the issues of identity formation, cultural adaptation, acculturation, displacement, alienation, and marginalization.

The complexity of locating oneself within the intersections of gender, race, ethnicity, class, and colonial/neocolonial politics involves, in each work, the projection of fictional autobiographical voices that inscribe the immigrant female myth-reality status within the emerging discourses of decolonizing cultures. Positioned at the borderlands of nations and cultures, each of the narrator-protagonists in the novels lives in various compelling ways; the wonder, despair, struggle, survival, dislocation, and transformation of the immigrant Asian and Asian American female subject in the process of claiming her space—her unique contested terrain. Focusing on the diasporic experience filtered through the consciousness of central women narrator-characters who traverse places and cultures, I examine the multiple sites on which female subjectivities are negotiated and renegotiated—sites where notions regarding homeland and host land, residence and domicile, self and landscape, inside and outside, converge and intersect across a terrain of movement, migration, cultural crossing, displacement, resettlement, hybridization, and reinvention. The multiple significations of identity formation, marginalization, erasure, and reconstruction are voiced by the speaking narrators in their unique responses to the dialectics of double perspective, difference, and otherness.

Shirley Geok-lin Lim and Amy Ling in their introduction to *Reading the Literatures of Asian America* emphasize that race and gender categories "are never unitary and separate" but are "historically and socioculturally embedded constructions" and "must be understood as interlocking and provisionally predicated terms" (7); this view is not unlike the views of Patricia Hill Collins and Carol Boyce Davies with regard to black women (Davies, in particular, notes the various deployments of the term black, in different geopolitical contexts; for example, a South Asian woman in the United States is categorized as a woman of color whereas in England she is black). Migration to the United States for women of color implies a certain relocating of self in a space where past identities (already complicated by experiences of colonization and/or imperialism) are simultaneously evoked and conflated in nameable categories of hyphenated ethnicity. It is interesting to note the ways in which Mukherjee and Kadohata deal with this remapping of the female migratory subject-self across boundaries that define national, racial, and cultural identities and trace historic links between specific past events and present cultural, social, political, and economic realities.

Mukherjee's Jasmine traverses boundaries defined by national borders and implicit in the politics of transnationalism. The differences between and intersections of her life as lived in Hasnapur, a feudal village in Punjab, India, and the various locations in the United States, from Florida backwaters to New York metropolis to the midwestern Iowa farmlands, are vividly captured at both the material and the conceptual levels of self-making and remaking. Further, the speaking voice reiterates the importance of her name changes as she moves from one geopolitical space to another. Her name changes range from Jyoti, meaning light and domestic bliss, to Jasmine, implying the blossoming of the inner self, to Jane, a typical common name in the Western world and associated with "Plain Jane" as well as the heroine of Emily Bronte's novel, and back to Jasmine, interspersed by appropriations of the Indian goddess name Kali to American contractions such as Jazzy, Jasey, and Jase. Woven into the symbolic significations of identity displacement and reconstruction are transformations of self in specific surroundings. Although these name shifts, ranging from symbolic domesticity to self-empowerment to heady adventure, trace the linear movement of grand epic narratives at one level, their regenerative power is undercut by the fact that the names are for the most part given by men. Jasmine negotiates her claim on naming herself through appropriating multiple perceptions of identity as simultaneously unfolding layers—she knows, unlike the men who name her, that Jyoti, Jasmine, and Jane as well as all other identities are enclosed within each other. Recalling her life as Jyoti, Jasmine ruminates: "I survived the sniping. My grandmother may have named me Jyoti, Light, but in surviving I was already Jane, a fighter and adapter" (35). These name shifts imply a fluid identity: "In the lamplight, ghosts float toward me. Jane, Jasmine, Jyoti" (18).

In my essay titled, "Narrative Voice and Gender Roles in Bharati Mukherjee's *Jasmine*," published in *Bharati Mukherjee: Critical Perspectives*, I examine in some detail the reinvention of the woman–centered oral tale in the narrative structure and thematic content of the novel. Jasmine's odyssey from post–independent India, triggered by political violence and personal choice, to the United States and the ensuing phases of violent upheavals in the process of reinventing the American female self, is itself a myth told in the language and voice that recovers spaces along borders and boundaries. And as myths go, there is the element of fantasy blended with truth. Recasting her roles from "silent woman" to "speaking person" to "teller of tales" implies not simply that America has liberated her; rather the silent woman in America is as susceptible to violent erasure as in the feudal Punjab of India. In the American context, however, Jasmine gains the economic opportunity, through her various jobs, to forge her reality along the lines of the American Dream—a dream which some postcolonial critics have problematized as "the dream of an urban, cosmopolitan freedom," the dream of "the upper–middle–class subaltern" (Roy, 129). In Jasmine's movement toward reinvention of self, these critics feel that Mukherjee has uncritically reproduced "the imperialist project of 'selving the Other' turning the Other into a self, giving the Other a voice, speaking for the Other" (Knippling, 147).

Mukherjee recreates the tension between the impulse for assimilation and the pain of letting go in the lives of immigrants who have, as she claims, "shed past lives and languages, and who have traveled half the world in every direction to come here and begin again" ("Immigrant Writing", 28). While Mukherjee centralizes Jasmine's quest, she also deliberately separates her from her community; Jasmine's contact with other Indians is limited to the Vadheras who are stereotypically caricatured as insular and self–absorbed. Later, noting the adopted Vietnamese son Du's links with his community, Jasmine admits how different they really are despite her constant attempts to align her experiences with those of other immigrants: "I am amazed, and a little proud that Du has made a life for himself among the Vietnamese in Baden and I hadn't had a clue. Aside from my Dr. Jaswani and from Dr. Patel in Infertility, I haven't spoken to an Indian since my months in Flushing. My transformation has been genetic; Du's was hyphenated" (198). The Jasmine-Jane subject tends to idealize the shared dilemmas of the immigrant masses as homogenous groups so that revelations of their differences come as a surprise to her. On the other hand, paradoxically, she also participates in the logic of hierarchizing difference by accepting Lillian Gordon's own brand of practical rationale regarding illegal aliens: "I was lucky, she said, that India had once been a British colony. Can you imagine being stuck with a language like Dutch or Portuguese? 'Look at these poor Kanjobal—they barely speak Spanish!' Lillian, of course, had taught herself Kanjobal. She felt it was the least she could do" (118); "At the end of a week, Lillian said in her brisk, direct way at the breakfast table, 'Jazzy, you don't strike me as a picker or a domestic.' The Kanjobal women looked at her intently, nodding their heads as if they understood. 'You're different from these others'" (120).

Jasmine, in her disturbingly conflicted space where the new choices of becoming are only superficially less threatening than older, feudally defined ones, renegotiates a space for herself. Rather than resisting, she participates in the neocolonial tendency to not only appropriate the third world subject for the purposes of inscribing a new history of the first world's "benevolent" hegemony, but also to layer it in a structural hierarchy, ensuring continuous cross-ethnic fractiousness. In doing so, Jasmine's course of reinventing a new self underscores the painful reality for many people of color who cross borders in search of a space to survive and in so doing find themselves pitted against other "minority" groups; the "American Dream" is an aesthetic commodity only for one who has bought into the system of capitalist neocolonialism. Jasmine finds herself implicated at the juncture of a new form of global colonization. Even at the end of the novel the question remains unanswered, not so much regarding her agency because agency itself is understood differently in different cultural contexts, but regarding the direction of her scrambling. Mukherjee, I believe, deliberately places the Jyoti–Jasmine–Jane persona at this juncture of geopolitical and ideological boundary–crossing, where past names are ineffectual: "I realize I have already stopped thinking of myself as Jane" (214). As Carol Boyce Davies articulates the female migratory subject's enterprise as one in which "at each arrival at a definition, we begin a new analysis, a new departure, a new interrogation of meaning, new contradictions" (5), so is the Jyoti–Jasmine–Jane subject poised for change and transformation, not in an absolute sense, but as part of the fluid remaking of the self.

Weaving across layers of Old World and New World colonial inscriptions, the "third world" immigrant female desire also becomes commodified within and across cultures. As an ostracized widow in Hasnapur, and later in Vadhera's Punjabi community in Flushing, Jasmine's sexuality becomes the site where compelling images of the traditional "Sati-Savitri" (the chaste and pure woman) are evoked. In feudal Hasnapur, it serves the purpose of maintaining cultural continuity (however irrational the practices may be) in times of sectarian strife: *A bull and a bomb have made them widows, mother and daughter! How they must have sinned to suffer so now!* My mother kept company only with other widows, bent old women of public humility and secret bitterness. I felt myself dead in their company"

(87). In Flushing the image ensures the comfort of "home" in a place of homelessness, while home itself is a place of exile for Jasmine. Thus women's sexuality—defined, controlled and policed—becomes the ground on which male definitions of nationhood and homeland find vivid and powerful expression. Jasmine's objective to commit voluntary sati (practice of widow immolation officially banned in 1829 in India) in the United States evokes, through temporal and spatial displacements, the absurdity of imbricated realities within old and new forms of colonization. Transformed from a potential Sati-goddess into the bloody-tongued Kali who self-preserves through destroying the evil Half-Face, Jasmine reclaims for herself a body on which scars (from early childhood), shame (of widowhood), and wounds (of perpetual loss of self) are located as sites where the violent politics of race, gender, sexuality, and nationality intersect. Negotiating a subject position among competing realities and ideologies across geopolitical boundaries, Jasmine wills her telling, despite doubts and questions, into the grand discourse of Americanization, capitalism, and feminism. By bringing together the temporal and spatial configurations of doing and not doing, Jasmine's final act defines "reinvention" in two ways: as the immigrant woman's creation of self by throwing open the new frontier, "pushing indoors through uncaulked windows" (214); and as a renegotiation within the defined parameters that prescribe and proscribe a certain subjectivity in the prevailing social order, "Watch me reposition the stars" (214).

On a different note, Cynthia Kadohata in *The Floating World* focuses on three generations of a Japanese family (the issei, nisei and the sansei) as they are impelled to traverse the American landscape in search of jobs, perceived through the mind and consciousness of the young Olivia Ann Osaka. Kadohata recaptures "the ukiyo, the floating world. The floating world was the gas station attendants, restaurants, and jobs we depended on, the motel towns floating in the middle of fields and mountains" (2). Commenting on the meaning of *ukiyo*, Gretel Ehrlich explains:

> The title is borrowed from the Japanese *ukiyo*, a word whose roots are *uki* (sadness or grief) and *yo* (world). At one time *ukiyo* referred to the world of prostitutes, as depicted in Utamaro's woodblock prints. But a pun on the word spun it into motion, connoting the sadness that comes from knowing that our sense of solidity and permanence is a dream. . . . The landscape is decidedly '50s America, but one cannot help thinking of the way Japanese literature—especially the *nikki no michi* (poetic diaries)-used the journey to hint at life's transience. Olivia's external journey to Arkansas and settlement there is an inward journey as well—toward comprehension of how the pieces of family history and geography-as-destiny fit together and why they come apart. . . . (6)

Kadohata's narrative moves beyond a number of immigrant writers' preoccupation with responding to the Western construction of the "other." Kadohata as a Japanese American writer delves into the contentious intrafamilial relationships in the context of larger sociopolitical and economic pressures that limit and circumscribe the space of cultural difference. With an insight and humor that is refreshing, Kadohata weaves in generational gaps and enclosures through a narration that connects the inner world of the migrants to the outer world of urban and rural American landscape as well as the socioeconomic and legal implications of racism in Japanese immigrant history. Olivia's figuration of these connections is through a narration that links personal experiences and identity registers with the political agendas of a white racist society. The family must undergo constant place changes because, as Olivia points out, "it could be hard even into the fifties and sixties for Japanese to get good jobs" (4). Name changes that occurred over time, from the issei generation to the nisei, is a legacy of racist laws that forcefully imposed a certain American identity, mainly white and Christian, as worthy of assimilation:

> Years later, in Hawaii at the start of World War II, the local school made my grandparents change their children's first names before they could enroll. Satoru, Yukiko, Mariko, Haruko, and Sadamu became Roger, Lily, Laura, Ann, and Roy. Today their original names are just shadows following them. My brothers and I all have American names: Benjamin Todd, Walker Roy, Peter Edward, and me, Olivia Ann. (2)

Suspended across the shifting terrain of rural and urban America as they crisscross into contours and shapes, the floating world of Olivia and her Japanese American family unfolds the raw nerves and quiet reveries, the silence and the noise, the pain and the pleasures of locating and relocating.

Olivia's narration counters the master discourse that linearizes history, thus enabling the female subject to return to its constructed rather than an essential point of origin—in locations, in relationships, and ultimately in experience. Shifts in time and place reflect not only memories of the past but also their persistence in shaping present subject positions. Laura (or Mariko), Olivia's mother, returns to the house of her second father only to hear from his second wife that he is dead; Laura is compelled to revive the security of her relationship with him through the possession of an enameled box she is sure belonged to her mother. Her obsessive need to maintain links with her dead father finds a foreboding replication in Olivia's experience with the ghost of her dead father, Jack. While Laura moves in a "private world of disappointment, unconnected to Charlie–O's love for her" (Edwards–Yearwood 12), Olivia learns to make that connection through memories of her grandmother, a woman of contrasts. Through reading her diaries, she works out the guilt of having let *obasan* die, and gains consciousness that events have multiple causes and that good and bad are not simple oppositions. Learning the "possibilities for 'bad'" in herself, Olivia extends a generous acceptance of others' imperfections. Olivia is guilty of having let her grandmother, *obasan*, die through not only her own inaction but mainly, as she believes, because of her hatred of *obasan*. The uneven and complex relationship between Olivia and *obasan* is evoked in apparently opposing ways in which Olivia describes her grandmother: "My grandmother has always been my tormentor. My mother said she'd been a young woman of spirit, but she was an old woman of fire" (1); she was "cruel, name-calling, quick-tempered" (7); "I was sick of her meanness, her insults, her hatred" (10). Yet *obasan* is ready to kill in order to protect Olivia; Olivia's "life is intertwined with (her) grandmother's" (7); they both even have "the same smooth skin all over" (10); like her, Olivia too hides her fears behind "a brave front" (19); they also share the same spirit not to be daunted and a sly sharpness to size up the Hakujin, the white people, "When I spoke with outsiders I was showing off, but they never understood this. I was trying to impress them, to make them like me. But at the same time I was always taunting them. See, I can talk like you, I was trying to say, it's not so hard. My grandmother didn't like that I wanted to impress them, but she liked the taunting part" (8). Eventually, Olivia becomes the teller of *obasan's* talk-stories after her death. Later, when Olivia is sixteen, her obsession with *obasan's* diaries leads her to view good and evil not as mere opposites, but as diabolically interconnected, even as her grandmother was and even as she herself is. Deconstructing the dialectics of Western epistemology, Olivia gains knowledge and awareness of the other realms besides the tangible and the material—the worlds of wooden roses, seven moon-clouds, ghosts and forebodings, worlds where fiction and truth coexist.

Her grandmother's diaries, written in English and Japanese, also become the means by which Olivia can understand the difference between the two clashing cultures, Japanese and Anglo-American, as a difference between two world views, contained in their language systems:

> And I liked the two languages, Japanese and English, how each contained thoughts you couldn't express exactly in the other. For instance, because you didn't use exact spaces between words in the same way in English and Japanese, certain phrases such as 'pure white' or 'eight slender objects' or 'how many people'—seemed to me like only one word in Japanese. Seeming to use only one word changed slightly the meaning of what I was saying. It made me think about what exactly was pure white and not merely white. (92)

Language is the means by which Olivia experiences the precise uniqueness of her bicultural reality.

Based on a concept derived from M.M. Bakhtin's discussion in *The Dialogic Imagination*, Betty Bergland's chronotropic analysis of immigrant women's autobiography in "Ideology, Ethnicity, and the Gendered Subject: Reading Immigrant Women's Autobiographies," focuses on "situating the autobiographical subject in the time and space of the narrative" and "placing the autobiographical subjects in their historical and discursive contexts" (104–5). As Bergland explains, "In order to understand an 'I' who speaks, especially the voice of the immigrant woman, we must appreciate not only the historical circumstances surrounding immigration but also the ideologies of the language systems in which these women were situated, including patriarchal ideologies of the old and new worlds" (104). In my analysis, I find this approach a meaningful strategy to understand not only how "ideology secures certain subjectivities within the prevailing social order," but also how the writings of immigrant and ethnic women who span two or more cultures and languages expose "multiple and competing ideologies represented by different languages and discourses," as well as multiple subjectivities, enabling us to see "relationships between culture and consciousness" (103–4).

Kadohata, throughout her novel, explores the process of arriving at the complex nature of female subjectivities as they are constructed across time and space, spanning generational and cultural differences and influences. There are at least two specific ways in which these female subjectivities are explored: through issei, nisei, and sansei communal interactions (at the Missouri hatchery in particular), as well as through the young Japanese American (sansei) female's questioning of the traditional paradigms regarding female sexuality and morality. Olivia observes, with a curious blend of attachment and detachment peculiar to the sansei generation, the way in which the Japanese-American community is operating within the larger system of American capitalism. Olivia contextualizes the process by which old world social bonds are replaced by the new world economic pressures that solidify loyalties within the group for the purposes of ensuring the larger profits of the hatchery:

> Sexers were hired not as individuals but as groups: the management hired and fired groups, not individuals, while the group hired and fired the individuals. . . . Unless you were with an agency, every group had a leader, who negotiated with the management in return for a commission from the rest of the workers. When one person did bad work, that put everyone's job in jeopardy. (100)

Mr. Tanizaki, who had worked sexing chickens for thirty years, becomes a problem when his productivity declines: "The rumours varied: he was taking too much Dexedrine; he was losing his mind; he was getting lazy," or as Olivia believes, "He just seemed tired" (100–10). Working within the system, Olivia unravels not only the counter–individual but ultimately the counter–communal group dynamics operating within the system: "It occurred to me their coolness and toughness hid an awkwardness they all felt with each other, and I really was one of them: being one of them was being an outsider. To be part of their group, you couldn't get close to them" (110).

While Olivia assesses her subject position within the larger socioeconomic forces of the 1950s America and the Japanese American communities, she also explores the consciousness of female sexual and moral agency through her grandmother. Her grandmother's diaries reveal the unconventional, even bold assertion of her *wants* above mere social conformity; she had a lover, not "someone she'd married" (96). She discovers and affirms her connection with her grandmother; she too seeks strength, not vulnerability, in a male–female relationship: "That's what I wanted, to feel the same strength, more than I wanted love" (96). But Olivia's mother constructs her own subjectivity in different terms; her relationship with Charlie-O, who married her while she was already pregnant with Olivia and was no longer in touch with Olivia's father, is riddled with a desperate tension to which Olivia is sensitive. Her attitude toward her mother is encased in a combination of quiet admiration for and incomprehension of her intractable serenity despite a rocky marriage, and her maturity compared to Charlie-O's boyishness. Olivia observes with uncanny clarity, "Yet I knew that sometimes my mother felt lonely and my father felt alone" (43). From desperate hopes of becoming the means by which their differences could be reconciled, Olivia moves to ultimately accept difference and dissonance as values in themselves.

In Kadohata's re-creation of a personal narrative and a communal history, the spatial markers between the ethnic communal borders and the larger American landscape are constantly blurred but not erased. Racial tensions, which were very visible in the post World War II period between the whites and the Japanese issei, nisei, and even sansei groups, are clearly present in the narrative unfolding of the temporal and spatial contingencies of the "Floating World" which the speaking "I" inhabits. Yet the narrative moves beyond a clear identification of aggressor–victim polarities by upsetting linearity of time and space. The past haunts the present, even as Japan and Hawaii pervade California, Wyoming, Nebraska, and Arkansas, and as evidenced in the temporal and spatial overlappings of the dead and living. The present revisits the past even as characters cross and re-cross geographical terrains through physical (the actual car traveling), mental (memories), and spiritual (supernatural events) journeys. Revealing so many ways of being Japanese–American, the narrative of the lives of *obasan*, Laura, Olivia, her adopted father, Charlie-O, as well as specific individuals and groups, represents the creation of both gendered and ethnic subjectivities. Passing in and out of alertness while the family travels across the American landscape, Olivia learns about life in "the floating world."

Susanna Moore notes that this world reminiscent of the older style of *ukiyo*, reflects the "Buddhist belief in the poignant, but seemly, impermanence of life" (5). She further points out that

> Kadohata also writes in the style of Japanese colloquial poetry, *haikai*, in which images—delicate, fragmentary and fleeting—float by. Watching the Osaka family as it travels by car across America is not unlike viewing the slow, horizontal unfolding of a picture-scroll. On a journey that invites a kind of macadam-realism, Kadohata has composed a meandering, anecdotal daydream. (5,7)

Through this haiku-like landscape, Olivia captures with a child's simplicity and resonance the complex circularity of life in America. The narrative scales the various tonalities between absence and presence, past and present, silence and language, death and life. This voice creates knowledge of truth perceived in bits and pieces as the speaking "I" experiences them subjectively. The glib piquancy of youth both echoes and counters the fierce awesome wisdom and the bitter peevishness of age in the relationships of characters that span the issei, nisei, and sansei generations.

Mukherjee and Kadohata both reveal their own perceptions of how specific Asian immigrant and Asian-American women engage themselves in the process of delineating a space for their presence on the American landscape, a presence that can only be inscribed through representations of the self against reductive and disabling culture registers of race, ethnicity, gender, class, and language. Jasmine's eventful, though uneven, odyssey across countries and states is often punctuated by her identification of a fluid, "becoming" self with an equally fluid, "becoming" America that is accepted by some but violently rejected by others. Realizing, within the parameters of her defined experience, how closely the identity of self is intertwined with the physical landscape and cultural ideologies of a place, both in a liberating and a constricting sense, the protagonist creates her space through forging her new reality onto her surroundings. She empowers her Old World "third eye" to guide her beyond the "potholes and rutted" driveway, and her blood-stained Kali-tongue to voice her "wants" and "hope" (214). While in Mukherjee the "third world alien" claims her place in the "first world," creating new epic/heroic narratives of female adventure, desire, and agency encoded within a neocolonial space, Kadohata's female subject discovers forms of collective truths that are written into her specific ethnic and communal history. Traveling across the "distant plains" of "Oregon, Wyoming, California, and

Washington" with brief periods in Nebraska, as well as Arkansas and Texas, Olivia identifies certain memories with certain places. It is out of these memories of all these different places that she grows and creates her inner topography of dreams and wants: "There was so much that I wanted. That's what kept welling up in me, disturbing my sleeping and waking dreams" (151). Both subjects, Jasmine and Olivia, in their construction of a viable worldview that sustains their fluid reality and identity, do not simply transform themselves; they also transform the American cultural milieu. Its very landscape is forged into a new shape and texture through their language and consciousness.

References

Bergland, Betty. "Ideology, Ethnicity, and the Gendered Subject: Reading Immigrant Women's Autobiographies." Pp. 101–21 in *Seeking Common Ground,* ed. Donna Gabaccia. Westport, Conn.: Praeger, 1992.

Davies, Carol Boyce. *Black Women, Writing and Identity: Migrations of the Subject.* New York: Routledge, 1994.

Edwards-Yearwood, Grace. "Growing Up Japanese–American." *Los Angeles Times Book Review,* 16 July 1989, 12.

13

GUS LEE, CHANG-RAE LEE, AND LI-YOUNG LEE: THE SEARCH FOR THE FATHER IN ASIAN AMERICAN LITERATURE

John C. Hawley

> As long as you can, you will please the father, the most holy and fragile animal.
> —Chang-Rae Lee, *Native Speaker* (285)

> The man who emigrated—my grandfather—carried within him the memory of home, the former world, the place where he was once "real." It tore at him, that memory, and yet it kept him anchored: he knew where his home was, knew that he had lost it. The son of that man—my father—believed he could make the new place his home. The task was probably impossible, but it kept him occupied. The son of that man—myself—realizes what? That the new home—in my case, a Jewish suburb—is no home; is, in fact, for me an absurdity, a sham, and that the old home is lost in unreality. (Mura, 32-33)

The increasing ambivalence in identity that David Mura here relentlessly narrates typifies the crisis that many immigrants, and children of immigrants, face in our nation. Who, they must ask, are they expected to be, who are they allowed to be, who do they choose to be? The anxiety ramifies in the lives of many Asian ethnic groups, who frequently enough become lumped together in the view of white Americans as "our" enemies from the second World War, the Korean War, or the Vietnamese War. As Shirley Geok-lin Lim notes, the consequence of this particular immigrant experience is pressure from within and from without: "when the internal subjectivized ambivalence is confronted by the sociopolitical, seemingly 'objectivized' ambivalence, the yeast of ethnicity or the virulence of racism takes place" (1992, 26). In what follows, the implications of Lim's observation play themselves out in three remarkably individual accounts of self-definition: Gus Lee's *Honor and Duty*, Li-Young Lee's *The Winged Seed*, and Chang-Rae Lee's *Native Speaker*.

In the past several decades a growing number of Asian Americans have been chronicling their experiences of assimilation and resistance, their struggles with equations of personal and social identification. Maxine Hong Kingston and Amy Tan have been the most successful in "crossing over" and finding a mass audience in America and beyond, and partly as a consequence of this popularity more attention is being paid to well-established writers from an earlier generation—Carlos Bulosan, for example, and Frank Chin. The field of Asian American literature, in fact, seems poised on the verge of a renaissance (see Wong).

It is not surprising that so much of this writing is autobiographical—either directly so, or in rather loosely disguised fiction. The theme of immigration and the need for roots is at the heart of these writers' concerns. In this paper I will examine three important male writers—Gus Lee, Li-Young Lee, and Chang-Rae Lee—who embody the classic struggles of Oedipus and Telemachus, seeking to discover their fathers without killing them in the process or losing a secure sense of themselves as significant individuals. As with Carlos Bulosan and so many immigrants, these writers recognize that the quest, once begun, cannot be abandoned. One's bridges to the past, while crucial to understanding the present, can lead only to the future.

Thus, David Mura visits Japan to find his "lost center" (33), but recognizes that that country represents only a portion of who he is:

> Japan helped me balance a conversation which had been taking place before I was born, a conversation in my grandparents' heads, in my parents' heads, which, by my generation, had become very one-sided, so that the Japanese side was virtually silenced. My stay helped me realize that a balance, which probably never existed in the first place, could no longer be maintained. . . . Either I was American or I was one of the homeless, one of the searchers for what John Berger calls a world culture. But I was not Japanese. (370)

What Mura calls "a balance" is, perhaps, what Lim refers to as "slippages of selves" (*Ambivalent American*, 27), national, racial, and existential, that allow for a gradual acceptance and publication of one's various—and potentially conflicting—components of personality. She cites Bulosan's dual identification with Walt Whitman's version of a utopian American future, along with his decision to integrate Philippine folklore into his struggle for liberty, as a typical instance of the immigrant's often unresolved negotiation of a dialogic of identity. The first and strongest impulse in most cases is an assertion of one's citizenship. As Sau-ling Wong argues,

> Asian American writers, however rooted on this land they or their families may have been, tend to be regarded as direct transplants from Asia or as custodians of an esoteric subculture. Thus it is incumbent upon Asian American critics to orient discussions away from exoticization and to ensure that the word American is not blithely excised from the term Asian American. (9)

But the next step (really, the concurrent step) is the search for the father.

Another ongoing negotiation in the lives of these writers is the one described by Wong (following Maxine Kingston and Ron Takaki) as "necessity" and "extravagance," two terms that shape her groundbreaking book: "The terms Necessity and Extravagance signify two contrasting modes of existence and operation, one contained, survival-driven and conservation-minded, the other attracted to freedom, excess, emotional expressiveness, and autotelism" (13). This struggle focuses on the protagonist's internal conflict between duty and self-expression, between, in some cases, patriotism and individualism.

In the literature under discussion in this paper, this struggle pointedly expresses itself in questions of masculine self-definition, questions which Wong considers characteristic of Asian American literature. "To the extent that being female (in Asian and white American cultures) and being Asian (in American society) both entail subordination," she writes, "race is a 'gendered' term of analysis" (99). This, at any rate, is at the heart of her analysis of Lonny Kaneko's disturbing short story "The Shoyu Kid": "The preadolescent narrator and his gang operate on an unstated syllogism distilled from the experience of political subjugation: being Asian means being weak; being female also means being weak; therefore being Asian is like being female" (99). The preadolescent response to subordination in this case is to assume the role of the bully, to empower oneself by brutalizing another.

At the heart of the works by Gus Lee, Li-Young Lee, and Chang-Rae Lee is the definition of self specifically as a man. Behind their idiosyncratic styles and notably individual story lines remains a remarkably similar quest. Which role model, they seem to be asking, is available to, and acceptable by, the Asian Americans in question? Is their biological father a heroic precursor for their struggle, or simply an albatross they cannot evade?

Honor and Duty gives an account of protagonist Kai Ting's four years at West Point. Gus Lee, who incidentally spent four years at the same institution, recognizes the iconic value of this most American of academies.

One cannot doubt that Lee's character voices much of the author's own uncomfortable experiences as a young cadet:

> I thought all the tall, broad-shouldered, straight-nosed blond guys with good grades in America had come. . . . I did not fit the profile. . . . An inch below six feet, I was a steady playmaking junior varsity basketball guard and a boxer. I was superstitiously Taoist and remotely Christian, ethnically Chinese, culturally quasi-Negro, trained to the table etiquette of Main Line Philadelphia, and blessed with a linguistic bouillabaisse of Shanghainese, Mandarin, and Spanish, African, and European English. I was physically strong, socially inept, intellectually underdeveloped, spiritually muddled, and politically untested. My father had come from wealth, but we were now of the economic underclass. I possessed a troubled conscience, hoped I was growing in height, and was clueless about girls. Actually, I knew a lot about girls; I had read Jane Austen and Jade Snow Wong and seen the Sears ads. . . . I was a Chinese colored boy with a Pennsylvanian Puritan upbringing who was fan toong, an overeater of Kwangtung food, who always wanted to be accepted, and would always have trouble finding people similarly situated. (54–55)

Maintaining one's honor and discerning one's duty serve as the backbone of the man Kai Ting is trying to build up, but the reader is struck by the literal nature of that growth: Lee's protagonist, a boxer for many years and a dedicated bodybuilder, repeatedly remarks on the reception he is given by long-lost members of his family, by casual acquaintances, and by his classmates at the academy. They all stand in awe of his massive size and his gargantuan appetite. He seems almost to be attempting to make his presence inevitable by its sheer bulk. He makes no attempt to become "more Asian" (nor does he attempt to disguise his obvious Chinese features), but he will not allow himself to be overlooked nor to be treated as a token representative of an alien race. In fact, by his determined affability, honesty, and hard work he is accepted as a leader; those bigots who rejected him ultimately find themselves on the margins of acceptability.

But this acceptance remains male-oriented. When he, in his last semester, ultimately defies the Asian stereotype by failing engineering he is unexpectedly dismissed from the academy and sent as an instructor to the Monterey language school. His return as an onlooker for the West Point graduation ceremony is the most emotionally wrought section of the novel: "I couldn't run from my heart. It had helped to come here, to lend my small applause and heart-bursting admiration to the graduating First Classmen of the USMA Class of 1968. I was proud to know them, proud to have been one of their brothers" (*Honor*, 402). This is not surprising in a novel that deals principally with the years spent in an all-male institution, but Kai Ting's relations with women in those four years are instructive. He remains a virgin throughout the novel. He tries to get his high school sweetheart, who is Caucasian, to return the love he feels for her, but to no avail ("I wanted to be American, and she was Miss America . . . . She was the yin, female, side of America, as much as West Point was the yang" [91, 93]). On the other hand, when a Chinese American woman who is wealthy, beautiful, and educated, tries to interest him in marriage, he demurs. Most readers would find his resistance strange and inadequately explained by Ting, who is the narrator.

There can be no doubt that Ting ponders the role of race in sexual relations; he is explicit in his questions in this area. Gus Lee sets up an interesting mirror situation between father and son, since Ting's father had first married a woman in China (Kai's mother), and when she died he remarried a Caucasian American—who is nothing less than the wicked stepmother in fairy tales, humiliating her stepson at every turn. Lee stacks the deck in favor of Asian women in the novel, in fact giving Kai's mother the last word by presenting the protagonist with a truly moving letter from her at book's end. She, at last, offers him the love that he had been denied, or could not accept, up to this point in the novel. One wonders if Lee is seeking to right the balance in the sexual politics that have cast Asian men as unattractive to Caucasian women, and Asian women as delightfully submissive to Caucasian men (see Mendez; Price; and Walsh). In any event, while Kai Ting is clearly interested in exploring the sexual realm, his real crisis during the years of this novel involves his relationship with his father.

More accurately put, Ting is caught between his Confucian uncle, Shim, and his father, who decisively turned his back on the ways of China when he came to the United States. Uncle Shim (and Kai's mother, we ultimately learn) wants him to become a peaceful scholar; his father wants him to be strong, a soldier, a man among men. Kai's father counts his own days at Fort Benning as the proudest of his life, even though in adopting this humble new identity he had had to give up his considerably imposing position in Chinese society. He wants more than anything for his only son to merit the American seal of approval that comes with a degree from a military academy.

Kai's father had had a patron in the army, a General Schwarzhedd (!), whose son, an instructor at West Point, becomes something of a Caucasian father for Kai. When Kai becomes too emotionally wrought to remain through the entire graduation ceremony he stumbles into the young Schwarzhedd and is thrilled when the teacher introduces him as "one of my men." Kai looks up at Schwarzhedd's full dress uniform and remarks, "He studied me, beaming, looking down while we shook hands, and he gently took his eyes from mine when he noticed mine were wet, that I was losing control. I had experienced an urge to hug him. . . . I enjoyed reviewing five banks of decorations, as if somehow they were mine as well" (400). Kai, hearing that Schwarzhedd has been ordered to Vietnam, worries that he might be killed ("Not you, please, not you" [401]), and learns a significant lesson from him as he is about to learn from his mother's letter:

> I'm not sure how long we were together, nor can I recall all that he said. It was too overwhelming for me to be back at the Academy, this strange and powerful school, founded by ancient Honor, Polish engineers, revolutionary Englishmen, Irish songs of strong ale, and the first political Americans, on this brightest and warmest day of all days bright and warm, with this officer who possessed so many connections to my family and to my heart. I basked in the vitality of my gahng and lun to him. The bonds were beyond my measure. He told me to forgive myself. I inhaled the river air, appreciating every moment. Life was full and I had no wounds, no injuring past, my heart clean and pure. (401–2)

This, it would seem, is the celebration of the young man who can finally identify himself as an American—of Asian ancestry. His is not the injuring past of his parents' generation.

His failure at West Point in fact frees him from the massive institutionalization of patriarchy that it represented. As one of the cadets tells him, "This whole place is filled with sons of ambitious fathers. We're all platforms for their hopes, their ambitions. West Point is a father's totem" (36). Having come to terms with the father figure it offered him in Schwarzhedd, almost as if he is lifting psychic barbells, he turns his attention to his real father:

> I had left a place that was all yang, male force, and the separation had brought my mother back to life in the bottom of my heart, where the most vivid feelings settle under the weight of living. I began to suspect that many of the deficiencies in my personality had arisen from the death of a mother I had forgotten. . . . My Mah-mee was telling me how to face my father. To face his harnessed fury with peace, to be of good courage where all I felt was fear, to hold tight to the good that lay somewhere in our relationship. (415, 416)

The balance he senses is, in fact, the consequence of his maturation and his confrontation with himself in all his cultural ambiguity. His new sense of self enables him to return to his father's house and confront what he has understood to be his father's weakness before his Caucasian wife, and intolerance of imperfection in his children. His father, at last, is released from the burden of protecting this child, and can allow his own "weaker" side to express itself. Lee centers the reconciliation of these generations around the father's confession of his own struggle to come to terms with the traumatizing pain involved in his own emigration and self-redefinition as an American.

Standing on their balcony, the father makes his first happy affirmation in the novel: "No . . . We not jumping. We climbing up American ladder!" (422).

Chang–Rae Lee's *Native Speaker* offers an amazing complement to the picture presented by *Honor and Duty*. Korean American Henry Park actually marries the sort of woman Kai Ting had described as "Miss America." Park describes Lelia Boswell as "the lengthy Anglican goddess" (Native 14); she describes herself as "the standard–bearer" (11); and Park describes Lelia's father as

> one of those tall, angular, self-embalming types . . . . Groton, Princeton, Harvard Business School. His neatly clipped silver hair and tailored suits and unmitigating stare of eyes and trim old body said it all over in simple, clear language: Chief Executive Officer. Do not fuck with this man. (111)

But the book opens on the day that Lelia has decided to leave her husband. She serves a function in this book somewhat similar to the role played in *Honor and Duty* by West Point: as the preeminent symbol for the protagonist for the essence of the traditional idea of America. Park's on–again, off–again relationship with Lelia nicely parallels his ongoing interrogation of his place in American society.

Chang–Rae Lee cleverly incorporates the stereotype of the inscrutable Asian into his plot and uses it to dismantle traditional notions of the benefits of assimilation. Park is an industrial "mole" for an unnamed group functioning something like the CIA. The duplicity involved consumes the protagonist and leads to a crisis of self-hatred that centers around questions of self-definition:

> Our clients were multinational corporations, bureaus of foreign governments, individuals of resource and connection. We provided them with information about people working against their vested interests. We generated background studies, psychological assessments, daily chronologies, myriad facts and extrapolations. These in extensive reports. Typically the subject was a well-to-do immigrant supporting some potential insurgency in his old land, or else funding a fledgling trade union or radical student organization. Sometimes he was simply an agitator. Maybe a writer of conscience. An expatriate artist.
>
> We worked by contriving intricate and open–ended emotional conspiracies. We became acquaintances, casual friends. Sometimes lovers. We were social drinkers. Embracers of children. Doubles partners. We threw rice at weddings, we laid wreaths at funerals. We ate sweet pastries in the basement of churches. Then we wrote the tract of their lives, remote, unauthorized biographies. I the most prodigal and mundane of historians. (*Native*, 16)

Park consciously becomes what many Caucasians in American society suspect him of being: a voyeur, an untrustworthy ingratiator who smiles and smiles and all the while is looking for information to use against the naive Caucasian. But Lee's genius is in using this stereotype to show the limits to which some immigrants will go to become fully identified with the new group. In effect, Park sets out to destroy his "own" people, whether they are Asian, Latin American, African, etc. It is a lesson he gradually learns, but with an acceptance of guilt comes an angry assertion of the value of his enforced role as outsider in American society:

> I think my father would choose to see my deceptions in a rigidly practical light, as if they were similar to that daily survival he came to endure, the need to adapt, assume an advantageous shape. My ugly immigrant's truth, as was his, is that I have exploited my own, and those others who can be exploited. This forever is my burden to bear. But I and my kind possess another dimension. We will learn every lesson of accent and idiom, we will dismantle every last pretense and practice you hold, noble as well as ruinous. You can keep nothing safe from our eyes and ears. This is your own history. We are your most perilous and dutiful brethren, the song of our hearts at once furious and sad. (297)

Having come to this complex assertion of a mixed identity, Henry Park leaves the agency—his life, like Kai Ting's, in some sense in a shambles, in some sense beginning afresh. To reach this point he has had to confront the fact that he is not simply American, and that the story of the immigrants that he is betraying is, in fact, his story as well:

> How I come by plane, come by boat. Come climbing over a fence. When I get here, I work. I work for the day I will finally work for myself. I work so hard that one day I end up forgetting the person I am. I forget my wife, my son. Now, too, I have lost my old mother tongue. And I forget the ancestral graves I have left on a hillside of a faraway land, the loneliest stones that each year go unblessed. (260)

Precipitating his crisis has been not only his wife's departure, but the death of their son, as well. Product of a mixed racial coupling, he is literally smothered to death by his white playmates. Looking back on this tragic, and ominous, death, Park admits that

> my hope was that he would grow up with a singular sense of his world, a life univocal, which might have offered him the authority and confidence that his broad half-yellow face could not. . . . The truth of my feeling, exposed and ugly to me now, is that I was the one who was hoping whiteness for Mitt, being fearful of what I might have bestowed on him: all that too-ready

devotion and honoring, and the chilly pitch of my blood, and then all that burning language that I once presumed useless, never uttered and never lived. (249, 265–66)

The issue of language is one to which we will return.

The self–hate that is implied in this rejection of his role as a biological father suggests his difficulty in accepting the role of his own father in his life. Henry Park's father is a self–made immigrant, the owner of several fresh produce stores in Queens. Henry recognizes the sacrifices that have been made, but he ultimately criticizes his father for imagining nothing bigger for himself than the wealth that results from slavish menial labor. When Henry is assigned to wheedle his way into the confidences of a rising Korean American politician, John Kwang, he thinks he has found a suitable alternative to the father who doggedly counts his pennies each working day. Kwang, on the other hand, appears to be wholly assimilated, envisioning himself as mayor of New York ("when the rest of us wanted only security in the tiny dollar-shops and churches of our lives" [304]). But he comes to recognize the price that Kwang has paid for this apparent assimilation: he has lost all sense of family, all sense of honor.

Henry's father is remarkably like Kai Ting's: both had to give up positions of influence in their native lands and to reinvent themselves in this new and unforgiving country. In doing so, both men had come to an accommodation with human limitation, recognizing that "the sky was never the limit" (309). Henry's duplicitous relationship with Kwang, involved in mutual betrayal, leads to the expulsion of a great many illegal immigrants who had been involved in Kwang's political campaign. A remorseful Park, imagining what it might have meant if his own father had somehow been one of those expelled, recognizes his father's true adaptive strength ("My father was a kind of trickster all his own. He'd keep me guessing with his storefront patois. Any moment I had him in square in my sights, he'd surprise me with a dip, a shake, a move from the street that I'd never heard or seen" [312]).

Unlike Kai Ting, however, Henry Park comes to this renewed respect for his father too late for a reconciliation. He does, though, begin once again to imagine himself taking on this role. One suspects the new role would offer far less accommodation to the melting pot theories that shaped John Kwang's life:

When I was young I would cringe and grow ashamed and angry at those funny tones of my father and his workers, all that English, Spanglish, Jive. Just talk right, I wanted to yell, just talk right for once in your sorry lives. But now, I think I would give most anything to hear my father's talk again, the crash and bang and stop of his language, always hurtling by. I will listen to him forever in the streets of this city. (313)

Park's mother had taught him that "San konno san itta. Over the mountains there are mountains" (309). And this is the principal characteristic he comes to embrace in his memory of his father: as Dylan Thomas wished for his own father, Mr. Park did not go gentle into that good night, but saw his life as a raging battle.

It is no accident that Li-Young Lee writes his memoir, *The Winged Seed*, when he is the exact age his father was when Li-Young was born. But when he writes the book his father has been dead eleven years. As with Gus Lee's novel and that of Chang-Rae Lee, this book centers its reflections on the protean image that the father played for the protagonist. Li-Young Lee's father also gave up a series of earlier identities and fought a constant battle in bringing his family to the United States. Beginning in China in the 1950s and moving to Indonesia, the older Lee ("Ba" to the narrator) became vice president at Gamaliel University. Eventually, however, in 1959 he was imprisoned by Sukarno. Li-Young was eighteen months old. Ba managed to escape and transport his family to Hong Kong, where he became famous as an evangelical preacher. They moved a final time in 1964 when the author was six; Ba became a Presbyterian minister to an all-white congregation in western Pennsylvania (the congregation referred to him as "their heathen minister" [82]). This was an ominous year to be Asian in the United States (it was also the time that Kai Ting was at West Point). Li-Young's father was the only one who spoke English at the time.

As with Kai Ting's mother and the mother of Henry Park, Li-Young's mother ("Mu") is very traditional in her understanding of her role in the family, and her support of the respect that must principally be shown to her husband. Like Henry Park's mother, she is from the landed gentry in her homeland. Like Kai Ting's mother, she is deeply respectful of education. The women stay in the background in the three books, like servants. But perhaps to offer them a contrast, the actual lot of servants is portrayed as far worse. *Native Speaker* describes a truly sad woman that Henry Park's father imports from Korea to tend house (and to hide in the back room), and Li-Young recalls the aged servant class in China who had been taught to see themselves as "a 'human to be used'" (177). Such descriptions silhouette the stark role of the father as viewed by these sons: remote, unapproachable, disapproving.

It is perhaps no surprise that his preacher father constantly referred to Christ as The Resurrected Man, since he possibly saw himself as one who had had to reinvent himself throughout his adult life. Li-Young Lee notes that he was never allowed to look his father straight in the eyes (60), a father whose appearance strangely resembled President Sukarno. But while he saw pictures of the president wherever he went, his father was in prison ("Ba was The Absent One" [63]). In his absence, "Ba had gradually become the object of our prayers as well, so that we were praying to him as well as for him" (64). Li-Young grew up speaking, first, Javanese ("the children's language" [122]), then Chinese, then finally English, which he found to be excruciating. While his father was in prison and his mother spent most of her day visiting her husband, Li-Young was entertained by the family's Javanese servants, who filled his head with wonderful stories of gods and goddesses. They planted the seed of metaphysical wonder in the child's head:

> We felt both less substantial and more, for we couldn't tell if we inhabited a world densely populated by three or four orders of beings, as the stories suggested we did, or if we were stranded on an island adrift in some old, measureless sea of anonymous powers which constantly threatened to overcome our finite ground. . . . We were convinced by the stories behind the stories that our island of cities and ice fields, forests, rivers, and volcanoes was The World. The greater stories persuaded us that our father being jailed, along with so many other fathers of Chinese households, had to do with something much older and darker than what could be explained by adult words like politics or economics. The greater stories called to some correspondent thing inside us that resisted a name, something barely apprehended and timeless. (122–24)

If Gus Lee and Chang-Rae Lee seem finally to salvage a great deal of respect for the fathers they portray in their novels, Li-Young Lee seems not to have come to a very peaceful accommodation with the father he remembers. He certainly understands the determination that it took to endure prison and constant emigration, but he portrays it almost as though it were a question of the survival of the fittest—with the unfit being various siblings who simply did not last all the way to America. Li-Young notes that his father spent four years building a cardboard and paper model of Solomon's Temple:

> And the real genius of the thing was not its true-to-life, full scale construction, nor its swinging doors complete with bolted locks, nor even the tenderness in the details of the faces of the seraphim, but its portability. For each piece could be gently dismantled, unfolded, spread flat, and put into a box to be carried across borders, barriers, into provinces, jungles, over seas and lands as language to language, landscape to landscape, we carried Ba's Temple of Solomon. (38)

Li-Young's implication seems to be that the temple was built not to honor Yahweh, but to honor the egomaniacal builder. He does not seem convinced by his father's insistence that "our seemingly incoherent and stray rovings across the horizontal plane of seemings and doings were, in fact, . . . a continuous unfolding of vertical and ultimate meaning" (39).

As respectful as Li-Young Lee remains in the face of his parents' trials, he recognizes that one of the many things that were jettisoned in his travels was The Past. He looks upon China and his father's generation as inescapably old and bound to the blood ties and traditions that he cannot embrace as self-defining.

> I've disavowed them one and all, all of them I never knew, and I've disavowed those from whom they were begot, all of them I never knew, and I've disavowed all those they begat, all but one, the one who immediately preceded me in life and who precedes me now on his longest flight down a very dark hall very subterranean. (164)

Instead, he has received from his father the sense of himself as the winged seed from which the memoir draws its title. He dedicates, and addresses, the book to his wife, and suggests that he carries within himself this seed, and from it will come his renewing sense of self that will result in fatherhood.

The three books, and many others like them, give voice to the generational anguish that defines the literature of immigration. The similarities are striking. Gus Lee's protagonist, intent on building up his muscles and becoming a man, nonetheless admits in a quiet moment that "for all the gahng and shiao, the math and Confucius, the hunger and hard times, I just wanted my dad to like me" (*Honor* 216). Li-Young Lee, bathing his father in his last days, sadly remembers that "my fear is he'll fall apart in my arms like a puzzle and I'll never get him put together" (158). So he, many years later, tries strenuously to put the pieces together. But his earlier remembrance surely offers a telling suggestion of why this quest is so necessary:

> Our sincerest wish was, I know now, too late, not, in fact, to be acknowledged by God, but to be seen, truly seen, seen once and forever, by our father, Ba, who was earlier than light and later than the last each night, whose bloody God exacted love exactly at the body, leveled the force of his divine affection precisely at the fatty heart and fibrous lungs. (*Seed* 44)

References

Lee, Chang-Rae. *Native Speaker*. New York: Riverhead, 1995.

Lee, Gus. *Honor and Duty*. New York: Ballantine, 1994.

Lee, Li-Young. *The Winged Seed: A Remembrance*. New York: Simon and Schuster, 1995.

Lim, Shirley Geok-lin and Amy Ling, eds. *Reading the Literatures of Asian America*. Philadelphia: Temple University Press, 1992.

Lim, Shirley Geok-lin. "The Ambivalent American: Asian American Literature on the Cusp." Pp. 13–32 in *Reading the Literatures of Asian America*, ed. Shirley Geok-lin Lim and Amy Ling. Philadelphia: Temple University Press, 1992.

Mendez, Carlos. "Those Controversial, Crazy, Calendar Boys." *Asian Week* 16 no. 5 (27 January 1995): 8–10.

Mura, David. *Turning Japanese: Memoirs of a Sansei*. New York: Atlantic Monthly Press 1991.

Price, Darby Li Po. "Asian Men, Caucasian Women." *Slant*, April 1992, 13, 23.

Takaki, Ronald. *Strangers from a Different Shore: A History of Asian Americans*. Boston: Little, Brown, 1989.

Walsh, Joan. "Asian Women, Caucasian Men." *Image* magazine, *San Francisco Chronicle/Examiner*, 2 December 1990, 11–16.

Wong, Sau-ling Cynthia. *Reading Asian American Literature*. Princeton: Princeton University Press, 1993.

14

"HALF FISH AND HALF F–O–U–L": KIBEI YOUTH, CONFLICTING ICONOGRAPHIES, AND JAPANESE AMERICAN INTERNMENT EXPERIENCES

James A. Wren

> Gone are the days of gaiety. . .
>
> Gone are the days of contentedness
>
> Of small childhood mischief. . . .
>
> "Gone," 28 April 1943

> A few hundred years hence, in this same place, another traveler, as despairing as myself, will mourn the disappearance of what I might have seen, but failed to see.
>
> Claude Levi-Strauss, *Tristes Tropiques*

> Here on my Army cot I lay
>
> Thinking about my home
>
> So far away.
>
> Tadashi Muranaka, Untitled

> VINCENT as MOTO: "What's wrong with you? You sickee in the head? What the hell is wrong with you? Why can't you hear what I'm saying? Why can't you see me as I really am?"
>
> Philip Kan Gotanda, *Yankee Dawg You Die*

Out of Japan and into the Fire

The Meiji Charter Oath of 1868 called on young Japanese intellectuals to travel abroad and return with the fruits of Western experience, educational and otherwise. But the act of calling complicity silences on at least two accounts. First, it propels a folk wisdom beyond the status of myth into the realm of fact, underscoring what everyone had "known" all along, that Japan had maintained a state of isolation until Commodore Perry forced it to open to the world and, as a logical consequence, tacitly serves to proclaim that there were *no* Japanese who had traveled beyond its borders since its closing until well into the middle of the nineteenth century. It is interesting to approach these contentions from the perspective of Japanese language education outside of Japan, since "no contact" would almost certainly have been met with "no language learners." To the contrary, there are a number of indicators that contacts were being made, from the publication of the *Ni-Po Jisho* (1603, *A Japanese-Portuguese Dictionary*) and Rodriquez's *Nihon Daibunten* (1608, *A Dictionary of Japanese Usage*), to the establishment of a Japanese language program in St. Petersburg, Russia (1705), and a journal dedicated entirely to Japanese studies at the University of Paris II (1856), to mention but a few. Further, we know that there were a number of Japanese, including the Christian *diamyô* Justo Takayama and Juan Narito (as they are remembered today), who fled Tokugawa, Japan, for the Philippines in search of religious freedom, as well as a number of Japanese who reportedly survived shipwrecks to make contact with Russia and the United States prior to Perry's mission to Japan. And second, such a calling gives the illusion of begrudging acknowledgment, claiming as it were that those who option to go abroad do so clearly with altruistic intent, namely to contribute to the construction of a "modern" state upon their return.

History, however, paints a wholly different story behind the exodus from Japan.

From 1869, with the establishment of the Wakamatsu colony to farm tea and silk in California, to the 1880s and the wake of political and economic upheaval on such an enormous scale that the Meiji government surely felt threatened for its very survival, emigration became but one of many devices of social engineering, with the bureaucracy relentingly recognizing its importance as a social "pressure valve," even encouraging its use. Under the terms of a treaty between the Hawaiian and Japanese governments in 1885, officially sanctioned emigration began. In less than a decade, some 30,000 Japanese, primarily from southern Japan, especially Kyûshû and the Okinawaan Islands, had entered Hawaii to work on the plantations (see Conroy; Takaki 1994b).

In fact, so great was the "outflux"—from the vantage point of government officials on both sides of the Pacific—that in 1891 an Emigration Bureau was established in the Japanese Ministry of Foreign Affairs, and the Emigrant Protection Act of 1896 placed emigrants solely under the protection of the Japanese government and its consulates abroad. In 1898, when Hawaii was annexed as a territory of the United States, there were well over 60,000 Japanese in residence in the islands. For these residents, annexation took on a different meaning: it facilitated, however ironically, a process already well under way and allowed for further movement onto the mainland without passports.

In the 1890s, private companies and labor recruiters, national government agencies and prefectural officials, all in like manner encouraged and capitalized upon such movements. Since the United States did not recognize labor contracts signed prior to entry, it witnessed the immigration of free, noncontracted workers. They came, this time, largely from the developed Inland Sea prefectures on the main island of Honshu and moved with relative ease from agricultural and entrepreneurial activities (see Hattori; Lukes, et al.; Pozzetta, et al.).

Narratives written from the internment centers some four decades later continued to reflect just such a trend.[1] As one youth remembers,

We had a ten acre ranch, mostly tomatoes was growed. And the tomatoes was sold at streets corner and also was taken to the markets.

My brother and I was the salesman of the tomato stand. Every time at night when we closed the stand, we count the amount of money we make each day.

We always make more money than we realized so we go to movies or shopping and have our fun. One night my father, mother and I was taking a load of tomatoes to markets on a small truck. Just before when we reach the market another vehicle came widely down the steep grade with a drunken driver. His truck smacked right into ours and turned Our truck upside down including the packed tomatoes. The tomatoes was all over the road. My father and I wasn't hurt but my mother was pretty bad injured and was rushed over to the hospital by an ambulance.

A few sadly days had passed after the accident had happened. My brother, sister and I was waiting at the hospital that day to see if my mother will recover from the head injury she received. The doctor had come out from my mother's hospital room to tell us the good or the bad news. It was the good news, boy I jumped and shouted cause of the good news. A few days had passed after my visit. Boy we sure had a good appetite cause of the good news. The afternoon my mother came home from the hospital, and had a party waiting for her.

Another youth's recollections underscore the economic prosperity that some found. Moving quickly away from the moment of his birth, he remembers, and what he remembers is embossed with larger notions of positioning and power: "Most of my time was spent on the Ranch. We had 1,000 acres of Sugar beets. On Saturday we all go riding horse back riding in Palos Verdes and Rolling Hill. There was a village to each person that worked for us. Village for Caucasian and Mexicans."

In fact, as the Japanese population grew along the West Coast, a number of nurturing communities indicative of a sophisticated, widespread social infrastructure essential to daily life sprang up around them. In 1898, the *Nichibei Times*, one of the first Japanese newspapers on the American mainland, was established in San Francisco to meet the needs of a burgeoning literate immigrant population. And other necessities were to be met as well. The story of one Issei is illustrative of this point:

> I was born in . . . County of Kumage, Yamaguchi Province. My father was the priest of a church, whose (sic) name is Jigokokuji. There were five other churches in that district and my father's was the dominating church. So I have had a pretty good time. Had that life continued, I might have become a spoiled child (sic), for in Japan, when you were born as a son of a rich man or a high class man, the people around you flatter and make you a spoiled child.

> But fortunately, for my sake, my father had been assigned to expand the Jodo Sect in Hawaii, so he and my mother left Japan to Hawaii. I was told to stay with my aunt, because I was too small. I was then only 7 years old. During my staying with aunt, I learned many things; she was a school teacher. Although the family was a well-to-do, she made me work hard, so I wouldn't become lazy.

> Then in 1934, when I was 10 yrs. old, a letter came from my father in Hawaii. . . . So I decided to see my parents. My friends said I wouldn't be able to go all by myself to such a far place. I sailed from Kobe, the second largest sea port in Japan, in January, and reached Honolulu in January 28th.

But in the face of emigration flew the wrath of prejudice, what has come euphemistically to be called the "Yellow Peril." A complex set of prejudices, this phenomenon owes if not its origin then its prominence in no small measure to the popularity of the racial theories of the Frenchman Count Arthur de Gobineau (1816–82), the main tenets of which are spelled out in his *Essai sur l'inegalitb des races humaines* (1853–55). In 1894, Ludwig Schemann, a professor at the University of Freiburg (Freiburg, Germany), established the infamous *Gobineau Vereinigung*, an "academic" society given to the propagation and reinterpretation of Gobineau's racial theories.[2] The effects should not be underestimated. During the same period that European émigrés are overflowing into America as a result of the Potato Famine, and the social upheaval accompanying the painful "birthing" of the German and Italian states, the baggage of European racism managed to stow away with them. As a result, the term "Yellow Peril" (in German, "Gelbe Gefahr") reached widespread use both in Europe and in the United States by the time of the Sino-Japanese War (1894–95). And its usage gave it a newfound respectability as an acceptable political stance—so respectable, in fact, that from 1900–1905, the term could be heard repeated time and time again by many a Western leader, including Kaiser Wilhelm II and Theodore Roosevelt (see Thompson).

The tentacles of such prejudice quickly moved out from the ghetto communities erected to shelter newly arriving European immigrants into the many "rooted" households of the American mainstream. The expansiveness of such hatred explains in part the reception Madame Hanako (1868–1945), the Japanese-born actress who was at the time enjoying an unparalleled following on the continent, found in America. The drama critic for the *Des Moines Register* (3 November 1907), as but one example, arrogantly flexes his critical acumen:

> I have seen such faces on oriental fans, vases and screens, and I recall some like them in nightmares; but hitherto have I not seen them alike. Hanako, the starred tragedienne of the company, enacts a belle supposed to be irresistibly charming; yet she could be no unsightlier woman unless her pygmy size were increased to ordinary size. . . . She dances awkwardly on stilts, and is clumsily blithesome in antics that make her and the three others look like decrepit, yet still tricky monkeys in a cage. (quoted in Sawada, 66–67)

With such strong condemnation coming out of the heartland, it was only natural—and not only in the American political arena—that such hatred ultimately found shelter on the steps of long-established governments, where prejudice was translated just as quickly into legislative action.

Australia moved first and forbade Japanese immigration in 1898. In 1900, the Japanese government and the United States embraced the first of two "gentlemen's agreements," the former announcing that no further passports would be issued to laborers bound for the U.S. mainland. By 1905, the Asiatic Exclusion League was meeting on a regular basis in San Francisco; the majority of its members were, not surprisingly, labor unions with large European-immigrant memberships. Following several widespread anti-Japanese riots in San Francisco in 1906–7, President Theodore Roosevelt issued an executive order barring the immigration of Japanese from Hawaii and other countries to the U.S. mainland (see Dyer; Hata; McWilliams). By 1908, a second "gentlemen's agreement" between Japan and the United States seemed in order. In accordance with this agreement, the Japanese government allowed only those with close relatives already in the United States to migrate there.[3] In return for curtailing the perceived influx, the U.S. government promised—but failed to follow through on—wide scale protection for those Japanese already residing in the United States.

Canada quickly followed suit and established its own limits in 1908 (see Sugimoto; Charles Young, et al.). Thereafter, a series of "anti–Oriental laws," as they were termed at the time, rapidly came into being. But the results were frequently comical (from our perspective), and almost always dismayingly ineffectual (from the perspective of the legislative bodies involved). Antimiscegenation laws were inadvertently countered with the influx of so called Picture Brides, Japanese men in the United States being prohibited by law from marrying non–Asian (i.e., Caucasian) women (see Ichioka, 1977, 1980, 1988). In 1913, the Alien Land Law prohibited "aliens not eligible for citizenship" from ownership or long–term leasing of land; an amendment in 1920 went one step further and prohibited purchases in the name of their Nisei children. A year later, Japan stopped issuing passports to Picture Brides. In 1922, in the landmark case of "*Ozawa v the United States*," the U.S. Supreme Court ruled that Takao Ozawa was not eligible for citizenship, for citizenship was by definition a right reserved for "free white persons" or an "African by birth or descent" only (see Ichioka, 1977b). With the Oriental Exclusion Act, the United States unilaterally ended Japanese immigration in 1924.[4]

"You Dropped a Bomb on Me": Pearl Harbor and Beyond

Against this neurotic backdrop—one country encouraging their departure, another taking moves to curtail their arrival—Japanese came to the United States, settled and established for themselves and their offspring some semblance of community, by no means static. Some came with the intent to return at some point in the future. Others arrived full of dreams of new beginnings. And still others found themselves swept up and carried along with the current, so to speak, as these communities began to grow. In spite of the external signs of prejudice and overt instances of racial discrimination, these communities came to represent stability, and that stability in turn contributed paradoxically to the spread of relative prosperity *and* relative isolation and invisibility to the gaze of a white America. Beyond the "unseen" but seemingly impenetrable walls of these hamlets, the Japanese and their offspring almost never ventured forth, were rarely seen, never heard. They eked out lives in the obscurity of silence.[5]

But that soon changed.

In the words of young Nisei, "Then came this terrible thing called 'war' between the United States and the Japanese Empire." Another youth expands upon this memory: "My days at Torrance were full of fun and laughter until the day of Dec. 7th 1941 when the treacherous enemies of America attacked Pearl Harbor. It came to me as a great shock. I never knew that Japan would do such things. Somehow, after the war broke out, I seem to be lacking in strength & energy which I had before." A young woman living in Honolulu at the time emphasizes the "personal horrors" she felt because of the bombing:

> On the morning of December 7, when Pearl Harbor was attacked, I was just having my breakfast. At first we all thought it was just a maneuver and didn't pay much attention to it. But when the radio announced that we were really being bombed, I was just scared to death. For a whole month after the bombing of Pearl Harbor, I couldn't sleep very well for I was afraid that we might be attacked again. . . . Much of our school time was devoted to gas mask drills, air raid drills and red cross work. We were all issued gas masks by the military office. When the air raid siren was sounded, we had to go into trenches and bomb shelters with our gas masks which we were required to carry to school everyday.

The moment is burned deeply into, permanently etched onto, the souls of Japanese-America. So pervasive is it that John Okada's *No-No Boy*, originally published in 1957 and often hailed as the first American novel written by a Nisei, begins with these very words. "DECEMBER THE SEVENTH" (vii). As its young protagonist Ichiro Yamada glimpses Eto Minato for the first time—note the hierarchy of power and position established with movement from "a couple of men in suits, half a dozen women who failed to arouse him even after prolonged good behavior, and a young Japanese with a lunch bucket" (1)—the latter remarks, off-handedly it seems, "Last time [we met] must have been before Pearl Harbor" (2). So monumental a date, it becomes seminal in the minds and souls of Japanese-America: more than the measure by which one's personal history is recorded or later recalled, it becomes that precarious means by which all must create a none-too-certain future.

Nor can the personal turmoil arising directly from President Franklin D. Roosevelt's words—"a day that will live in infamy"—easily be ignored. "I graduated my Junior High (sic) at 1941," a Hawaiian-born Nisei recollects, "and in summer I helped my father with the canefield . . . such as planting, weeding, and fertilizing, and then on December 7th Pearl Harbor was attacked and we were very much to surprise and then my father was interned by the U.S. Government and on December 24, 1942 we have to evacuate to Mainland. . . ." Or as a young woman laments,

> Dad and I were always great friends and I never dreamed that someday we would have to be separated. But on that unforgettable morn of December, we heard that Japan had bombed Pearl Harbor. I saw that queer look on Dad's face and did not realize what it meant until a week later, he was interned. At first I was very lonesome, but after awhile I got used to living without Dad.

In short order, the national tragedy of war had reached into their "invisible" homes and in doing so became a wholly personal one. Further, it focused the world's attentions on these communities. Suddenly the very brunt of the war and its consequences were being shouldered squarely by the few. "These were the disconsolate months," one high school student succinctly recalls. "'Remember the Main,' the battle cry of the Spanish American War had been changed to 'Remember Pearl Harbor.' Even our graduation wasn't the same as the former ones."

And if the synthetic vibrations of the bombing of Pearl Harbor sent shock waves throughout these previously unseen communities, then the ensuing reverberations of evacuation and relocation were felt even more violently. Without trial, without evidence, without a single instance of verifiable sabotage, American citizens and permanent residents alike were herded together and summarily branded as traitors in the eyes of white America. Families were forced to sell hurriedly their homes, farms, and properties for a pittance of their real worth. They arrived—"stripped of dignity, respect, purpose, honor" (Okada, 12)—to hastily built, wholly unfurnished stables or, sometime later, barracks.

The various narratives from this period written by interned youth underscore vividly the feeling of the times. "After 16 years on the farm," one man begins, "we had to evacuate our home because there was an Aircraft factory about two miles away from where we lived. So departing from some of my best friends in Inglewood, we left our dear home and moved to our friend's place in Redondo Beach." Later came evacuation en masse. "After the war had broke out," according to a young Nisei, "plenty of rumor had been going around, such as the Japanese people had to go to camp. Well, it did come true and. . . in March a notice was delivered to each Japanese home to report to the train station. . . ."

The stories are largely the same. "On March 31, 1942," one youth recalls, "we were notified that we were to be evacuated into Santa Anita Assembly Center. We stayed in Santa Anita for over six and one half months and had to live in horse stables. . . ." Retold by another young man, "leaving Redondo, we had to go to the Santa Anita Race Track which later became the temporary home of approximately 19,000 Japanese. While in Santa Anita, I worked in one of the six mess halls which served approximately 3,700 persons a day." Or again in the words of another young Nisei, "I found myself along with many Southern Californians of the same race as I herded into a temporary military assembly center hastily set up in the Santa Anita Racetrack. There, for six and a half months, our family, my parents, two elder brothers, a younger sister and I, lived in a crowded barrack . . . , away from the pleasures of home, confined to a restricted area, not free as before." As an integral part of the strategies by which these narratives are presented, verb usage is remarkable as much for what is said as for what is left unsaid. Both the passive construction of the former ("that we were to be evacuated") and the obligatory stance of the alter ("we had to go") pay homage to the presence of an "outside" agency, thereby providing markedly different perspectives on what the War Relocation Authority (WRA) argued was a "voluntary" program.

One fact remained always in the fore for all interned. As one youth pointedly ends his story, "Here were sent aliens and citizens. A deaf ear was turned to our plea for a stand . . . because of a military need. Here I lived only for the morrow which was to be the same as the one before, no different. We all shared the same showers, same mess hall, ate identical meals and soon all was to dress identically with the issuing of 'GI.'"

"Rearing Their Ugly Heads": The Emergence of Icons

A term wildly appropriate to the situation from the point of view of those interned, considering that their Government had placed them in stables, this "branding" justified ex post facto to those in Washington or at home in front of their radios that a massive relocation had been of vital necessity. In the words of one young man, "I had planned on going to college in 1943 but evacuation dashed my hope. My ambition is to become a chemical research engineer".[6] These innocent people were yet again herded together onto trains and "relocated" to ten inhabitable camps spread throughout America's interior (see table 1). The unsettling nature of these actions was not missed by Okada, who would later recount, "The war had left its mark . . . , like trying to find one's way out of a dream that seemed real most of the time but wasn't real because it was still only a dream" (5). The end result, people were transported to "camps with barbed wire and ominous towers supporting fully armed soldiers in places like Idaho and Wyoming and Arizona, places which even Hollywood scorned for background" (ix). On the literal and figurative levels, the barbed wire made their isolation complete. It kept them from college, from freedom, and for some even from the *dreams* of freedom. It preserved intact "an emptiness that is more empty and frightening than the caverns of hell" (12). A number of studies repeatedly lay bare the sordid details.[7]

Table 1. Relocation Centers and Populations

Relocation Centers
    Population as of 1 April 1943

Central Utah	7,984
Colorado River	17,386
Denson (Jerome, Arkansas)	8,399
Gila River	13,244
Granada	6,833
Heart Mountain	10,470
Manzanar	9,497
Minidoka	9,138
Rohwer (Rohwer, Arkansas)	8,379
Tule Lake	14,534

Source: adapted from the War Relocation Authority's "Community Analysis Report No. 5: Evacuee Resistance to Relocation," 8 June 1943. The report is clearly marked "NOT FOR PUBLICATION."

"I was an American citizen," Miné Okubo writes in the 1983 preface to her *Citizen 13660*, "because of the injustices and contradictions nothing made much sense, making things comical in spite of the misery" (ix). In fact, the need for some sort of vindication for using race as the sole determining factor to explain the mass evacuation and the subsequent relocation of an entire population played an increasingly important role in the behavior of governmental institutions at this time. But as Okada would observe—in another context perhaps but wholly applicable to this situation—"the overwhelming simplicity of the explanation threatened to evoke giggles which, if permitted to escape, might lead to hysterics" (9).

Even members writing on behalf of the WRA were aware of the "surreal" nature of the events unfolding. They clearly anticipated at least three possible "objections" to their actions, noting that "most of the aliens and citizens of Japanese ancestry in the United States are going to continue living in this country after the war," that "the rights of citizenship and the rights of law-abiding aliens are closely associated with what we are fighting for in this war," and that "assimilation, which includes the development of attitudes of loyalty, cannot develop in an atmosphere of hate, suspicion and fear" (8 June 1943). Having recognized as much, the obvious remained: people were interned, their internment deemed useful insofar as it edified a particular view of the world.

The terminology subsequently used as justification was to be found in the history of Japanese immigration, in an acute—arguably pathological—awareness of difference that had arisen within Japanese-American communities over a number of decades. The WRA was well aware that in any particular reading of these events, in fact, the white reader would in effect ally himself with a particular figure of authority, would accept his point of view—and consequently his system of norms. Thus, it went about establishing its authoritative voice, most often characterized as contrasts to those interned. The WRA's voice became, then, a sort of framing device that facilitated strategies of "discontinuity" between the narratives themselves and the context within which they were narrated, through which the anticipated audiences (arguably two, inside and outside the camps) were to view a particular narrated world. As Katherine Galloway Young understands this strategy in general:

> . . . implication is a matter of context and their distinctness is a matter of frame. Contexts are the continuities between stories and some aspects of their surroundings, and of other relevant events. Frames mark the discontinuities between stories and other present or pertinent contexts . . . Stories can be seen as contextual events that are situated and occasioned or they can be seen as discrete objects that can be detached and resituated. (121)

To this, she cautions how "story" provides a background upon which ideology might be seen:

> Storytelling is about both messages and relationships. The story consists in the message level of acts and events by characters inside the Taleworld, the realm evoked or invoked by the story. But the message is itself an act or event delivered for and with other persons as part of the Storyrealm, in a way that bears on the relationships among participants in that realm. On this occasion, presentations of self are undertaken by one person in the form of two presentational routines, one in each realm, these presentations having an elegant relationship to each other. (157)

The WRA opted for such a traditional narrative strategy since it permitted—even encouraged—its target audiences to see through its eyes, thereby permitting strong identification. In this way, the American people were to participate, and in participating were to embrace those characteristics and qualities deemed appropriate by their authority. Through such an illusion, the American people as a singular entity assuredly would overcome any obvious feelings of resistance to the particular unsavory "details." But what they had not anticipated was just how "untraditional" an event the internment would be.

Certain of the perceived differences being resurrected and redirected for public consumption, having origins in the immigrant groups themselves, were classifications based upon "space" and "time," namely origin (land of your ancestors) or generation, whether an individual was "Issei" or "Nisei" (or later still, "Sansei," or "Nikkei").[8] Still others came about in reaction to the collision of two completely different cultures, the us/them dichotomy that translated however loosely into Japanese/Caucasian or Caucasian/Japanese, depending upon positioning and perspective. It is again helpful here to recall the words of Miné Okubo:

> . . . I was working on mosaics for Fort Ord and for the Servicemen's Hospitality House in Oakland, California. I was too busy to bother about the reports of possible evacuation.
>
> However, it was not long before I realized my predicament. My fellow workers were feeling sorry for me; my Caucasian friends were suggesting that I go East; my Japanese American friends were asking me what I would do if all American citizens and aliens of Japanese ancestry were evacuated. Letters from a sister in Southern California informed me that Father had been whisked away to an internment camp. (10–11)

In hindsight, the pervasiveness of these binary oppositions comes as little surprise. Nor is it surprising to us that these structures invariably privileged one group over the other. The director of the Denson Center (Jerome, Arkansas) recalled in a speech before a "white" Arkansas audience: ". . . the War Relocation Authority was set up by Executive Order by the President. The first Director of the WRA was Milton Eisenhower, a brother of General Dwight Eisenhower" (ca. 1944). It is tempting to balance—if not to temper— his words with those of a Japanese–American woman interned: "Day and night Caucasian camp police walked their beats within the center. ["Caucasian" was the camp term for non-evacuee workers.] They were on the lookout for contraband and for suspicious actions" (Okubo, 60). Another internee recalls precisely these sentiments: "My first opinion of this camp life was one that I guess all the other Nisei's also thought—Exciting—Something New. But as the days went by–It became difficult to explain. You missed the Caucasians, so much. Well we saw a few—Heads of various departments—but, shucks—they didn't mean anything—what we wanted was to be back at our hometown going to school, planning and playing with those we use to go around with." What is interesting about these images is that they become institutionalized and appropriate as purpose for maintaining the dominant political and social system. That is, they become icons; once removed from the "reality" of "image," they served to propagate and perpetuate the dominant sociopolitical ethos.

Life in the camps added to the stratification of icons available and in full use. Several usages arose from without to describe situations within. The Japanese American Citizens League (JACL), an organization whose membership was heavily Nisei and therefore American citizens, suddenly found itself polarized and often at odds with the larger Japanese–American community for its stand to submit willingly to the mass evacuations.[9] Their actions, prudent or otherwise, may be read as futile attempts at convincing a dominant white citizenry that they, too, were worthy of their status of citizens (see Hosokawa, *JACL*; Masaoka). Another group, the "No–No Boys," arose and were quickly branded as "disloyal," in no small part because they refused for whatever reasons to fight in the American military or to swear allegiance to the country that was responsible for their current predicament.

For the individual, it began with a number. As Miné Okubo poignantly recalls, "A woman seated near the entrance gave me a card with No. 7 printed on it. . . . The woman in charge asked me many questions and filled in several printed forms as I answered. As a result of the interview, my family name was reduced to No. 13660" (19). An interesting strategy is at work here, as well: when depersonalization begins, the individual is immediately robbed of the ability to control the force of her words. In essence, the power of the word is appropriated by the dominant, the Other. The result is, most often, silence. In Okubo's rare case, however, she put a drawing pen to paper and gave her silenced words a wholly unanticipated spatiotemporal physicality. She illustrated the muteness of her time in the camps.

Internees silenced for the most part, the War Relocation Authority thereafter constructed and spent a considerable amount of their time on the perpetuation of its construction of an elaborate "iconography" of these Japanese Americans. By use of image, borrowing freely from the worlds of metaphor and symbol, it encouraged the discernment of previously unapprehended aspects of a reality–under–construction. Through its creative reorganization, their authority to initiate a discourse intact, it "startled" its captive readership into fresh insights, jostling—stretching almost to its limits—the capacity to think symbolically, relationally, and mythically. As Mircea Eliade observes of this strategy in general: "[To] translate images into concrete terms is an operation devoid of meaning: . . . the reality they are trying to signify cannot be reduced to . . . concrete references . . . Images by their very structure are multivalent . . . It is therefore the image as such, as a whole bundle of meanings, that is true, and not any one of its meanings, nor alone of its many frames of reference" (14).

In fact, everything in these camps revolved around a keen awareness of, and appreciation for, these icons, from the overall physical layout down (see figure 1). In the case of the Denson Center, for example, the only clearly discernible "center" is represented by hallmarks of a dominant Caucasian administration: baseball and softball fields flanked by an elementary and high school. As the Director of this center relates without hesitation, there was

> an enormous American flag proudly floating from the top of each high flag pole in the center of each of the school blocks. Each morning when school takes up each student in school pledges allegiance to the flag of the United States of America and each student is taught and sings American patriotic songs.

> The schools are taught, as you might judge, only in English. The teaching of schools in any other language than English is forbidden. (ca. 1944)

Dispersed out from the center, pushed to the periphery, are the people themselves. Again, there is an obvious strategy at work here. As a symbolic exercise in controlled and manipulated distance, the physical layout mirrored the ongoing construction of a variety of icons, served as a template whereby acceptable norms, i.e., the observable criteria for judgment and value, were manufactured for center consumption.

Other obvious examples can be found in Victoria, the high school yearbook brought out by the Denson Center in 1944. The very first images we see are those of Caucasian administrators. Next are photographs of envelopes received from the outside—letters written by Japanese-American volunteers who adhered to the acceptable criteria for judgment and were in the active service of their country. These are followed by faculty photographs, the Caucasian faculty appearing on the printed page "above" their interned counterparts, a practice mirrored in the printing of names, as well: non–internees "above" internees. Authority and authorization are, without fail, primary issues in the presentation of any of the images of life in the center. Taken to an extreme, we cannot help but remark upon the symbolism inherent in the coronation of the high school beauty queen: head bowed (or so we are told, since no photographs of the coronation were published), she receives her crown from the director of the center, an obvious act of submission by an internee to a dominant Caucasian. The implication here could not be clearer: reality itself is shaped *in* and *by* the experiences of individual characters—but only after having been transformed to meet acceptable criteria as narrated by the Dominant.

Figure 1: The Denson Center

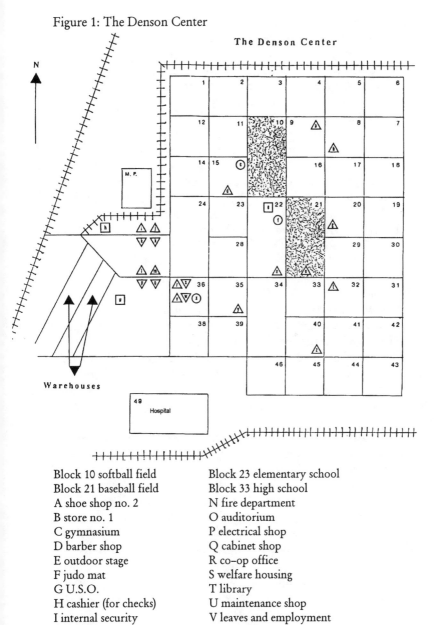

The Denson Center

Block 10 softball field	Block 23 elementary school
Block 21 baseball field	Block 33 high school
A shoe shop no. 2	N fire department
B store no. 1	O auditorium
C gymnasium	P electrical shop
D barber shop	Q cabinet shop
E outdoor stage	R co–op office
F judo mat	S welfare housing
G U.S.O.	T library
H cashier (for checks)	U maintenance shop
I internal security	V leaves and employment
J post office	W community activities
K administration buildings (2)	X *Tribune* newspaper
L refrigeration and plumbing	Y dry goods
M store no.	Z shoe shop no. 1

Following this line of reasoning, we cannot overlook the obvious. These icons work as a system of conventions and codes, a set of structures dictating and circumscribing the ultimate possibilities of the individual narratives. Narrative constructions, then, are the result of linking such icons together to create connections and continuities not found in the pre-narrative reality. Meaning, if there can be any, arises from separate entities by a kind of accumulation forced by the contiguity and the logic of the icons appropriated. In other words, meaning arises from the relationships within the context of the icons; icons in turn arise from a meaning-generated set of signs. The ideology permeating the iconography, then, arises not simply from the content of the icons but in the signifying practices of the medium itself.

Interestingly, Okada's *No-No Boy* preserves in miniature just this sort of practice. The preface to this novel introduces in rapid succession a cast of non-Japanese-American characters as they react to news of Pearl Harbor, the evacuation, and subsequent internment. We first see a college professor, "conviction lacking" (vii), presented in relief to a drunk, himself full with the conviction that he "never thought much about the sneaky Japs" (vii). We stumble quickly over him and into the arms, spread eagle-like, of the welcoming whore Jackie, for whom "the news made. . . unhappy because she got two bucks a head and the Japanese boys were clean and considerate and hot and fast" (viii). At the end of the line, so to speak, we find "horse-trading" Herman Fine, who "cried without tears" for "bombs had fallen and, in less time than it takes a Japanese farmer's wife in California to run from the fields into the house and give birth to a child, the writing was scrawled for them. The Jap-Jew would look in the mirror this Sunday night and see a Jap-Jew" (viii).

As Nicos Poulantzas cautions us to remember, "Dominant ideology does not simply reflect the conditions of existence of the dominant class,...but rather the concrete political relation between the dominant and the dominated classes in a social formation" (203). The result? Within the context of life in these centers, the various internee groups themselves were likewise made busy with the construction of competing iconographies wherein "only the meaning got lost" (Okada, 34)—appropriating as it were the various labels superimposed upon them by government authorities. Put differently, these iconographies provided a ready source of definition in their search for self, especially for those youth interned. "Where was the slide rule . . . ?" a young man was given to question. "Where was the shaft of exacting and thrilling discovery when I needed it most?" (Okada, 53).

For these youth, self became either a reflection of—or more often the carefully orchestrated negation of—prevailing icons. In turn, we as an audience become painfully aware of competing definitions for the same things. To heed Mikhail Bakhtin's caveat, meaning is revealed through encounter with another, foreign meaning, the resultant dialogue laying bare the essential closed nature of individual cultures (86–ff). Only undialogized language when all is said and done is authoritative, absolute, primary, is the proverbial slide rule by which all things may be measured and given some sort of logical position within a greater whole. It is little consolation that such language does not, indeed cannot, exist. We are left with nothing more than an act of mediation.

The process whereby such icons were internalized is laid bare time and time again with the progression of images in Okada's *No-No Boy*. We watch as the "real Japanese-Japanese," in particular, diplomats, businessmen, or visiting professors, are "put on a boat and sent back to Japan" (ix). Quickly moving from this event, we watch in silence as the "alien Japanese,...ones who had been in America for two, three, or even four decades," are summarily rounded up and "transported to the hinterlands and put into a camp" (ix). But then, quite unexpectedly, the narrator jars us loose from our complicity, our comfortable acceptance of such preconceived notions of "reality." As readers, we are *defamiliarized*. Our attentions are, however sudden and as if by accident, focused on an "old man, too old, too feeble, and too scared." We learn that he "had been a collector for the Japan-Help-the-Poor-and-Starving-and-Flooded-Out-and-Homeless-and-Crippled-and-What-Have-You Fund." And as unexpectedly, we watch agape while innocent bystanders whose only crime is a monthly act of charity were "whisked away from their homes while weeping families wept until tears must surely have been wept dry, and then wept some more" (ix).

We ourselves are forced, if somewhat unwittingly, to participate both in the argument as it unfolds and to submit in the inevitable acceptance of its conclusion:

> The Japanese who were born Americans and remained Japanese because biology does not know the meaning of patriotism no longer worried about whether they were Japanese-Americans or American-Japanese. They were Japanese, just as were their Japanese mothers and Japanese fathers and Japanese brothers and sisters. The radio had said as much. (viii–ix)

The only defense in the face of such an argument is equally unsatisfying. Denial. As we overhear Eto Minato remark to Ichiro Yamada: "Lotsa Japs coming back to the Coast. Lotsa Japs in Seattle. You'll see 'em around. Japs are funny that way. Gotta have their rice and sake and other Japs. Stupid, I say" (2). His remarks are evidence of his utter dissociation, the schizophrenic disintegration of self brought about both by the guilt associated with and the ultimate denial of, these icons. We later learn to what degree such internalizations are obviously pathological, for they had in his case landed him first in a military hospital and later back on the streets of Seattle. Equally telling is Ichiro Yamada's despair–ridden response: "God in a pair of green fatigues, U.S. army style . . . [as if saying] . . . Beseech me, . . . throw your arms about me and bury your head between my knees and seek pardon for your great sin" (4). As the narrator takes pains to preface:

> And so . . . the only Japanese left on the west coast of the United States was Matsusaburo Inabukuro who, while it has been forgotten whether he was Japanese–American or American–Japanese, picked up "I am Chinese"—not American or American–Chinese or Chinese–American but "I am Chinese" button and got a job in a California shipyard (x).

Ultimately, we conclude that there is little "reality" inherent in any of the various icons in use. Instead they should be approached as signs that deceive by concealing, of necessity distorting an underlying process of ideological representation. As icons, therefore, instructive only insofar as they illuminate their "creators," be they government–aligned or interned. Ideology within the environment of these icons, unlike its external counterpart, clearly has abstractable form, is perceptible upon analysis, and is therefore explicable as the result of particular narrative strategies employed. Moreover, the confusion, the utter chaos created by the existence of the various conflicting, competing images as they evolved into fully formed, self–sustaining icons, found its most poignant expression in the lives of youth in the centers.[10]

Who are YOU?

"Then he got so mad his face went white and he said: 'How do you know you're you? Tell me how you know you're you!'" (Okada 22) These words, spoken amidst the whirling frenzy accompanying Ichiro Yamada's release from prison and his subsequent reencounter with "home," are telling of a greater conflict pervading the narrative weave of the novel as a whole. In a not entirely unrelated event, the director of the Denson Center, in presenting a history of his center, confronts the judicial problem of who controls the centers (i.e., under whose jurisdiction these centers fall), and by association, under whose jurisdiction camp residents fall. He recounts the following story:[11]

> When the Supreme Court of the State of Arkansas said that the two projects were under exclusive federal jurisdiction, which decision the Revenue Department, The Bureau of Vital Statistics, and the Circuit judges promptly ignored, I wrote to Washington . . . that the jurisdiction in these two projects

ignored, I wrote to Washington . . . that the jurisdiction in these two projects were half fish and half fowl—my secretary, a Japanese girl, spelled fowl f-o-u-l and at that she might have been more than half correct.

This observation, too, may be widely applied. For in discussing how ideology necessarily permeates and embeds itself within any act of narrating the self—that is, participating however unwittingly in the establishment of a particular set of icons, submitting to their authority, and eventually internalizing them as the definitive self—the individual simultaneously is condemned to live in a world, the essence of which is dictated by and wholly pre-occupied with the very constituents of any narrative strategy. For those interned, the most frequently encountered strategies involved the manipulation of traditional concepts of representation, the translation of competing notions of reality, the disjointed nature of unity, and the ever-shifting perception of what and who constitutes knowledge.

Passing the Torch: Issei to Nisei

The Issei, many of whom sought assimilation into and acceptance as what they perceived to be American, were all too often left with little more than depression and humiliation for their labors (see Ichioka 1988; Kimura; Mori). For them, the only hope for the future was what they might be able to pass on to their American-born children, the Nisei. One longtime resident recalls,

I came from the fair island across the Pacific called the Garden Island or Kauai. I lived there for the past 14 and 1/2 years, although I was born at Hiroshima, Japan. . . . I am the second eldest in the family and have three sisters and no brothers. I live with my mother at Block 38-11-F. My father was held as an internee after the war started and he is now over at Lordesbury, New Mexico for about half a year.

The present situation only complicating and obscuring any thoughts of the future, a young Issei only recently arrived writes, "I came from Japan in I can not understand English very much I went Narbonne High school one semester and 8 week I took special English two per. a day." Compare the humility, the humanity behind these declarations of self with the brazenly self-confident words spoken by the Director of the Denson Center before a non-interned audience:

As for their ability to read and write the Japanese language the Nisei just simply don't have it. They can understand a few simple words in the Japanese language but so far as being able to read the Japanese language they can't do it.

students, hard working and try to make excellent grades. It is nothing unusual for a Japanese student to memorize whole sections of a book rather than try to get the "gist" of it and write his impressions of it on a test. (ca. 1944)

The former speak only of what they know to be true, namely of origins and personal history; the latter continues the tone of authority, ironically betraying his arrogance, his cultural ignorance, and seeming self absorption. He speaks of matters about which he is at least twice removed. Furthermore, the adoption of the heterodiegetic (third person) voice is likened to an overt attempt to erect the facade of Truth throughout his meditations of reality. Important in overcoming the objections of an audience to such manipulations (and in part responsible for drawing the wrath of dissenting voices) is that the director-as-narrator begins with an authoritative stance.

In contrast, the Nisei most often adopt "authenticity" as a narrative strategy, speaking only about that which they had directly experienced. They waste no time in idle speculation, virtually never cast aspersions against their captors, and never adopt an authoritative voice in matters where they have none. In this light, Miné Okubo's recollections take on special import:

We had not believed at first that evacuation would affect the Nisei, American citizens of Japanese ancestry, but thought perhaps that the Issei, Japanese born mothers and fathers who were denied naturalization by American law, would be interned in case of war between Japan and the United States. It was a real blow when everyone, regardless of citizenship, was ordered to evacuate. (17)

The seeming isolation of the Nisei point of view is deceptive, and has deceived many a critic: in reality it establishes a sense of authority for the speaker, even in instances where there seems not to be an authority, in a nonauthoritarian world. It gives the speaker a sense of authority without authoritarianism. Moreover, in adopting the homodiegetic "I," the narrator avoids the tone of objective authority. The autobiographical mode, for example, enables the author to make a variety of statements concerning self-image, and does so without regard for, or need of, an outside (heterodiegetic) authoritative voice. The frequent reliance on first person voices by internees underscores their distrust of ideology of the authority. The rejection of the heterodiegetic voice is the simultaneous rejection of the very political, economic, and social systems that bind—an act that becomes, in a word, ideological.

Let us then focus our attention on other recollections in which similar narrative strategies are being employed, this time by Nisei at the Denson Center. As a young woman writes,

On the morning of June 7, 1927, in a large house on Keawe Street in Hilo, Hawaii a chubby looking baby girl was added to the family of. . . . That was my very first appearance to this world. Since I was born in the month of June Mother named me June. . . . a terrible sickness of the intestines overtook me in the summer of 1934 before I was to enter the 2nd grade. All doctors gave up hope for me but I think it was the will of God that pulled me through. I rested in the hospital for three long, weary months and learned to walk again like a baby. . . . I went to school during the week and to the movies or the Christian Church or traveled around the Island during the week–ends. I went for my first joyous camping trip to the Volcano when I joined the six grade Girl Reserves . . joined the school band as a clarinet player and also was a member of the Junior Auxiliary.

Or another young woman recounts, perhaps somewhat humorously from our vantage point,

I enter Grammar school in 1930–1936. Then I went Marbonne Hi school which is located in Lomita. . . . What I was looking forward was our graduation. Every body was so excited that day. Everybody had corsages, nice looking clothes, hose, felt so big & proud when I went to receive my diploma. I also had banquet too. The theme I never forget the "Palrtosim."[12] Everything was fixed in red, white & blue. Even our flower arrangement was in palrtosim too.

Or in the words of another young woman,

I was born in a small "hick" town, as so many Californians would call it, although it is much better town than towns here in Arkansas. It's called Gardenia and I was born at a Japanese doctor's home. This doctor is now a famous specialist on nose, ear, and throat. Before I knew anything we moved to Keystone, and then Wilmington. And finally when I was able to tell anything apart, we moved to Long Beach where my actual schooling began. . . . My most saddest moment was also mixed with a most happy experience. That time was when my grandmother died suddenly of paralytic stroke. Also I had my first "crush" on a person that certain night.

"My name is Jiro," writes one young man,

which means in Japanese, second son. . . . While I was just nine years old my father died of the flu and my mother was faced with bringing up four young children alone. It was during this period that I became very independent and unlike other boys who had a father. I began to form my own ideas. That is probably the reason why my opinion differs radically from those of . . . [my] . . . friends.

Or ". . . our neighbors were (sic) mexicans, Americans and Japanese. Where I lived it was nothing but farming. So we made our living by helping our neighbor's ranch. Our home was located between Alamida and Santa Fe Street, Long Beach, California. . . . Just below our house was the City dump. I found lots of valuable articles and spent most of my time there, too."

And still another internee relates,

> For a blissful seventeen years I lived in the American way in what to me was the whole world, my home. . . a homey cottage situated along California's busiest highway in Wilmington. Here in the home where my parents started from scratch many years ago and built after years of sweat and toil, I was born on a cold January morning in the year 1925 and christened. . . . There I was among my Caucasian friends and subsequent years were spent among them. I have dates and jitterbugging were my main interests and indeed I lived a life of the average American girl.

But not all lives need be quite so "average." As a young man recollects, vividly and with an overwhelming sense of the poetic:

> I was born in Fresno March 14, 1926. I was brought up in the rowdiest section of the city.

> I remember one night there was a fight out in the mexican Saloon where a man was cut in the throat and a few minutes he died. I witnessed many other fight and knifing of people.

> I can't forget the day a police car and a sedan collided at the corner of my house. We all ran out to see the wreck and the sedan was on the sidewalk upside down.

> There was a woman pinned under the car; so everybody lifted up the car and when they dragged her out, she was dead.

> There was lots of trouble in that town, pinball games, lottery, vice and burlesque (which I saw couple of times) and many others. When I was the age of 12 I got in a fight with a drunk who kicked my bicycle. I knocked him down and was going to hit him. My father came out and pulled me off.

> My father gave me a bawling out that night which I shall never forget.

> I almost got expelled from school one day because I acted smart, but they gave me another chance. After that I was quieter than a mouse.

> I went to Fresno Technical High School and took up machine and mechanic shop.

During summer vacation my friend's and I went to the country and got a job on a peach farm.

I was passing out newspaper early in the morning and after I finished I went out in the ranch an (sic) worked.

From these voices we are able to ascertain at least in outline the primary narrative strategies used by Nisei as they attempted definitions of self-identity. First and foremost is the reliance upon "sincerity" as the sole criterion for judgment (e.g., "To tell you the truth . . . ," "I can't forget the day . . ."). Second is the almost universal observance that sincerity somehow equates with authenticity, thrusting us as readers into the moral conundrum of these narrated worlds (e.g., the dead woman became so because of a collision with a police car). Theirs was, prior to internment, a world of the "homey cottage," or "cold January morning," moments when deep sadness might suddenly become tinged with a bittersweet "crush." All of these details serve to inscribe their narrators with the semblance of normalcy—but a normalcy that would easily be recognized by the white Other.

And when there is an attempt at establishing authority of any sort, its motivation must be suspect. Even an action as simple as identifying the "origin" and "meaning" of one's name may serve another unspoken agenda. Take, as example, the young man's seemingly innocent self-introduction. The Japanese name for "second son" is commonly Jiro, spelled with a long vowel sound; such sounds are lost as names become Japanese-American. The presence or absence of such markings in the orthography has ideological implications, and is one clearly demonstrable measure of distance. In this particular instance, he makes two points very clear: he is not the "first son," inheritor by definition of certain birthrights, and as important, he is also *not* Japanese. Indeed, as Edward Said notes, narrators as homodiegetic informants wield an extraordinary authority (35-ff). The first-person voice is a rhetorical, as well as a theoretical, strategy. At stake in the choice of this strategy is the distinction between personal and political. The invocation of the first-person is itself a nostalgic move, which acts to "create an inviolable moral space." The authority associated with "personal" experience—with those of the "I"—may serve to "pre-emp" further discussion. Or the invocation may assume a strategic political weight within certain contexts. In short, the narrative "I" is *meant* to problematize the very terms "first person," "personal," "private" that might conventionally be used to dismiss a particular voice and its discourse.

These discourses also betray in concrete terms something more of the times. One young woman is quick to relate the "patriotic" fervor by which her adolescent worldview is wholly consumed—she might not be able to spell *patriotism*, but she certainly understood its value! Another is as quick to record, however unintentionally, the role that racism had played on the West Coast prior to the internment. Note the prism-like structuring of power and domination established through the movement and usage of capital letters, from "Mexican," up to "Japanese," but only after through the "Americans." In the final discourse, a young man postures with what to contemporary sensibilities is readily identifiable as machismo. But behind this stance cum method acting, mirrored in the quick, thrust-like jibes of his sentences as they penetrate, as they erect and stand alone as paragraphs, is the equally obvious erection of a *persona*. The poetic sensibility inherent in this discourse betrays the acute pain and vulnerability of a young man torn from a world, the rules of which he had learned to understand, only to find himself thrown into a wilderness providing no obvious means of protection, no shelter. Like all the Nisei youth interned, he must on a metaphorical level provide that shelter himself. He does so by fashioning a world of memory within which he can retreat and about which he can take solace as needed.

Kibei

Against the backdrop of these historical events, a final category of conflicting, competing icons of Japanese-America arose, however, and it is this category that became the cornerstone in the War Relocation Authority's continuous effort at self-justification. A particular government document from the period, for example, underscores these machinations. It begins with a deceptive, seemingly simple question:

> What happened to a boy or girl who grew up for awhile in a California town, then went to school in Tokyo or Kumamoto, and finally returned to the California town? What effect did living and going to school in two such different places have on his speech, his manners and daily behavior, his family and friendship relations, his purposes in life, and his sense of national loyalty?[13]

These individuals were summarily labeled "Kibei," a quasi-Japanese term composed of the characters "ki" ('return') and "bei" (the first character in the term "Beikoku," the then accepted term for the United States).[14] In hindsight, the argument employed seems terribly naive. We now accept that "meaning" is mediated through and embedded in ideological constructs, no matter how partial or unstable they may be. What we witness here is the concrete practice of creating such meaning. The image of the Kibei served as a correlative by which other icons might successfully be constructed. But the historical icons was none too easy. At times, officials were forced to "reconstruct" images and thereby erect new icons to fit a particular camp reality (e.g., the sudden transfer of the "disloyal" to Tule Lake).

So concerned, so preoccupied was the government that it attempted to survey the entire Nisei population (see table 2), in order to demonstrate that a statistically significant number of Kibei "really did exist."[15] But what is most disturbing about the result of this survey is its obvious misappropriation of details. The format appears on the surface simple enough, but there are several noticeable flaws in design. For example, there is no explanation about the "differences" implied between residence and educational experience, no explanation as to how these two variables articulate with issues of (external) assimilation and (internal) "loyalty." Further, while we know the number of individuals surveyed (n = 17,956), we do not learn how the overall population breaks down into distinct groups. Put differently, how many individuals under twenty years of age had never been to Japan? How many from this same subgroup had received none of their education in Japan? How many had received more than three years? The usage of a percentage without explaining just what it is a percent of does nothing but betray its abuse.

Table 2. Survey of Nisei Residential and Educational Experiences in Japan (n = 17,956).

Residence/Education in Japan	Total	Age in Years		
		< 20	20–39	> 40
Born in the U. S.	100%	100	100%	100%
Never in Japan	72.7	86.8	54.1	46.9
No education in Japan	14.2	11.1	18.6	25.8
1–2 years	0.7	0.3	1.3	0.5
3 or more years	12.2	1.8	26.0	26.8
(Adapted from data in WRA, Community Analysis Report no. 8, 28 January 1944)				

centers, realized. On the offensive, the government was forced to justify its actions. The obvious target became the majority, the American–born, about whom some sort of distinguishing characteristic seemed necessary. Hence, authorities introduced a new suspicion via questions of residence and education. That is to say, from the Nisei majority, how many *might* be Kibei? But even this strategy proved neither efficient nor persuasive. So, they were forced finally to resort to question 28, the question of loyalty, and to the practice of segregation of "disloyals" to Tule Lake (see Christgau; Collins). But even this strategy failed. In short, what are left over are the traces of an elaborate rhetorical process that made full use of whatever means available— Aristotle used the word *dynamis* in another context—to persuade the widest possible audience to accept a particular worldview.

Juxtaposed to these processes are the multifarious voices of the Kibei themselves. Unable to deny previous contacts with Japan, many set about negating their importance. As one young man cleverly points out, "I went to Lincoln Grammar School in Fresno when I was 5 years old. I did not do so well in school. In 1937, I went to Japan for brief visit and as soon as I came back, I found myself about a year behind where I should be." Another relates, "About an year after we moved to Lomita. . . . I enter to Lomita Elementary School. My study in there didn't do any good to me. I was taken to my parents country, Japan. Everything was new to me. It was my first time I learned to take off my shoes and go into the rooms. . . . I had to start all over with my English."

In this light, the act of relegating any contact to "a visit" takes on new meaning. Having related the details of her birth, one young woman remembers as an afterthought lacking in any particular importance: ". . . the following year we went to Japan. Riding in the boat for about two weeks were rather fun. During this two years in Japan, we visit lots of interesting places such as famous mountains, hot springs and many other places. We came back when I was eight years old."[16] She maintains the "afterthought," juxtaposing her tourist related activities with other details from her daily life: "I, of course, attend school and liked it very much. . . my hobbies is collecting movie stars pictures and reading about each one of 'em. Best actress I enjoyed watching is Ann Rutherford and Deanna Duskin. The actor is Ronald Reagan and his family." "A trip to Japan and a Girls' Reserve Conference at Lake Tahoe, Nevada," as another young woman succinctly concludes, "were the only two times I've been away from home."

There are also attempts at underscoring the "likeness" or "similarity" to the authoritative gaze. "That's where you were born, Mary," ventures another. From there, she moves quickly to position her birth within an "acceptable" world of values:

Tahoe, Nevada," as another young woman succinctly concludes, "were the only two times I've been away from home."

There are also attempts at underscoring the "likeness" or "similarity" to the authoritative gaze. "That's where you were born, Mary," ventures another. From there, she moves quickly to position her birth within an "acceptable" world of values:

> . . . Sometimes we would see a plump lady in front chatting with other ladies— perhaps a neighbor, and mom says—"That little chubby one was the midwife." Mom was always telling us things like that. . . . She was an excellent English speaker—living in this country so long, living among Caucasians all that time till this evacuation started. . . . in 1934 Mom became ill. . . . So this time we were sent to another aunt & uncle in Tokyo Japan. In the year 1934, Summer at the age of 9—I had to experience an all together different life. Didn't no how to speak Japanese—I guess all we knew how to say at that time was "yes" & "no." Every time at school or when we were with our cousins at home and a quarrel starts—We couldn't speak Japanese so we blabbed off some bad words in English, and they in Japanese—It sure sounded like at mad house.—But eventually, we were learning and getting accustomed to the way of living and the weather. Although we [as]ked if we could come back to the U.S. it [was]n't until 1936 that we're able. . . By that time Dad had started an farm of his own so we could be together. This time it was vice versa—because we could hardly say anything in English—at school we had a hard time. But, since we use to know English It all came back to us and a year later—We spoke only English and our Japanese was poor. . . .

And there is the invocation of external agency, laying any "blame" for having traveled to Japan at someones else's doorstep. "I don't know why," a woman argues,

> but we are a moving family. So although we moved within Los Angeles, I attended many schools, Japanese as well as American. Hideo, my youngest brother is 13 years old and is living in Japan with my grandparents, next comes Freddy who is 15, living with my first father in Denver, Colorado, I'm 17 and here in Arkansas with my mother and step-father and my sister who is 19 lives near her soldier-husband at Minnesota with their baby.

The functional role of illness falls within this strategy. Still another woman declares matter of factly, "In 1937, I was taken to Japan and there I had another mastoid operation. I was continuously sick during my stay in Japan." Or as another youth elaborates, "We left Seattle, Washington on November, 1927, so that our mother could be with her sick mother who was then in Japan (the last time we heard from her was from Manchuria. If she is

. . . In about an hour we just started to see just the blue ocean and the blue sky we went on looking at the ocean and sky for 5 days on the boat we played hockey played ping pong once in a while the ball would fly into the ocean and then it would cost us another $.10 for another ball. . . . Later when we got off of the boat women and children welcoming us with Leis, putting them around our neck boy was I really surprised seeing an island pretty as Hawaii. I thought I could never see the Hawaiian Islands in my life. Soon as we went to town we went to get some good old American food, on the boat all we ate was Japanese food, then in the evening we went to Waikiki. . . . Then when morning came every body was back because the ship was leaving at 8:00 from Japan bound when the ship started to pull out they started to sing Aloha Ohe and you couldn't stop from crying . . . they would tell us not to throw any orange peelings or any kind of garbage because they wanted to keep the ocean pretty like it always was, except Leis they could throw away On the 10th day early in the morning we started to see the mountains and fishing boats Japanese fishermen fishing every body was ready to leave. . . . The next day we went to Tokyo stayed for a couple of days and then went home where my brother had been . . . and then about a week later he passed away at 12:30 in the morning. After that we had the funeral 2 days later they went to cremate him and then took him to the cemetery. After that was all over I started school on and on going to school a year and a half and then we came back to America. Then I went to school over here, started in the 8th grade and went to school a year and a half, then we started to evacuate to Assembly Center in Santa Anita.

Representative of the autobiographical discourses of Kibei youth in general, he introduces the role of an external agent (e.g., "I had to go to Japan with my mother. . . "); as if that agency were not enough, he couples obligation with an incident completely beyond his (or anyone's) control, the illness and eventual death of his brother. Further, his reliance on run-on sentences (much like the reliance on the dash, seen earlier) emphasizes a past sense of the urgency, inherent to the moment, that compelled his family to make such a long journey. As technique, they also indicate the immediate compelling necessity of getting the words on the page, of getting the truth out as quickly as possible before silence sets in and all becomes mute, before "the walls had closed in and were crushing all the unspoken words back down into his stomach" (Okada, 3). And finally, there is the relationship between "detail" and its temporal narration. The considerable amount of narration spent on short intervals of time (the majority of his reported memories are of the trip between the American mainland and Hawaii) underscores further their relative significance. Little time is given over to narrating his life in Japan, indicative as it were that the "value" of such experiences are by association minimal, barely worthy of repeating.

Reading these narratives in this way and having dismantled the process whereby images become icons and icons become part of a cultural short intervals of time (the majority of his reported memories are of the trip between the American mainland and Hawaii) underscores further their relative significance. Little time is given over to narrating his life in Japan, indicative as it were that the "value" of such experiences are by association minimal, barely worthy of repeating.

Reading these narratives in this way and having dismantled the process whereby images become icons and icons become part of a cultural iconography, all that is left for us now is to direct our attention to the pernicious nature of such iconographies. We accept without question that a text cannot be separated from its function. Charles Altieri and Martha Craven Nussbaum, among others, conclude that even when not overtly didactic in form, the text can and is used by its audience to gain a fuller understanding of life. Taken a step further, we understand that icons, and iconographies within which they are subsumed as cognitive representations, are both historically and linguistically mediated. It is in this light that we should examine Momoko Iko's *The Gold Watch* (1971). In doing so, we are left to question just to what degree interdigitation occurs between these iconographies and the emergence of subsequent Japanese–American discourses of self.

Family Heirlooms and Pernicious Iconographies

A powerfully compelling drama, Momoko Iko's *The Gold Watch* took the East–West Players Playwriting Award in 1971. Some quarter of a century removed from the Second World War and the internment experiences, it is an "American action" set in "the house and yard of [Masaru] MURAKAMI's forty acre farm in the Pacific Northwest, fall of 1941 and summer of 1942." As the drama unfolds, we as audience become increasingly aware, however, that its meaning does not adhere to or originate from the play as an essence: it is the result of positioning and perspective—simply put, is historically and linguistically mediated. The way in which the dramatic text positions itself in relation to a wider cultural discourse of which it forms a part is simultaneously encoded in systems of signification built upon these textures. We are then confronted with a system of signs that acquire meaning through the interpretive codes attached to them by socially and culturally constructed "discourses."

Perhaps most obvious about this work are the disparities between what the playwright writes and the words as they are spoken. The paucity of Iko's characterizations are worthy of remark in this respect. For example, we are told only that Masaru Murakami is "given to mimickry, expansive gestures, and displays of emotion." Tanaka seems his opposite, is described as a man who "tends to scurry along, duck his head before speaking, is somewhat the stage. Further, the drama in which they are involved quickly reveals itself to be part and parcel bound up with the cultural iconographies of Japanese-Americans that emerged during the internment period.

Most notably, we have the characterizations that emerge on stage in the words of and in the interactions between characters. Take, for example, the opening scene in which Tanaka, a wealthy storeowner, attempts to give Murakami's wife a bolt of cloth. Unfortunately, times being what they are, either the crops fail or the political climate turns cold. In either case, the Murakami family finds itself, quite literally, dirt poor and unable to afford even the barest of necessities. The following dialogue ensues:

Masu: Hoh' Tane-san, you're just in time for some sake before supper. Cocksacca' What have you got there? (He eyes the cloth bolts elaborately.)

Tanaka: (Embarrassed, trying to change the subject). Potatoes? This late?

Masu: Found them . . . clearing the fields. They're still good. What's new in town?

Tanaka: It gets chillier every year. Let's go inside. I planned to come earlier. . . . I didn't mean to bother you at dinner. How are they? The diakon?

Masu: Kimi' Get Tanaka sake!. . .

Tanaka: No, no more . . . just one, I have to go back for dinner myself.

Masu: Tanakasan, you come here, you ask how are the crops . . . you have our sake and now you are leaving. For a visit it's too short. If it is business, it hasn't been started.

Tanaka: You know the wife. . . . I must get going. . . . Masu, I was clearing my summer stock. I found these clothes, yes? Who is going to buy cotton now, I say to myself . . . I am right, No? Perhaps Kimikosan might be able to use them. There's no harm in that? It's eehh my cu-i-s -ma-su pu-resants to you. Yes, that's right. A early gift.

Later, after Kimiko has been reduced to begging her husband to accept this act of charity, Masaru and Tanaka retire to the front porch. Away from the wife and unable to be overheard, they cease participating in what has become a time–honored "ritual" and begin to speak freely:

Masu: Give me another tobac. Why does she have to do it, like this?

Tanaka: You're too stubborn, a stupid male, what else can she do?

Masu: Was I asking you?

Tanaka: Don't talk so loud within my hearing. . . . If you were just a little bit more reasonable. Masu . . . you know, you have credit with me.

Masu: (With joking irony) Still? Is that so? I still do?

Tanaka: Masu.

Masu: To pay you off, all I need is a rainbow, stretching from waaay over there . . . to right here. And I will need that rainbow five years running.

Or later still, Tanaka gone home and Masaru gone inside, the family prepares for dinner. As everyone approaches the table, Masaru becomes aware of his son's absence. Kimiko cautiously ventures an explanation: "He said he was going to play . . . football?" Her words betray both her own unease with the situation and unfamiliarity with the subject matter. At that point, Tadao enters and the education of father by son gets under way.

Masu: Football? What is that? (. . . Tadao enters, carrying some books. He is feeling kind of good.) You're late for dinner!

Tadao: Sorry . . . got held up at school.

Masu: Playing footsubalu?

Tadao: Yes,

Masu:	What is football?
. . .	
Tadao:	It's a game . . . where . . .
Masu:	With a foot and a ball?
Tadao:	(Laughing but upset). Right papa, with a foot and a ball There's some checks you have to sign, papa.
Masu:	What!
Tadao:	Bills . . .
Masu:	For what? . . . Fifteen dollars. For what?
Tadao:	For food, school . . . (quieter, hesitant) shoes.
Masu:	Shoes? Food? We have everything right here.
Tadao:	No we don't . . . papa. You have to buy meat and sugar and salt and eggs . . .
Masu:	Who eats all these eggs?
Tadao:	You do . . . over rice . . . in the mornings . . .

Or later still, after dinner as Masaru and his son retire to the front porch, they begin to talk. Masaru is neither angry nor lacking in compassion for his son's situation. He is, instead, a concerned parent who loves his son but who because of the current political—and therefore economic—crisis is unable to give him anything more than that love. They begin to talk:

Masu:	You are going to high school soon?
Tadao:	Yeah Papa, next fall.
Masu:	What kind of classes are you going to take?
Tadao:	I don't care. What they give me, I guess.
Masu:	You have no special interests? What do you want to do?

Tadao:	I don't know.
Masu:	You have to decide. What? You want to be a farmer, like me?
Tadao:	The farm's okay. But I don't really want to be a farmer. Is that okay?
Masu:	Sure.
Tadao:	I want to . . . I want to fly airplanes . . .

In all four interactions, Masaru distinguishes himself as a man who questions. It is less that he does not understand than that he is in the process of actively seeking answers. But such a characterization is wholly simplistic and unsatisfactory, is reductionalist. It fails to account for the depth of his character.

We witness an entirely different side to Masaru's personality when Tanaka's family comes to visit. During the encounter, we learn that Tanaka's son Hiroshi is Kibei. Only recently returned from Japan, he was sent there four years ago for a proper education because, as his mother argues, "These American kids, no respect, no self-control, flighty . . . plain flighty . . . Ah, Kimikosan understands what I'm talking about. Isn't that so, Kimikosan?" The interaction between Masaru and Hiroshi displays a keen affiliation with, nods its head in passing awareness to, the Kibei icon so prevalent during the internment period. With all of the passion, all of the vigor, all of the arrogance of youth, Hiroshi attempts to justify the bombing of Pearl Harbor.

Hiroshi:	It had to be the embargoes. Japan was slowly being starved to death.
Masu:	Certain death to possible starvation, huh?
Hiroshi:	The Imperial Way cannot be defeated. It is the only way! Still, I was not prepared for Pearl Harbor. I believe . . . Pearl Harbor was Japan's way of letting America know that she will not be dallied with. What are these white countries screaming about? We, I mean, Japan does in Asia only what Westerners do all over the world. Asia belongs to yellow people. The bitter struggle is with China. Who will lead the yellow people of Asia? (During this entire exchange, Tanaka is trying

> to take pictures with his new camera so that Hiroshi's lines can be broken up.)

Masu: Asia belongs to yellow people or yellow rulers? (Pose, snap.)

Hiroshi: Japan's rulers think only of their people. . . . Murakamisan . . . do you question integrity for yellow people?

Masu: No . . . but what has integrity to do with the conquest of China?

Hiroshi: The Chinese will smother us to death if we . . . (realizes, perhaps, that he has no reasonable answer.) They are worthless swine anyway . . .

Masu: Then we must be swine too. They have been our teachers for centuries.

There are two important points regarding characterization to be noted here. First, Hiroshi's speech is verdictive in its force. He passes judgment; as a man in possession of all of the necessary answers, only he is able to lord them out. He is stereotypical Kibei (from a WRA perspective). Masaru, in contrast, continues to ask questions, but suddenly the nature of his interrogative takes on the force of interrogation. And second, the role of the posed shot is important. This scene is the only one in the entire play where the camera is used. It reduces the durative to a single moment, freezes and preserves actions and motivations as still images. In short, it simultaneously reduces the temporal coordinate while overcompensating for the spatial; in its preservation, it violently promotes the image to cultural icon and assists in its perpetuation. It focuses as it were our attention on the nature of character as image and conversely of image as character.

But even this explanation is not wholly reliable. Later, as sons and fathers go their separate ways, we see another side to Hiroshi. Tired of the poverty, tired of the scarcity of opportunities for Japanese–Americans, tired of the outright discrimination that he faces every day in town and in school, Tadao finds in Hiroshi both an "older brother" and mentor, as well as the promise of a brighter future. He begins his own inquiry thus:

Tadao: What is Tokyo like?

Hiroshi: The Imperial Way, how can I explain it . . . You know
                what is happening. . . . Them, (indicating Masu and
                Tanaka) they are stupid, behind the times. . . . Japan was
                fated to rule Asia. There is no . . .

Tadao: I mean, if, if a guy went to Tokyo, what would it be
                like for him? What do you do at school? What's it like?

Hiroshi: (Hesitant about personal feelings). Well . . . we have
                drills . . . and economics . . . history. . . . I am fluent in
                Japanese now. I didn't like it at first . . . lonely . . . and
                everyone always jumping to attention. (Angry at
                revealing this.) You become a real man. Now I can't
                believe that I could have been so weak!

Tadao: Do they have art? . . . I mean . . . I'm interested in
                airplanes. I like to draw them.

Hiroshi: The Zero is the best fighter plan in the world . . . even
                better than the Messerschmitt.

Tadao: Better than the Spitfire?

Hiroshi: Easy!

Still, Hiroshi holds out verdicts, but masked by these words—indeed, the
words are no more than his mask—are the feelings of isolation, of loneliness,
of belonging nowhere. He is a young man formal and judgmental because he
can be nothing else. With Tadao, he is able to maintain this stance while at
the same time revealing a certain childlike innocence, even now untainted by
the adult realities of the ongoing war between his two worlds.

   In the closing scene, Tadao and Masaru have once again returned to the
front porch. For the first time in many years, Masaru acknowledges how
much he values their relationship. It is during this interaction that we
overhear that Tadao, too, is Kibei—in truth, we are apt to miss this detail,
since it is couched in a discussion of his mother's one excursion back to Japan.
A young man in pain looking for placation, for solace, he turns to his father
for answers. It is his turn to ask the questions—indeed, the act of questioning
becomes a right of passage into the adult world.

Tadao: Papa . . . do you ever think about going back to Japan?

Masu:	No . . . Why?
Tadao:	Nothing, doesn't matter.
Masu:	Tell me.
Tadao:	(A sudden angry burst . . . or slow, deeply concentrated voice). I hate it here.
Masu:	You don't know Japan . . .
Tadao:	That's not fair . . .
Masu:	I wasn't making light of what you said . . .
Tadao:	. . . You think because I can't read the Japanese papers . . . I can read . . . the *Herald* . . . and those signs in town . . . and I can hear what they say. . . . If they hate us so much, why don't we go back to Japan?
Masu:	Sa. . . . I was the black sheep in my family. Everyone who comes here is a black sheep . . . of their family, of their class . . . of their country. They were not wanted where they were. . . . You like this watch, one day I'll give it to you.
Tadao:	Was it your father's?
Masu:	No, I bought it in a pawnshop . . . off the wharf in Seattle. It's pure gold . . . see . . . pure gold. . . . When you were six, Mama went back to Japan. . . . Don't you remember? . . . This land was still uncivilized and unpopulated. It still is, Tadao. Every act still had no name and every piece of land and sky were still not spoken for. I guess it is different for you. You were born here so when other people tell you that you don't belong, it must hurt. That didn't hurt me. I knew I didn't come from this land. I knew where I came from. It cannot be helped. We are born, Tadao, to different times, so our lives are different, must be different if we are to survive.

Tellingly, in a moment of profound depth and intensity, Masaru answers Tadao's questions by revealing to him his inheritance. As an Issei, he can but hope that his son's future will be brighter than his own; he has nothing more to give him than a gold watch. His son's response, "Was it your father's?" is equally insightful, for he perceives the watch to be a family heirloom, by definition something passed down from one generation to the next. Neither flippant nor unappreciative in its intent, his response is in thought and in deed wholly American. Within the frame of the drama, there is pathos as Masaru concedes that the watch came from a pawnshop; by association his only keepsake, the only thing he is able to pass on to his son in this land is something not his own, something he values but which its previous owner had held in so little regard. In balance, there is hope in the recognition that "heirlooms" can be created *sui generis*; by association that Tadao's future awaits him, is a matter of his own creation. This watch signifies Masaru's rejection of the past while paradoxically showing us as audience ultimately that we must refine our sensibilities by augmenting our pasts and by realizing that these pasts bear on our present—and our futures.

Lurking outside of the frame are those pernicious icons. Momoko Iko's strategy is instructive. There is the obvious acknowledgment that such icons do exist and remain potent and alluring. When the artistic imagination confronts an iconography, it is either ironically "trapped" or "imprisoned" by the struggle for understanding or liberated by the very act of confrontation. In this instance, the act of acknowledging simultaneously attempts to silence. We witness "stereotypical" depictions, suddenly transformed and Mobius–like in their contortions, immediately deconstruct before our very eyes. We listen as patent verdict suddenly is turned on its ear and gives way to admissions of innocence, inexperience, questioning. In short, under Iko's pen, the icon becomes, if not its own iconoclast, then the portent that such iconoclasts are forthcoming, imminent.

Conclusion

The power of the image cannot be underestimated, for once the seed of an image is planted it tends to grow; and growing with sufficient fertilizer, it is often violently picked from the level of latency to become a fully functioning cultural icon before those who willingly—or otherwise—view it. When that fertilizer is the hate and discrimination we witnessed during the Second World War, the icons become seemingly all powerful. By December 1945, only 368 internees, ill and elderly, remained behind in Denson Center. On 2 December, they boarded Western–bound trains and left the Center forever

(*Arkansas Gazette*, 2 December 1945). But their stories would not end there. It would take well over four decades for *all* Americans—not only Japanese Americans—to get beyond the stranglehold of these particularly powerful, even alluring and seductive foes in order that they might demand justice.

But justice has a way of taking its time. There can be do doubt of the numerous, invaluable contributions made by Japanese Americans to the war effort; what remains doubtful, however, is how effective their actions were in initiating worthwhile changes on the home front. A small but important step in laying bare the deceptive nature of these icons—and in doing so breaking their stranglehold. The McCarran Immigration and Naturalization Act of 1952 finally allowed the Issei citizenship and for all intents and purposes canceled out the 1924 Oriental Exclusion Act. The next order of business proved none too easy and took substantially longer, for it involved instigating change "on the inside" of now amorphous Japanese American communities, once dispersed and evolving across the United States.

Amid lingering distrust and outright acts of hatred by their neighbors, amid the insensitivity of unresponsive employers and educators alike, internees scattered after the war to rebuild their lives. They suppressed their humiliation with, to borrow John Okada's words, "teeth clamped together to imprison the wild, meaningless, despairing cry which was forever straining inside" (12). Throwing themselves into the more immediate struggle to survive, they simultaneously strove to become "200 percent American" so that none might ever question their loyalties again. But at what price? A deafening silence. A part of this silence was almost certainly the willful negation of what they had witnessed, but in larger measure it represented the pathological internalization, the acceptance of the "validity" behind an us/them opposition. And such silence cannot help but be tinged with guilt and shame. The only possible cure for these ails involved the dismantling of the very distinctions that had for so long provided them with a sense of definition.

But how to do so? The pain, the injustice of it all, would somehow have to be diagnosed and treated if newly emerging Japanese–American communities were to survive. Again, time becomes a sore point. As early as 1970, JACL member Edison Uno had publicly proposed seeking redress through Congress, but it would take almost a decade to break through the lethargy and convince the JACL membership at large to move to action. In 1978, it adopted a resolution calling for government redress for all Japanese Americans interned during World War II (see Daniels, et al. 1986; National Committee for Redress). In the meantime, in 1976, recalling none of the hoopla or fanfare that had welcomed it in, Executive Order 9066 was formally rescinded. On 28 November 1979, Representative Mike Lowry (D–Washington) introduced the first in a long series of bills aimed at redress. On

17 September 1987, the U.S. House of Representatives passed HR 442, the Civil Liberties Act of 1987, by a vote of 243–141. Calling for public apology from the U.S. Government for the evacuation and imprisonment of Japanese-Americans, this bill also included a $20,000 one-time payment to surviving internees as compensation in part for their wartime losses. The U.S. Senate passed S. 1009, the companion bill to HR 442, by a vote of 69–27, on 20 April 1988. After four months of deliberation and soul-searching, President Ronald Reagan signed the Civil Liberties Act into law on 10 August.

One might hope that justice had been done. But justice is a fragile and short-lived thing. One hopes against hope that the lessons of this tragic chapter of American history have been learned, the ramifications understood fully. At the risk of exposing the cliché, it is helpful to remember the words of a young Nisei poet, written during his internment:[17]

> Look to the future, my son,
> Past is past, what is done is done. . . .
> The past may be dark.
> But future, like a flying dart,
> Will bring light and glow, my son;
> Someday to you it will come.

Acknowledgments

Over the years, I have benefited immeasurably and often from the support of those around me. At this time, I wish to express my continuing appreciations to them (in chronological order only): To Dr. Frank K. Robinson who firmly supported my including Japanese American literature as a course toward an M.A. in English literature; to Peter Bacho, instructor, mentor, and friend, who tirelessly supported the inclusion of Asian American literature toward a Ph.D. in comparative literature and who as often spent hours on end talking with me about my interests; to Shawn Wong, who patiently served as my examiner in Asian American literature; to Dr. Ken Goings, friend and colleague, who encouraged me to probe beneath the surface of material artifacts to reveal the very important mechanisms *behind* the production and consumption of Asian American icons; and to Berna Love, Curator of The Arkansas Museum of Science and History (Little Rock, Arkansas), who spent many an hour on the telephone discussing with me the available documentation for the Denson Center. To each of these people, I heartily express my gratitude. Of course, I take sole responsibility for any shortcomings herein.

Notes

1. This essay focuses on Miné Okubo's *Citizen 13660*, John Okada's *No-No Boy*, and the various narratives written by youth interned at the Denson Center (Jerome, Arkansas). Put differently, placing historical retrospection and fictional recollection on the same podium encourages new and intriguing readings off of each other. From these works, the essay moves with these insights to a particular reading of Momoko Iko's drama, *The Gold Watch*. Because of the traumatic nature of the internment experience, many internees have preferred to remain silent. That is, they have not spoken of these events even to their children. In respect of their privacy, I have chosen not to "name" the speakers (those who were writing while interned) directly within this essay. Rather, a complete list of authors is available in the bibliography. Those who find the original words so compelling as to want to learn the identities of their authors are encouraged to turn to this listing.

2. The *Gobineau Vereinigung* boasted an elite membership of sorts. Among its members were Elizabeth Forster–Nietzsche and H. S. Camberlain (1855–1922). The latter is the younger brother of the renowned Japanologist Basil Hall Chamberlain as well as the husband of Wagner's daughter Eva. See, for example, Biddiss and Gollwitzer.

3. Japanese novelists, ironically or complicitly, appear naively unaware of such sentiments, and in fact emigration came to be a not unfamiliar theme in certain representative works of this period. *Hakai* by Shimazaki Tôson (1872–1943), depicts the story of a man of outcast origins who emigrates with his hard-earned lover to Texas. *Aru onna* (written during the interval 1911–19) by Arishima Takeo (1878–1923), features Satsuki Yoko, a heroine who voyages from Japan to Seattle and back again. And *Sôbô* (1935), by Ishikawa Tatsuzo, depicts the lives of a group of Japanese who had sailed from Kobe to South America in search of a new home. Interestingly enough, this novel was the first recipient of the prestigious Akutagawa Prize for Literature.

4. From 1923 on, the Japanese government provided financial assistance to emigrants who were booking passage to Brazil. The Brazilian Constitution of 1934 countered by specifying limits. Certainly, emigration to the Asian mainland in the 1930s came about as the result of attempts by the Japanese government at "colonization" there. But it had little demonstrable effect on alleviating the agricultural crises in Japan. No more than 10.3 percent of the Japanese emigrants to Manchuria were involved in some way in the

agricultural sector. Fewer than 1 percent of Japanese in China could be found making their livelihood from the land.

5. This fact is born out ironically by the large number of scholarly studies of these communities, clearly indicative of their "unusual" nature from an academic perspective. See, for example, Bell, Daniels (1988), Fujita, Glenn, Kitano, Knaefler, La Violette, Levine, Matsumoto (1946), Miyamoto, Modell, Murase, O'Brien, Shindo, Suehiro, and Yanagisako.

6. The use of verb tense (the past perfect is juxtaposed with the present) in this passage is important to the narrative as a whole. Clearly while the present (indicated by a past perfect usage) remains bleak, the belief in a brighter future (indicated by a present usage) remains resolutely intact.

7. See, for instance, Anderson, *The Arkansas Gazette* (3 June 1942), Bearden, Blicksilver, Bosworth, Cully, Daniels (1981), Dorr (N.D.), Drinnon, Friedlander, Girdner and Loftis, Grodzins, Hansen, Huston, James, Kogawa, Matsumoto (1984), Mossman, Myer, Nakagawa, Nakano, Spicer, Tateishi, Taylor, Uchida, Vickers, and Weglyn. This list is far from exhaustive.

8. *Issei* were Japanese born in Japan, as the Sino–Japanese characters indicate. *Nisei*, second–generation, were American–born and therefore citizens. *Sansei*, third generation, are their children. *Nikkei* ("Ni," from the first character of "Nihon," Japan, and "kei" meaning "relation" or "background") refers to anyone of Japanese ancestry who resides outside of Japan. These terms are frequently used in Japan by native speakers.

9. As a result, members affiliated with this group often suffered humiliation at the hands of their peers. In fact, at Manzanar, a group of JACL leaders were removed for their own safety because of overt hostility toward them by other internees (see Embrey, et al.; Hansen and Hacker).

10. One may ask why I have chosen to focus on such an out–of–the–way center as the one in Jerome, Arkansas. The answer is just that: as an "outpost" (to borrow from the patois in use at the time), the internees of the two Arkansas camps have all but been ignored, even by scholars of the camps.

11. This story is related in a copy of the center director's speech (ca. 1944, p. 12), available in the Special Collections of The University of Arkansas Libraries.

12. From context and the sequence of consonants, the word must be "patriotism."

13. War Relocation Authority, "Japanese Americans Educated in Japan." Community Analysis Section Community Analysis Report, No. 8, 28 January 1944, 1. Interestingly enough, the title betrays—or at least concedes—the fact that those interned were "American" by birth or on principle.

14. The term "Kibei," however Japanese its origins may appear on the surface, is not a widely used term among Japanese living in Japan. It does appear in Nelson's *Japanese-English Character Dictionary*, designed with a nonnative audience in mind and not for the Japanese native speaker. Japanese dictionaries for Japanese users do not ordinarily recognize the usage. Further, while the characters might be pronounced correctly by a native speaker were they encountered within a document, the very meaning of the individual character would undoubtedly serve to obscure the meaning of the whole.

15. Certainly, some efforts were made to develop a sort of zoology of Kibei, the "good," the "bad," and so on. But such distinctions did not in any way substantiate the need to intern anyone. Further, these attempts appeared only in the War Relocation Authority's "Community Analysis Report No. 8" (28 January 1944), a report neither widely circulated nor intended to be.

16. Interestingly, there are no remarks about visits to temples or shrines, the absence of which may be read as yet another strategy to construct her particular worldview while, simultaneously, moving consciously around matters that might have fueled disapproval from Caucasian authorities. It should be pointed out that these center narratives were written as assignments for an English class, taught by Virginia Tidball.

17. Sky Komatsu, "To the Future." The Virginia Tidball Collection. This poem may be read in at least two ways: as the words of an Issei *persona* spoken to his son, or as a Nisei *persona* speaking to *his* son, representative of the adoption of a narrative stance more clearly associated with Issei discourses. The latter case offers new insights into the life of Nisei youth within the camps.

Japanese American Bibliography

Manuscripts

Ando, James. "My Autobiography." The Virginia Tidball Collection (hereafter VTC). The University of Arkansas Libraries Special Collections Division, 1943.

Aoki, Sally. "My Autobiography." VTC, 1943.

Arakawa, June. "My Autobiography." VTC, February 1943.

Aoto, Mary. "Autobiography of Mary Aoto." VTC, 1943.

Arata, Joe M. "Introductory Sketch of Myself. " VTC, 10 January 1943.

Denson High School. *Victoria* (Yearbook). Special Collections of The Burrow Library, Rhodes College, Memphis, Tenn., 1944.

Embree, John. "Causes of Unrest at Relocation Centers." Community Analysis Section Community Analysis Report No. 2.. The University of Arkansas Libraries Special Collections Division, February 1943.

Enokida, Isako. "My Autobiography." VTC.

Fukuda, Lillian. "My Autobiography." VTC, 18 January 1943.

"Gone. " VTC, 1943.

Hatashita, Rumiko. "My Autobiography." VTC, 11 January 1943

Hata, Mary Jane. "My Autobiography." VTC, 11 January 1943

Hayashida, Stella. "My Autobiography." VTC, 1943.

Hino, Masayoshi. "My Autobiography." VTC, 1943.

Hatashita, Murako. "My Autobiography. " VTC, 1943.

Hirata, Masako. "My Life." VTC, 1943.

Hitomi, Takeshi. "My Life." VTC, 1943.

Horie, Showph. "Autobiography." VTC, 17 January, 1943.

Ikeda, Margaret. "Biography of Myself. " VTC, 1943.

Iguhara, Kay. "My Biography." VTC, 1943.

"Jerome" (a historical presentation by the director of the Denson Center). The University of Arkansas Libraries Special Collections Division, ca., 1944.

Komatsu, Sky. "Autobiography." VTC, 12 January 1943.

———. "To The Future." VTC, ca., 1943.

Kumamoto, Shigeko. "My Autobiography." VTC, 1943.

Muranaka, Tadashi. "Untitled." VTC, ca. 1943.

Nakanishi, Haru. "Who Me?" VTC, 14 January 1943.

Nakayama, George. "Autobiography." VTC, 11 January 1943.

Nishimoto, Jeanne. "My Autobiography." VTC, 1943.

Odate, Michiko. "Autobiography." VTC, 1943.

Osako, Kunio. "Biography." VTC, 1943.

Oyama, Jiro. "My Autobiography." VTC, 1943.

Rowher Outpost. *Lil Dan'l: One Year in a Relocation Center*. The University of Arkansas Libraries Special Collections Division, 1943.

Shiotani, Akiko. "An Autobiography of Myself." VTC, 1943.

Tabata, Jack Hitoshi. "Autobiography." VTC, 1943.

War Relocation Authority. "Evacuee Resistances to Relocation." Community Analysis Section Community Analysis Report No. 5. The University of Arkansas Libraries Special Collections Division. 8 June 1943

———. "Japanese Americans Educated in Japan." Community Analysis Section Community Analysis Report No. 8. The University of Arkansas Libraries Special Collections Division, 28 January 1944.

Yamaura, Mary. "My Autobiography." VTC, 1943.

Yonemura, Haruo. "Autobiography." VTC, 1943.

Articles, Books, and Dissertations

Altieri, Charles. "From Expressivist Aesthetics to Expressivist Ethics." Pp. 134–66 in *Literature and the Question of Philosophy*, ed. Anthony J. Cascardi. Baltimore: The Johns Hopkins University Press, 1987.

Anderson, William Cary. "Early Reaction in Arkansas to the Relocation of Japanese in the State." *Arkansas Historical Quarterly* 23 (autumn 1964): 195–211.

Ano, Masaharu. "Loyal Linguists: Nisei of World War II Learned Japanese in Minnesota." *Minnesota History* 45 (1977): 273–87.

Arakawa, Hidetoshi. *Ikoku hyoryu monogatari*. Tokyo: Shakai Shisosha, 1969.

Arkansas Gazette (Little Rock, Arkansas). "10,000 Japs to be Removed to Arkansas Camp." 3 June 1942, p. 1, cols. 2, 3.

Bakhtin, Mikhail. *Speech Genres and Other Essays*. Trans. Vern W. McGee. Ed. Carly Emerson and Michael Holquist. Austin: The University of Texas Press, 1986.

Bearden, Russell. "The False Rumor of Tuesday: Arkansas Internment of Japanese-Americans." *Arkansas Historical Quarterly* 41 (winter 1982): 327–39.

———. "The Internment of Japanese Americans in Arkansas, 1942–1945." Master's thesis, University of Arkansas, 1986.

———. "Life Inside Arkansas's Japanese-American Relocation Centers." *Arkansas Historical Quarterly* (summer 1989): 169–96.

Bell, Reginald. *Public School Education of Second Generation Japanese in California.* 1935. Reprint, New York: Arno Press, 1978.

Blicksilver, Edith. "The Japanese American Woman, the Second World War, and the Relocation Camp Experience." *Women's Studies International Forum* 5 3/4 (1982): 351–53.

Biddiss, M.D. *Father of Racist Ideology: The Social and Political Thought of Count Gobineau.* London: Weidenfeld and Nicolson, 1970.

Bosworth, Allan R. *America's Concentration Camps.* New York: Norton, 1967.

Brooks, Charles Wolcott. *Japanese Wrecks Stranded and Picked Up Adrift in the North Pacific Ocean.* 1876. Fairfield, Wash.: Galleon Press, 1964.

Broom, Leonard, et al. *The Managed Casualty: The Japanese American Family in World War II.* Berkeley: The University of California Press, 1973.

Christgau, John. "Collins versus the World: The Fight to Restore Citizenship to Japanese American Renunciants of World War II." *Pacific Historical Review* 54 (1985): 1–34.

Chung, L.A. "Upholding the Constitution." *Rice* 2 (1989): 5, 15, 24, 34.

Collins, Donald E. *Native American Aliens: Disloyalty and Renunciation of Ntizenship by Japanese Americans during World War II.* Westport, Conn.: Greenwood Press, 1985.

Commission on Wartime Relocation and Internment of Civilians. *Personal Justice Denied: Reports of the Commission on Wartime Relocation and Internment of Civilians.* Washington, D.C., 1982.

Conroy, Hilary. *The Japanese Frontier in Hawaii, 1868–1898.* New York: Arno Press, (1953) 1978.

Cully, John J. "World War II and a Western Town: The Internment of the Japanese Railroad Workers of Clovis, New Mexico." *Western Historical Quarterly* 13 (1982): 43–61.

Daniels, Roger. *Asian America: Chinese and Japanese in the United States since 1850.* Seattle: The University of Washington Press, 1988.

———. *Concentration Camps: North America, Japanese in the United States and Canada during World War II.* Malabar, Fl.: Robert E. Krieger Publishing Co., 1981.

Daniels, Roger, and Harry H.L. Kitano. *American Racism: Exploration of the Nature of Prejudice.* Englewood Cliffs, N.J.: Prentice–Hall, 1970.

Daniels, Roger, Sandra C. Taylor, and Harry H.L. Kitano, eds. *Japanese Americans: From Relocation to Redress.* Salt Lake City: The University of Utah Press, 1986.

Davis, Horace. *Record of Japanese Vessels Driven Upon the Northwest Coast of America and Its Outlying Islands.* Worcester, Mass.: Charles Hamilton Palladium Office, 1872.

Dorr, Guy E. "Issei, Nisei, and Arkansas: A Geographical Study of the Wartime Relocation of Japanese Americans in Southeast Arkansas (1942-1945)." Master's thesis, University of Arkansas. 1977.

Drinnon, Richard. *Keeper of Concentration Camps: Dillon S. Meyer and American Racism.* Berkeley: University of California Press, 1987.

Duus, Masayo Umezawa. *Unlikely Liberators: The Men of the 100th and the 442nd.* Trans. Peter Duus. Honolulu: University of Hawaii Press, 1987.

Dyer, Thomas G. *Theodore Roosevelt and the Politics of Racism.* Baton Rouge: Louisiana State University Press, 1980.

Eliade, Mircea. *Images and Symbols: Studies in Religious Symbolism.* New York: Sheed and Ward, 1969.

Elliot, Albert H., and Guy C. Calden. *The Law Affecting Japanese Residing in the State of California.* 1929. Reprint, New York: Arno Press, 1978.

Embrey, Sue Kunitomi, et al. *Manzanar Martyr: An Interview with Harry Iyeno.* Fullerton, Calif.: California State University at Fullerton Oral History, 1986.

Flowers, Montaville. *The Japanese Conquest of American Opinion.* 1917. Reprint, New York: Arno Press, 1978.

Friedlander, E.J. "Freedom of Press Behind Barbed Wire: Paul Yokota and the Jerome Relocation Center Newspaper." *Arkansas Historical Quarterly* 44 (winter 1985): 303-13.

Fujita, M. "The Japanese Associations of America." *Sociology and Social Research* 14 (1929): 211-17.

Girdner, Audrie, and Anne Loftis. *The Great Betrayal: The Evacuation of the Japanese Americans during World War II.* New York: Macmillan Co., 1969.

Glenn, Evelyn Nakano. *Issei, Nisei, War Bride: Three Generations of Japanese American Women in Domestic Service.* Philadelphia: Temple University Press, 1986.

Gobineau, Count Arthur de. *Essai sur l'inegalite des races humaines.* Paris, 1853-55.

Gollwitzer, H. *Die Gelbe Gefahr.* Gottingen, Germany: Vandenhoeck and Ruprecht, 1962.

Gotanda, Philip Kan. *Yankee Dawg You Die.* New York: The Playwrights' Press, 1986.

Grodzins, Morton. *Americans Betrayed: Politics and the Japanese Evacuation.* Chicago: University of Chicago Press, 1949.

Gulick, Sudney. *The American Japanese Problem: A Study of the Racial Relations of the East and the West.* New York: Scribners, 1914.

Hansen, Arthur A. "Cultural Politics in the Gila River Relocation Center, 1942–1943." *Arizona and the West* 27 (1986): 327–62

Hansen, Arthur A., and David A. Hacker. "The Manzanar 'Riot': An Ethnic Perspective." Pp. 41–79 in *Voices Long Silent: An Oral Inquiry into the Japanese American Evacuation,* ed. Arthur A. Hansen and Betty E. Mitson. Fullerton: California State University, 1974.

Haruna, Akira. *Hyôryû, Josefu Hiko to nakamatachi.* Tokyo: Kadokawa Publishers, 1982.

———. *Nippon otokichi hyôryûki.* Tokyo: Shobunsha, 1979.

Hata, Donald T., Jr. *Undesirables; Early Immigrants and the Anti-Japanese Movement in San Francisco, 1892–1893.* New York: Arno Press, 1978.

Hattori, Itsuro. *77-nin no samurai Amerika e yuku.* Tokyo: Nozeki Shoichi, 1968.

Hosokawa, Bill. *JACL: In Quest of Justice.* New York: William Morrow and Co., 1982.

———. *Nisei: The Quiet Americans.* New York: William Morrow and Co., 1969.

———. "Our Own Japanese in the Pacific War." *American Legion Magazine,* July 1964, 15–17, 44–47.

Huston, Jerry. "History Haunts: Japanese Internment Remains Painful." *The Commercial Appeal* (Memphis, Tenn.), 4 April 1991, 1, col. 2–4; 11.

Ichioka, Yuji. "*Amerika Nadeshiko:* Japanese Immigrant Women in the United States, 1900–1924." *Pacific Historical Review* 48 (1980): 339–57.

———."*Ameyuki-san*: Japanese Prostitutes in Nineteenth Century America." *Amerasia Journal* 4, no. 1 (1977a): 1–21.

———. " The Early Japanese Immigrant Quest for Citizenship: The Background of the 1922 Ozawa Case." *Amerasia Journal* 4, no. 2 (1977b): 1–22.

———. *The Issei: The World of the First Generation Japanese Immigrants, 1885–1924.* New York: The Free Press, 1988.

Iko, Momoko. *The Gold Watch.* Act I, pp. 89–114 in *AIIIEEEEE! An Anthology of Asian-American Writers,* ed. Jeffrey Paul Chan, Frank Chin, Lawson Fusao Inada, and Shawn Hsu Wong. Washington, D.C.: Howard University Press, 1974.

Irons, Peter. *Justice at War: The Story of the Japanese Internment Cases*. New York: Oxford University Press, 1983.

Iwata, Edward. "Japanese Americans: A Vanishing Community." *Rice* 2, no. 5 (1989): 11–14, 21–22, 51, 75, 79.

James, Thomas. *Exile Within: The Schooling of Japanese Americans, 1942–1945*. Cambridge, Mass.: Harvard University Press, 1987.

Kachi, Teruko Okada. *The Treaty of 1911 and the Immigration and Alien Land Law Issue between the United States and Japan, 1911–1913*. 1957. Reprint, New York: Arno Press, 1978.

Kawakami, K.K. *The Real Japanese Question*. 1921. Reprint, New York: Arno Press, 1978.

Kikumura, Akemi. *Issei Pioneers: Hawaii and the Mainland, 1885–1924*. Honolulu: Japanese American National Museum, 1992.

Kimura, Yukiko. *Issei: Japanese Immigrants in Hawaii*. Honolulu: University of Hawaii Press, 1988.

Kitano, Harry K.L. *Japanese Americans: The Evolution of a Subculture*. Englewood Cliffs, N.J.: Prentice Hall, 1969.

Knaefler, Tomi Kaizawa. *Our House Divided: Seven Japanese American Families in World War II*. Honolulu: University of Hawaii Press, 1991.

Kogawa, Joy. *Obasan: A Novel of the Nisei in Wartime Canada*. Boston: Godine, 1982.

La Violette, Forrest E. *Americans of Japanese Ancestry: A Study of Assimilation in the American Community*. 1945. Reprint, New York: Arno Press, 1978.

Levine, Gene. *The Japanese American Community: A Three Generation Study*. Westport, Conn.: Praeger, 1981.

Lukes, Timothy J., and Gary Y. Okihiro. *Japanese Legacy: Farming and Community Life in California's Santa Clara Valley* (Local History Studies, vol. 31). Cupertino, Calif.: The California History Center, 1985.

McCormick, Frederick. *The Menace of Japan*. Boston: Little, Brown and Co., 1917.

McWilliams, Carey. *Prejudice: Japanese-Americans: Symbol of Racial Intolerance*. Boston: Little, Brown and Co., 1945.

Masaoka, Mike, with Bill Hosokawa. *They Call Me Moses Masaoka*. New York: William Morrow and Co., 1987.

Matsumoto, Toru. *Beyond Prejudice: The Story of the Church and Japanese Americans*. 1946. Reprint, New York: Arno Press, 1978.

Matsumoto, Valerie. "Japanese American Women during World War II." *Frontiers* 8 (1984): 6–14.

Mears, Eliot Grinnel. *Resident Orientals on the American Pacific Coast: Their Legal and Economic Status.* Chicago: University of Chicago Press, 1928.

Mills, H.A. *The Japanese Problem in the United States: An Investigation for the Commission on Relations with Japan Appointed by the Federal Council of Churches of Christ in America.* New York: Macmillian, 1915.

Miyamoto, S. Frank. *Social Solidarity among the Japanese in Seattle.* 1939. Reprint, Seattle: University of Washington Press, 1984.

Modell, John. *The Economics and Politics of Racial Accomodation: The Japanese of Los Angeles, 1900-1942.* Urbana: University of Illinois Press, 1977.

Mori, Toshio. *Yokohama, California.* Seattle: University of Washington Press, 1985.

Morimoto, Joy K. "S.F. Sansei Speaks Out on Spirituality." *Asian Week,* 9 February 1990a, 100, 106, 112.

———. "Spirituality in the Nikkei Community (sic) Today." *Asian Week,* 9 February 1990b, 96, 98, 100, 112-13.

Moriyama, Alan T. *Imingaisha: Japanese Emigration Companies and Hawaii, 1894-1908.* Honolulu: University of Hawaii Press, 1985.

Mossman, Robert A. "Japanese-American War Relocation Centers as Total Institutions with Emphasis on the Educational Program." Master's thesis, Rutgers University, 1978.

Murase, Ichiro Mike. *Little Tokyo: One Hundred Years in Pictures.* Los Angeles: Asian American Studies Center, 1983.

Myer, Dillon Seymour. *Uprooted Americans: The Japanese Americans and the War Relocation Authority During World War II.* Tucson: University of Arizona Press, 1971.

Nakagawa, Gordon Wayne. "The Politics of Narrative: Stories of Japanese-American Internment." Ph.D. diss., Southern Illinois University at Carbondale, 1987.

Nakahama, Akira. *Nakahama Manjiro no shôgai.* Tokyo: Fuzanbo, 1970.

Nakano, Takeo Ujo. *Within the Barbed Wire Fence: A Japanese Man's Account of His Internment in Canada.* Seattle: University of Washington Press, 1981.

National Committee for Redress (Japanese American Citizens League). *The Japanese American Incarceration: A Case for Redress.* San Francisco: Japanese American Citizens League, 1978.

Nussbaum, Martha Craven. "Finely Aware and Richly Responsible." Pp. 169-191 in *Literature and the Question of Philosophy,* ed.

Anthony J. Cascardi. Baltimore: Johns Hopkins University Press, 1987.

O'Brien, Robert W. *The College Nisei.* 1949. Reprint, New York: Arno Press, 1978.

Ogawa, Dennis, ed. *Jen Ken Po: The World of Hawaii's Japanese.* Honolulu: The University Press of Hawaii, 1973.

―――. *Kodomo No Tame Ni: For the Sake of the Children.* Honolulu: The University Press of Hawaii, 1978.

Okada, John. *No-No Boy.* 1976. Reprint, Seattle: University of Washington Press, 1980.

Okubo, Mine. *Citizen 13660.* Seattle: University of Washington Press, 1983.

Plummer, Katherine. *The Shogun 's Reluctant Ambassadors: Sea Drifters.* Tokyo: Lotus Press, 1985.

Poulantzas, Nicos. *Political Power and Social Classes.* Trans. Timothy O'Hagan. London: New Left Books, 1973.

Pozzetta, George E., and Harry A. Kersey. "Yamato Colony: A Japanese Presence in South Florida." *Tequesta* 36 (1976): 66–77.

Quiason, Serafin D. "On Historical Committees and Early Japanese Relations with Manila." *Solidarity 95* (1983): 63–67.

Said, Edward W. *Beginnings: Intention and Method.* New York: Basic Books, 1975.

Saiki, Patsy Sumie. *Early Japanese Immigrants in Hawaii.* Honolulu: The Japanese Cultural Center of Hawaii, 1994.

―――. *Gambare! Internment of Hawaii's Japanese.* Honolulu: Kisaku Inc., 1982.

Sakamaki, Shunzo. *Japan and the United States, 1790–1853.* Wilmington, Del.: Scholarly Resources Inc., 1973.

Sawada, Suketaro. *Chiisai Hanako.* Nagoya, Japan: Chunichi, 1984.

Shapiro, H.L. *Migration and Environment: A Study of the Physical Characteristics of the Japanese Immigrants to Hawaii and the Effect of Environment on their Descendants.* 1939. Reprint, New York: Arno Press, 1978.

Shibutani, Tamotsu. *The Derelicts of Company K.* Berkeley: University of California Press, 1978.

Shindo, Kaneto. *Hokubei imin (Nihon gendaishi 16).* Tokyo: Iwanami, 1992.

Shirley, Orville C. *Americans: The Story of the 442nd Combat Team.* Washington, D.C.: Infantry, 1946.

Spicer, Edward H., et al. *Impounded People: Japanese-Americans in the Relocation Centers.* Tucson: The University of Arizona Press, 1969.

Steiner, Jessee Frederick. 1917. *The Japanese Invasion: A Study in the Psychology of Inter-racial Contacts.* New York: Arno Press, 1978.

Suehiro, Shigeo. *Hokubei no nihonjin.* Tokyo: Nishodo, 1915.

Sugimoto, Howard Hiroshi. *Japanese Immigration: The Vancouver Riots and Canadian Diplomacy.* 1966. New York: Arno Press, 1979.

Tachiki, Amy, et al., eds. *Roots: An Asian American Reader.* Los Angeles: Asian American Studies Center, UCLA, 1971.

Takaki, Ronald. *Iron Cages: Race and Culture in Nineteenth-Century America.* London: Oxford University Press, 1990a.

————. *Issei and Nisei: The Settling of Japanese America.* New York: Chelsea House, 1994a.

————. *Pau Hana: Plantation Life and Labor in Hawaii, 1835–1920.* Honolulu: The University of Hawaii Press, 1983.

————. *Raising Cane: The World of Plantation Hawaii.* New York: Chelsea House, 1994b.

————. *Strangers from a Different Shore: A History of Asian Americans.* New York: Viking Press, 1990b.

Tateishi, John. *And Justice for All: An Oral History of the Japanese American Detention Camps.* New York: Random House, 1984.

Taylor, Sandra C. "Japanese Americans and Keetley Farms: Utah's Relocation Colony." *Utah Historical Quarterly* 54 (1983): 328–44.

Thompson, Richard A. *The Yellow Peril, 1890–1924.* 1957. Reprint, New York: Arno Press, 1978.

Toby, Ronald P. *State and Diplomacy in Early Modern Japan: Asia in the Development of the Tokugawa Bakufu.* Princeton: Princeton University Press, 1984.

Treat, Payson J. *Japan and the United States, 1853–1921.* Palo Alto: Stanford University Press, 1928.

Uchida, Yoshiko. *Desert Exile: The Uprooting of a Japanese American Family.* Seattle: The University of Washington Press, 1982.

————. *Picture Bride.* Seattle: Northland, 1987.

United States Department of War. *Final Report on Japanese Evacuation from the West Coast, 1942.* 1943. Reprint, New York: Arno Press, 1978.

Vickers, Ruth Petway. "Japanese American Relocation." *Arkansas Historical Quarterly* 10 (summer 1951): 168–76.

Wakatsuki, Yasuo. "Japanese Emigration to the United States, 1866–1924: A Monograph." *Perspectives in American History* 12 (1979): 387–516.

Wax, Rosalie H. "The Development of Authoritarianism: A Comparison of the Japanese–American Relocation Centers and Germany." Ph.D. diss., University of Chicago, 1951.

Wilson, Robert A., and Bill Hosokawa. *East to America: A History of the Japanese in the United States.* New York: William Morrow and Co., 1980.

Weglyn, Michi. *Years of Infamy: The Untold Story of America's Concentration Camps.* New York: William Morrow and Co., 1980.

Yanagisako, Sylvia Junko. "Explicating Residence: A Cultural Analysis of Changing Households among Japanese–Americans." Pp. 330–52 in *Households: Comparative and Historical Studies of the Domestic Group*, ed. Robert C. McNetting, et al., Berkeley: University of California Press, 1984.

Yatsushiro, Toshio. *Politics and Cultural Values: The World War II Japanese Relocation Centers and the U.S. Government.* New York: Arno Press, 1978.

Yoneda, Karl. *Ganbatte! Sixty-Year Struggle of a Kibei Worker.* Los Angeles: Asian American Center, University of California at Los Angeles, 1983.

Young, Charles H., et al. *The Japanese Canadians.* 1938. Ed. H.A. Innis, New York: Arno Press, 1978.

Young, Katherine Galloway. *Taleworlds and Storyrealms: The Phenomenology of Narrative.* Martinus Nijof, Philosophy Library #16, 1986.

15

HOME(S), FAMILY(IES), AND IDENTITY(IES) IN MUKHERJEE'S *JASMINE*

David Goldstein-Shirley

The struggle to forge a new identity recurs as a central theme in the literature of all American immigrant groups. Caught between the customs and values of their old world and the lifestyle and conflicting mores of the United States, immigrants turn to literature to express their difficulties. Each group—in fact, each individual—handles the conflict in a different way, which accounts for the rich variety of immigrant stories available to us. Fiction by and about Asian immigrants, which differs from tales by and about white ethnic immigrants who never faced American racism, adds an important perspective to our understanding of the immigrant experience. Out of the understudied body of Asian Indian immigrant literature comes Bharati Mukherjee's novel, *Jasmine* (New York: Grove Weidenfeld, 1989). This exemplary piece of literature by a naturalized American citizen centers on the title character's journey through several identities as she attempts to find her essential self. Because the novel deals explicitly with the theme of identity change, it is an ideal model of immigrant literature, enriching our knowledge of that most American experience: formulating one's own identity among new homes, families, and communities in the face of innumerable challenges.

The novel's opening sentence, "Lifetimes ago, under a banyan tree in the village of Hasnapur, an astrologer cupped his ears—his satellite dish to the stars—and foretold my widowhood and exile" (3), immediately establishes the vicissitudes to come. It emerges that the narrator, the novel's protagonist, is recalling this tale from an immense temporal, geographic, and cultural distance: from her perspective as a thirtyish woman in America's heartland, the young, obedient, innocent girl she had been in the Punjab might as well have been someone else entirely.

When the second chapter opens, the narrator reveals that her lover Taylor, in New York, had not wanted her to go to Iowa, her current home. Already the shifts in locale have jarred the reader, a narrative strategy employed by Mukherjee to emphasize the radical changes undergone by her protagonist. Rather than present the story chronologically, Mukherjee unravels the tale by flashing forward and backward through time and locations. The reader's resultant vertigo mirrors the challenges to a sense of belonging experienced by the character herself; the novel's structure thus creates empathy between the reader and the character. A truer portrayal of the chaotic immigrant experience is conveyed in this manner. "The zigzag route is the straightest," Jasmine notes (101).

Within the first two chapters, the reader learns that the narrator has been called Jyoti Vijh, Jane Ripplemeyer, and Jasmine, and has lived in India, New York and, of all places, Elsa County, Iowa. By the novel's end, the reader has witnessed more names and more identities, each different in outward personality and each with a different, mitigated sense of home. Not until the closing pages, when she becomes fully American in America, does she entirely overcome her foreigner's feeling of not belonging, not being truly home.

As a young girl in the Punjab, she is Jyoti, the obedient, powerless girl whose destiny is to be married young, and without a dowry. Although Hasnapur was the only home she had known, even in her childhood she felt displaced, opening in the novel the theme of challenged sense of home. Her parents spoke continually of the family's roots in Lahore, a large city where they had been wealthy. Chased away by Muslims during the Partition Riots, Jyoti's parents mourn their exile to "a village of flaky mud huts" (41), and Jyoti learns early that fate is cruel. "Life shouldn't have turned out that way! I've never been to Lahore, but the loss survives in the instant replay of family story: forever Lahore smokes, forever my parents flee" (41).

She skirts her own destiny several times in the novel, first by marrying Prakash, a young, idealistic man with dreams of immigrating to the United States. She first falls in love with him, sight unseen, when she overhears him telling her brothers of his plans. "When I go to work in another country, it'll be because I want to be a part of it," he tells them (67). He calls her Jasmine, and with her name change comes a new personality: Prakash treats her as an equal, and shares with her his dreams of starting a business, Vijh & Wife, in America. This first identity shift is not instantaneous, however, and for a while she feels "suspended between worlds" (76). She states, "Jyoti, Jasmine: I shuttled between identities" (77). Subsequent identity shifts, however, are more complete, and she endeavors to sever her ties to her past(s).

She internalizes his dreams of emigrating, but for a different reason. She believes that emigration will allow her to escape her destiny of a lifetime of bad luck. "If we could just get away from India, then all fates would be canceled. We'd start with new fates, new stars. We could say or be anything we wanted. We'd be on the other side of the earth, out of God's sight," she says (85). As they work toward their dream, she realizes that her metamorphosis from "feudal" Jyoti to Jasmine is complete. "My life before Prakash, the girl I had been, the village, were like a dream from another life" (91). They do not escape in time, however. Prakash is murdered by a Sikh extremist, but Jasmine nevertheless has been changed forever. Although a young Hindu widow, she does not return permanently to her family. She imagines her husband exhorting her, "Don't crawl back to Hasnapur and feudalism. That Jyoti is dead" (96). Prakash eradicated Jyoti's sense of home in India, but she and Prakash had created Jasmine, a new life, and she determines to fulfill their shared dream of a home in America.

True to her husband's dream, Jasmine illegally immigrates. The smuggler who brings her ashore in Florida brutally rapes her, and she murders him in a seedy motel room. She burns her old clothes in a trash can behind the motel, symbolically and dramatically discarding her history. Severing ties with her past becomes necessary for survival. "For me, experience must be forgotten, or else it will kill," she states elsewhere (33). This act begins her journey toward a genuine American identity, passing through several others as she changes and is changed by her environment, creating, as best she can, a home wherever she finds herself.

That moment of horror also marks the beginning of her flight from her pasts and from memory which constantly threaten what sense of home she manages to achieve. Her rescuer, a compassionate but unsentimental Quaker woman named Lillian Gordon, understands her frightened charge's need to cast off her past, one of many kindnesses for which Jasmine remains grateful. Lillian's home is a sanctuary for many of the poor, undocumented immigrants who come ashore in Florida, and she receives and aids them without judgment or excessive sentimentality. In the space of two weeks, Jasmine has experienced two extremes of America: in her rapist she survives its worst and most cruel; in her protector she sees its best and most benevolent.

After healing and learning how to look like (although not yet how to become) an American, Jasmine departs from Lillian Gordon's generosity to New York's indifference. There, she locates her husband's former teacher who is living in Flushing, Queens. She stays with him and his family in an insular Punjabi neighborhood for five months, rarely leaving the house. There, her transformation into an American had already begun. Already accustomed to American clothes (they "disguised my widowhood" [145]), she thinks of America as "real life" (143), as opposed to her earlier lives that seem to have been merely dreams. Although she feels safe there, she begins to stifle. In Flushing's "fortress of Punjabiness" she "was a prisoner doing unreal time" (148). She is grateful for the imaginary brick wall that "cut me off from the past," but the same wall prevents her from "breaking into the future" (148). She leaves one morning without a goodbye.

Fleeing to Manhattan, Jasmine finds Lillian Gordon's daughter, who arranges for her an au pair position uptown. She is to care for Duff, the adopted daughter of a young professor and his wife. In their home, amid their modern, American, shockingly warm and openly loving relationships, Jasmine takes enormous steps toward her own Americanness. In her first encounter with her new employers (who were to become her family), Jasmine feels obligated to pick up their pet iguana, something that would have terrified her in her former lives. "Truly, I had been reborn. Indian village girls do not hold large reptiles on their laps," she notes (163). Yet she is not entirely free from her past, as her unspoken comment to the lizard reveals: "Sam, I thought, we're both a long way from home, aren't we?" (163–64). Although she still thinks of India as home, she understands that she can never go back.

Moving in with this family who, to her enormous surprise, treats her with respect and dignity, she jumps at the opportunity to change into someone she herself could respect. "I wanted to become the person they thought they saw: humorous, intelligent, refined, affectionate. Not illegal, not murderer, not widowed, raped, destitute, fearful," she says (171). She succeeds, noting, "The squatting fields of Hasnapur receded fast" (174). In her two years with Taylor, Wylie, and Duff Hayes, Jasmine recalls, she developed self esteem, achieved happiness, and "became an American" (165). The unselfconscious ease with which her new family relates to her—as an equal, not as a servant—nurtures in her a new personality and, with it, a new name: Taylor begins calling her Jase. Spending too much of her generous weekly salary, Jasmine notes that her old selves would have been saving money. "But Jyoti was now a *sati*–goddess; she had burned herself in a trash can–funeral pyre behind a boarded–up motel in Florida. Jasmine lived for the future, for Vijh & Wife. Jase went to movies and lived for today" (176).

Jasmine quickly learns that nothing is permanent in America. Wylie falls in love with another man and leaves with him to Europe. Although the ephemeral nature of everything in this new country disturbs Jasmine, she also finds that it opens doors for her. Jasmine takes Wylie's place in Duff's nightly bedtime ritual with her father and, foreshadowing the novel's conclusion, Jasmine states that the trio "became a small, self sufficient family, and I told myself, guiltily, that everything might really work out all right. . . . I, the caregiver, was eager to lavish care on my new, perfect family" (183). In that new role, she "bloomed from a diffident alien with forged documents into adventurous Jase" (186). The adventurous Jase falls in love with her new life, and with Taylor. Jasmine's world crashes once again when she sees her husband's murderer in Central Park. That he sees her, too, terrifies her even more. She suddenly realizes that the walls that she had carefully constructed between lives were vulnerable. Perhaps, she fears, she has not really escaped her awful fate. On the spot, she decides to flee to a place she can only imagine, chosen solely because her beloved charge Duff was born there. She flees to Iowa, and again adopts a new identity: Jane.

In Baden, Elsa County, Iowa, she enters a relationship with a farmer/banker, Bud Ripplemeyer. Although Bud and Jane are unmarried (unbeknown to the townsfolk), they adopt a Vietnamese refugee, Du. This is her new family, and Baden County, Iowa, becomes her new home. Again, she undergoes a transformation; as simple Jane, her violent history is left behind. "I rip free of the past," she says (208). This transformation is total, as she immerses herself in her new home, new family, new Midwestern world. So distant are her old lives that she refers to her younger self as "a girl I once knew" (222). When Bud is left paralyzed and wheelchair-bound after a distraught borrower from Bud's bank shoots him, Jane's role becomes one of caregiver as well as lover, and she assumes the role with pleasure and comfort. Although she is not in love with Bud, she does love him, and she again regains a sense of home. The farmhouse and its add-ons "cozy me into thinking that all of us Ripplemeyers, even us new ones, belong," she says early in her tale (13).

Again, however, Jane's comfort is short-lived. Her adopted son, Du, suddenly announces that he is moving to California to be with a sister of whose existence Jane had not even known. He had always been private, she realizes in retrospect. Earlier, she had recalled that "I've told him my stories of India, the years between India and Iowa, hoping he'd share something with me. When they're over he usually says, 'That's wild. Can I go now?'" (18). It occurs to her that Du had entered an expatriate Vietnamese community in Iowa, while she herself had not even spoken to another Indian since she left Flushing. She has much in common with Du: "Once upon a time, like me, he was someone else. We've been many selves. We've survived hideous times" (214). This latest discovery of Du's private activities, however, forces her to face their differences. "My transformation has been genetic; Du's was hyphenated" (222), she realizes. Unlike herself, Du has added a new identity to one he already had; she has become a new person altogether. His response to his immigrant experience differed from hers to a degree she had failed to recognize. Du could never have felt a sense of home when he had a sister 2,000 miles away. In different circumstances, she notes, Du could have had an ideal, robust father and a place to call home. "This, I realize, is not it" (224), she reflects sadly as Du leaves.

Out of the blue, Taylor, with Duff in tow, tracks Jasmine down and asks her to run away with them. At this point, the narration shifts for the first time into present tense, creating a sense of immediacy and dramatic tension. Jasmine suddenly faces a fateful choice. Duty dictates that she remain in Iowa to care for Bud. Jyoti or Jasmine certainly would make that choice; they would not even recognize an alternative. Leaving with the man with whom she is in love, however, might mean a lifetime of happiness rather than one of contentment. "I am not choosing between men. I am caught between the promise of America and old-world dutifulness," she says (240). At last, she breaks entirely from her past.

At the novel's conclusion, she leaves with Taylor and Duff, having put, in genuine American fashion, her own happiness before her sense of duty. She is, ultimately, adventurous Jase again. "I realize I have already stopped thinking of myself as Jane" (240), as she slips from the fate foretold to her decades ago in India. For the first time, she dares to think of her future. "Time will tell if I am a tornado, rubble-maker, arising from nowhere and disappearing into a cloud. I am . . . greedy with wants and reckless from hope," she says (241).

The value of ethnic literature as a window into America has long been recognized. Mukherjee's novel merits attention for this alone. It depicts this land as a place of staggering contrasts—the brutality of Jasmine's rapist and the kindness of her Quaker rescuer—and also of change: Jasmine notes the "fluidity of American character and the American landscape" (183). Perhaps it takes an outsider to describe this tabula rasa quality in America:

> In America, nothing lasts. I can say that now and it doesn't shock me, but I think it was the hardest lesson of all for me to learn. We arrive so eager to learn, to adjust, to participate, only to find the monuments are plastic, agreements are annulled. Nothing is forever, nothing is so terrible, or so wonderful, that it won't disintegrate. (181)

Jasmine's outsider perspective also teaches the reader about Americans, from the cruelty of some to the kindness of others. She recalls the accuracy of Lillian Gordon's parting advice to "walk and talk American" so Americans will think she was born in the United States. "Most Americans can't imagine anything else," she says (134–35).

Jasmine also lifts the veil on the darker aspects of America, the parts about which native-born, white Americans are ignorant. When Du's history teacher tells Jasmine that he, a Vietnam veteran, "tried a little Vietnamese" on Du and was surprised at Du's terror, she is disgusted at his insensitivity. Of course street Vietnamese coming from his ostensibly innocuous, white history teacher would strike fear in the boy; how could this reaction surprise the teacher? "This country has so many ways of humiliating, of disappointing," she says (29). When a man in a bar, noticing her foreignness, calls her a whore, Jasmine tells the reader, "I wish I'd known America before it got perverted" (201). Most Americans are unaware of these daily insults against those who occupy the country's secret, liminal spaces. "I wonder if Bud even sees the America I do," she says (109). Of course, he does not.

Jasmine also clarifies the process by which one's environment—family and home—alters and is altered by one's sense of self: although her various identities are partly self-created, her various names came from her different families and communities. One way in which Jasmine creates a sense of home amid numerous challenges is to make her environment bend a little. Hers is not a wholesale assimilation; rather, it is an arranged compromise between herself and her surroundings. At its most subtle, the environmental alteration might be as simple as introducing Indian food to Iowans: "I took gobi aloo to the Lutheran Relief Fund craft fair last week. I am subverting the taste buds of Elsa County" (19). At its most significant, the alteration involves the lives of the people around her. She becomes half of Prakash's dream, and fulfills their shared destiny after his death. Although she leaves Bud in the end, he remains indebted to her for spiritually saving him after his paralysis. Ultimately, she completes the Hayes family and achieves happiness for all three of its members

Jasmine's agency in the story—her depiction as one who not only is changed by her environment but also changes it—marks one of the novel's strengths. Mukherjee, like her protagonist, does not subscribe to environmental determinism. Despite her belief in fate, Jasmine at several junctures in the plot chooses her own path. Amazed at the turns her life has taken, she asks, "Who lays out the roadways of our futures?" (174), but the answer is herself. She believes that the human soul is "like a giant long-playing record with millions of tracks," bringing its bearer from one life's destiny to the next, but she also believes that "extraordinary events can jar the needle arm, jump tracks, rip across incarnations, and deposit a life into a groove that was not prepared to receive it" (127). In many cases, particularly in her ultimate decision to leave with Taylor and Duff, her own hand jars the needle arm.

Despite Jasmine's many identity shifts, she has not abandoned her essential personality; in fact, her odyssey brings her into touch with it. Her identity at the novel's conclusion, adventurous Jase, is not so different from her childhood self, Jyoti. On the book's opening page, Jasmine recalls that, at age seven, she was "fast and venturesome" (3), and she recounts her courageous encounter with a rabid dog (56-57). Like the leaves and thorns that scratched her in her youth, the challenges and conflicts she surmounts in her extraordinary life (or lives) scrape from her sense of self the burdensome identities imposed upon her by others—by family and by cultures.

As this novel demonstrates, identity, family, and home are infinitely mutable in the unlimited possibilities represented by America. The fluidity of her own identity—and the endurance and preservation of her core personality—as she struggles with the creation of new homes in new communities makes Jasmine an emblematic immigrant. *Jasmine* fits into the tradition of American fiction that captures the timeless theme of new world expectations colliding with old world habits. Because Mukherjee addresses the struggle so artfully and so explicitly, *Jasmine* is an ideally representative immigrant novel, which is to say, in this nation of immigrants, a supremely American novel that reveals as much about America as it does about those who come to it from distant lands.

16

BUTTERFLIES AT SEA: THE THEME OF MIGRATION IN CONTEMPORARY CHINESE POETRY

Clayton G. MacKenzie

In Ai Qing's poem "A Young Man's Voyage" (1945), a disenchanted youth declares tetchily:

> I dislike that village—
> It is as common as a banyan tree,
> As dumb as a water buffalo.
> I spent my childhood there.
> Those stupider than I laughed at me;
> I kept silent but cherished a wish in my heart:
> To go to the outside world to learn more,
> To go far away—to places unseen even in dreams. (li. 5–12)

The imperatives of departure are strong in the literatures and art of many rural communities. In Western cultures, for example, the Scottish Highland clearances and the famine exodus of nineteenth century Ireland found poignant expression through pen and brush alike. In African writing, Ngugi, Achebe, Aidoo and others explore the tensions between the old ways of the village and the new and alluring ways of the city, tracing and identifying the spiritual decimation concomitant with rural–urban patterns of movement.

Ai Qing's poem, though, challenges fundamentally the more traditional emotional backdrop to departure. Here is no forlorn young man, hanging his head sorrowfully, as in Thomas Faed's masterly "The Last of the Clan"; here is no M'ma Asana, in Ama Ata Aidoo's "Certain Winds from the South," despairing of the necessity of village emigration. On the contrary, Ai Qing's young man *wants* to leave, *needs* to leave, *longs* to leave. The customary despairing of the necessity of village emigration. On the contrary, Ai Qing's young man *wants* to leave, *needs* to leave, *longs* to leave. The customary notion of pastoral well being and benignity is expressly and emphatically disavowed. Leaving the village for the undreamed of destination becomes a pietistic expression of cleansing, a rite of redemption and even of near-deification:

> There will be far better than here.
> People live like immortals (li. 13–14)

Of course, part of the power of the poem is that it captures so compellingly the unquenchable and unreachable optimism of youth. It is the prerogative of each new generation to presume, albeit erroneously or otherwise, a superior knowledge to its antecedent. Even so, that sense of "purification" the young man envisages as the destination of migration is arrestingly extravagant—and, importantly, it is one that is replicated and reworked in the writings of other contemporary Chinese poets.

Gong Liu's "The Shadow of a Departing Sail" (1987), for instance, at once expresses the worthiness of migratory dreams and goes on to explore the contradictions and confusions that they inevitably arouse. The poem moves beyond youthful imaginings of near-deification through migration, and engages the harsh consequences of communal and geographical disengagement:

> Do not ponder
> Why the lost good dreams
> Get taken to the ends of the earth
> Yet pester each other in the ear. (li. 13–16)

Though dreams may be "good," they yet may be lost in the transmigrations of culture and place. Gong advocates no search for certainty—in fact, counsels against it with a succession of negative imperatives ("Do not inquire . . . "; "Do not investigate . . . "; "Do not comment . . . "). Just as the dream is the stuff of mystery, so the failure or success of dreams is equally elusive. The important thing is to *have* good dreams and to strive to live them out in the face of all the adversities that life will throw in their way. As in Ai Qing's "A Young Man's Voyage," the migratory dream assumes a speculative importance beyond its factual possibilities. The dream comes to encapsulate the imaginative essence of human aspiration, an almost religious intuition of faith in not only the potential betterment of time and place, but in the progress toward a mysterious and ultimate perfection.

envisions in the guise of the planting and propagation of wild flowers a purificatory migration toward sanctity,

> One night
> I sowed stars as flower seeds
> In the tranquil mountain valley . . .
> One after another
> The wild chrysanthemums
> With their little feet pattering along
> Have walked into the heart of the mountains. (li. 1–3; 12–15)

The sowing of stars becomes a figure for the dream of an idealized destination. The familiar polar images of darkness and light, of the void and the stars, are reworked through the metaphor of planting into a new scheme of possible harmony. The planter–dreamer becomes the creator of stars—but, more than that, the initiator of a process of purification which begins with the planting of stars and continues with the spreading advancement of the chrysanthemums into the mountains:

> Range after range of mountains:
> Have been washed clean by the streams
> Their shapes are so lean and vague
> That they look somewhat translucent (li. 8–11)

The journey of "star" flower heads becomes a pilgrimage, a migration to–ward the purity and unity of the mountains which stretch up into the vast reaches of heaven. Zhou Xiaoping's wild chrysanthemums come to represent a spiritual odyssey in the search for perfection, echoing Ai Qing's notion of the journey as a passage toward perfection, toward immortality.[1] Significantly, the planter–dreamer is not some incidental voyeur to this process, but is in fact instrumental to its initiation: "I sowed stars. . . ." Zhou Xiaoping's envisioned perfection may be a mystical one, but she asserts that it stems from a very human dream, that it could not begin the journey towards realization without the intercession of the human agency.

The religious refrain in the preoccupation with what one may call a state of "otherness" is not unusual. It composes part of the homiletic quest of most religious belief systems. Nor is the sense of "journey" an unfamiliar vehicle for the expression of that quest, for it is a theme reiterated frequently in Western art forms, from Mallory's *Morte D'Arthur* to Bunyan's *Pilgrim's Progress* to Coleridge's *Rime of the Ancient Mariner* to Spielberg's *Raiders of the Lost Ark*. What distinguishes the notion of "quest" in contemporary Chinese poetry is the potential for layered significances—and, in particular, political and social commentary that function sometimes subliminally, sometimes poetry is the potential for layered significances—and, in particular, political and social commentary that function sometimes subliminally, sometimes translucently, and very occasionally obviously, as part of the discourse of the poem. The young emigrant in Ai Qing's "A Young Man's Voyage" initially gives as his reason for departure the commonness and dumbness of his village, but he goes on to describe his ideal world as one where, unlike his "poor village" (li. 29), one does not have to

> . . . hear the heartbreaking sound of mortars
> Or see the deplorable faces of monks and nuns. (li. 15–16)

The poetry is not simply about the idealizations of youth. It is also a social and political statement on the state of prerevolutionary China. On one level it is about a young man leaving home; on another it is about the poverty of subsistence survival (the "heartbreaking" pounding of the mortar and pestle used to husk rice by peasants struggling to eke out a living) and of life constrained by a corruptive religious order which leads the young man to "feel sorry" (li. 26) for his village.

Acclaim for Ai Qing's work has not been diminished in post-revolutionary China, partly because it consistently addresses the very issues that underpinned the theoretical discourse of the 1949 revolution itself. Inevitably, that discourse, like Chinese politics, is subtle. Outright poetic propagandizing was unwise and unwelcomed in prerevolutionary China. In postrevolutionary China, the poet's role as social and political critic has proved rather more ambivalent: occasion-ally countenanced as in the "Hundred Flowers" period of 1956–57, at other times discouraged as during the Cultural Revolution of the 1960s and 1970s. On political issues in particular, most contemporary Chinese poets tread a judicious line.[2] An interesting illustration of this can be found in the work of the Chinese-born Taiwanese poet, Yu Guangzhong, who has used the idea of spatial distance to reiterate political separations between the mainland and Taipei: [3]

> When I was very young
> Homesickness was a little postage stamp
> I was on this side
> While mother was on the yonder side
> After I became an adult
> Homesickness was a narrow strip of steamer ticket
> I was on this side
> While my bride was on the yonder side
> Alas, sometime later
> Homesickness was a low tomb
> I was outside

While mother was inside
But at the present time
Homesickness is the shallow Taiwan Straits
I am on this side
While the mainland is on the yonder side. (li. 1–6)

Yu Guangzhong prudently titles his poem "Homesickness," suggestive more of emotional rather than political nostalgia. "Homesickness" articulates the tragedy of the emigrant: the personal and familial dislocations caused by physical geographical separations. Though not obviously political, the poem is yet inherently so. The personalization of the hardships of migration moves inevitably against the factual backdrop of ideological "separations"—in this case, between the communist People's Republic of China and pro-American Taiwan. It is a disjunction that Yu Guangzhong chooses not to engage overtly in the poem and yet without it there is the certainty that the lifetime it delineates would have been very different.

The theme of the sea as the route of migration, such as the Taiwan Straits in "Homesickness," is one picked up by a succession of contemporary Chinese writers: Ren Hongyan in "A Boat," Wu Bengxing in "Farewell," Ngaleg in "A Journey on the Highland," Bei Dow in "A Dream of the Harbor," Zheng Ling in "At a Ferry." But perhaps its most powerful expression is to be found in the work of Niu Han. "Butterflies at Sea," a poem written in 1981, expresses with beguiling power the imperatives of migration:

It may be said
That whatever flies over the sea
Must have hard wings
To pit its strength against the thunderstorm.
Yet I have seen
(As true as true may be)
Small, yellow butterflies
Skimming the boundless billows of the Gulf of Bohai,
Not coast clinging
But flying far out away and away!
Soaring and dipping
As vigorous as gulls. (li. 2–13)

On one level this is simply a puzzling causal observation: butterflies migrating in the face of tumultuous elemental threat. And, indeed, the first line of the poem, a lank and prosaic statement, suggests a superficiality of interpretative intention: "I have encountered many inexplicable wonders over the decades." Yet other features of the poem encourage the reader to move beyond the faunal facade of understanding and into a more politicized domain of significance. The poem starts on the precept of a generalization: "whatever" flies across the sea must have "hard wings." Immediately, therefore, it invites broader comparisons and associations. The precise example of the small yellow butterflies is both moving and instructive. Having established the parameters of successful migration (hard winds, strength), the poem then bluntly instances a migrating creature that in no regard meets the criteria for migration, save in its determination to leave. The strength of objective is endorsed by the repetition of "away" and by the certainties of action ("Not coast clinging"; "as vigorous as gulls").

Though the spectacle does fill him with wonderment, at no point does Niu Han counsel the futility of the butterflies' endeavors. What emerges from the poem is rather the absolute desire for removal and, in the phrase "Not seeming lost," the suggested premeditation of action:

> Small, yellow butterflies
> Glimmering like flames
> Not seeming lost
> Not obviously alarmed
> Flying ever farther
> As the coast melted away. (li.14–19)

The poem establishes a double paradox. First, it presents migrating creatures that are, by normative physical standards, unsuitable for migration. Second, it establishes a dichotomy of understanding: the poet marvels at the enigmatic motive behind the creatures' departure, but the butterflies themselves do not hesitate to dare safety and to move against the threatening void with an unnerving sense of calmness and assured self-comprehension.

In the final couplet, images of fragility and determination are woven together exquisitely in the first and only question of the poem:

> Tiny butterflies,
> Why do you not look back? (li. 20–21)

Why, indeed. It is this question that runs to the very heart of the poem. What is it that drives a creature, so delicate and vulnerable, to these extravagant and dangerous ends? What is it that provokes the butterflies to abandon the sanctuary of their native habitat and to embark on this perilous odyssey? To these questions there is no obvious answer. All that can be said is that whatever imperatives demanded migration, they were extreme enough to encourage an unambiguous incisiveness of action. In the images of departing butterflies, there is an implication of ambiguous flight—they are "flying far out," but they are also "fleeing." It is upon the second significance that Niu Han builds the question, "Why do you not look back?" The inherent assumption is that what is behind them is less alluring or more fearful than what is beyond.

"Butterflies at Sea" mythologizes the act of departure. It encapsulates not simply a mysteriousness of purpose but also the indomitable spirit and courage of the voyagers. Their action is valorized into an exemplary framework of potential conduct. For the poet this is an important and decisive condition. The poem, deliberately Sinocized through reference to Bohai, seeks to express not the determination and courage that butterflies have shown, but the determination and courage that people *could* show.

Angela C. Y. Jung Palandri, writing in 1972, argued that "mainland poets, isolated from all contact with the outside world because of fervent nationalism and xenophobia, are forced to look to their indigenous past for literary theories and inspirations"(4). It is perhaps a measure of the changes that occurred in China that by the late 1970s this judgment no longer holds sway.[4] By way of example, one may look to the mythologization of politically motivated migration in "Song of a Little Mermaid," where the poet Zheng Ling deliberately and pointedly selects a Western mythology (Andersen's fairy tale "The Little Mermaid") as her mode of expression. Exiled herself from Hunan Province on the charge of being a "rightist" during the Cultural Revolution, Zheng Ling explores the mysterious nature of her exile:

> I didn't know where this unexpected disaster came from,
> Which destroyed my joy in the twinkling of an eye.
> Yes, I remembered,
> Oh, how terrible!
> It must be that monstrous witch
> I knew her from Andersen's fairy tales,
> She emerged from beneath the winding stairs
> The moment I entered the palace,
> Her gruesome black cloak trailing on the floor,
> Her blood red fingernails half hidden. (li. 25–34)

Andersen's tale of the tragic, muted mermaid parallels obliquely the experiences of a poet who was exiled and silenced on the accusation of "having ulterior motives" (li. 65). Zheng Ling has spoken of the considerable comfort she gleaned during the period of her exile in the reading of Western classics smuggled to her mountain retreat (140). It is perhaps not surprising, therefore, that "Song of a Little Mermaid," written shortly after her official exoneration in 1979, is defiant in its use of a Western vehicle for the statement of enforced migration. In one regard, her choice of Western fable as the agency of protest and free statement is an act of ex post facto protest itself, accentuating the implication that those who tormented her are really the "evil" (li. 63) ones. Migration, therefore, is not simply a physical disjunction, but it is further echoed in intellectual and cultural terms. Alienated from her home, Zheng Ling articulates, as well, an alienation from the pervading culture that precipitated her exile. While the poet has physically returned from exile, her ideological perspective remains foreign.

"Song of a Little Mermaid" chooses to reject the considered reticence of "Butterflies at Sea," and in this regard the two pieces, written within a few months of each other, reveal varying attitudes towards the creation and utilization of migratory mythologies. As readers we may not be able to decipher the considerations, political or otherwise, that determined the creative choices made in the construction of these poems. What can be said is that the compulsion of absence is represented quite differently. In "Song of a Little Mermaid," parting is a physical compulsion, an obligation enforced upon the unwilling subject. In "Butterflies at Sea," departure remains a compulsion but one undertaken with a certitude of determination and desire by the subjects.

Zheng Ling's forthright approach in "Song of a Little Mermaid" remains untypical of modern Chinese poetic writing. The tradition of cautious understatement on political matters is one traceable in this century at least to Feng Zhi's "The Silkworm Horse" (1925), which draws upon Chinese folklore to explore the condition and tragic consequences of separation:

> She did not know where her father had gone—to the land's
> end or to the sea's edge?
> There was still the same wind, still the same rain.
> But the fields, they were more wasted every day.
> "O father, when will you come back?
> Separation is indeed like a vast boundless sea.
> Horse, could you take me to the other shore
> To find my father's smiling face?" (li. 21–28)

To a degree the poem typifies the important disjunction that has come to characterize contemporary Chinese poetry: a willingness to articulate the state of separation but a calculated reserve in the expression of those causal elements that have precipitated the state of separation. Even when subject matter promises to offer a more translucent personalized testimony, addressing the *detail* of cause remains tentative. For instance, Ai Qing's archetype of the young man leaving for the city because his village is "common" or "dumb" seems a readily recognizable developing world motivation. And yet it survives little introspection. What does "common" and "dumb" actually mean, and why may village life be so characterized? What are the factors—political, social, economic—that derogate the worth of the village and aggrandize the virtues of urbanized environments?

Even poetic discourse that traverses in a more overt manner the political boundaries of debate, still tends to engage the substance of causal dissatisfaction obliquely. This is understandable, partly in terms of the poet's consideration of personal and family well-being and partly in terms of the symbolic traditions of the poetic genre itself. Undoubtedly, the "marginal status of poetry and the poet" (Yeh, xxvi)[5] in modern and contemporary Chinese writing has encouraged a certain caution and reticence. This factor may seem inhibiting since one might expect that constrictions of context and genre would limit the adventurousness of poetic content and debate. In practice, however, the effect has been liberating. The blurring of significances, and the imprecisions of commentary, particularly in the work of the so-called "obscurist poets," has enabled Chinese poetry to explore some of the less accessible recesses of con-temporary Chinese life. There is a price. Symbolic gesturing must take the place of literal explication. But that, of course, is the natural milieu of the poet. And it is for this reason that the theme of migration provides such a valuable and versatile medium of poetic expression, allowing the poet to move beyond primal statements of dissatisfaction toward an exploration of more complex considerations of consequence and amelioration.[6]

Notes

1. It should be noted that Ai Qing would probably not enjoy the comparison—since he has firmly denounced the "obscurantism" of much contemporary Chinese poetry. See *The Red Azalea: Chinese Poetry Since the Cultural Revolution*, ed. Edward Morin, with an introduction by Leo Ou-Fan Lee (Honolulu: University of Hawaii Press, 1990), 3.

2. It is, of course, a mistake to think that Taiwanese poets (as opposed to poets from the People's Republic of China) are entirely "free." See, for example, the "Translators' Introduction" to *Bo Yang: Poems of a Period*, trans. Stephen L. Smith and Robert Reynolds (Hong Kong: Joint Publishing Co., 1986), iii–vi.

3. For a comprehensive consideration of Taiwanese poetry, see *Modern Verse from Taiwan*, ed. and trans. Angela C. Y. Jung Palandri (Berkeley, Los Angeles, and London: University of California Press, 1972).

5. The phrase is Michelle Yeh's: "The self in modern Chinese poetry is more often tragic than triumphant, possibly because of the marginal status of poetry and the poet."

6. Julia C. Lin, in *Modern Chinese Poetry: An Introduction*, has characterized modern Chinese poetry as having provoked "more hostile criticism and fierce opposition than any other form of modern Chinese literature" (3).

References

Ai Qing. "A Young Man's Voyage." In *Anthology of Modern Chinese Poetry*, ed. and trans. Michelle Yeh. New Haven: Yale University Press, 1992.

Feng Zhi. "The Silkworm Horse." Translated by Julia C. Lin. *Modern Chinese Poetry: An Introduction*, ed. Julia C. Lin. London: Allen & Unwin, 1972.

Gong Liu. "The Shadow of a Departing Sail." *Chinese Literature* (spring 1990): 148–49.

Lin, Julia. *Essays on Contemporary Chinese Poetry*. Athens: University of Ohio Press, 1985.

Morin, Edward, ed. *The Red Azalea: Chinese Poetry Since the Cultural Revolution*. Honolulu: University of Hawaii Press, 1990.

Niu Han. "Butterflies at Sea." Trans. Simon Johnstone. *Chinese Literature* (summer 1988): 19–20.

Palandri, Angela C.Y. Jung, ed. and trans. *Modern Verse from Taiwan*. Berkeley: University of California Press, 1972.

Smith, Stephen L., and Robert Reynolds, eds. and trans. *Bo Yang: Poems of a Period*. Hong Kong: Joint Publishing Co., 1986.

Yeh, Michelle, ed. and trans. *Anthology of Modern Chinese Poetry*. New Haven: Yale University Press, 1992.

Yu Guangzhong. "Homesickness." *Chinese Literature* (spring 1994): 149.

Zheng Ling. "Song of a Little Mermaid." Trans. Hu Shiguang. *Chinese Literature* (summer 1994): 140.

Zheng Ling. "Song of a Little Mermaid." Trans. Hu Shiguang. *Chinese Literature* (summer 1994): 140.

Zhou Xiaoping. "Wild Chrysanthemums." Trans. Hu Shiguang: *Chinese Literature* (summer 1992): 138.

SELECT BIBLIOGRAPHY

Ahmad, Hena. "Kamala Markandaya and the Indian Immigrant Experience in Britain." Pp. 141–48 in *Reworlding: The Literature of the Indian Diaspora*, ed. Emmanuel Nelson. Westport, Conn.: Greenwood Press, 1992.

Allen, Sheila. *New Minorities, Old Conflicts: Asian and West Indian Migrants in Britain*. New York: Random House, 1971.

Andryszewski, Tricia. *Immigration: Newcomers and Their Impact on the United States*. Brookfield, Conn.: Millbrook Press, 1995.

Arnold, Fred, Urmil Minocha, and James T. Fawcett. "The Changing Face of Asian Immigration to the United States." Pp. 105–52 in *Pacific Bridges: The New Immigration from Asia and the Pacific Islands*, ed. James T. Fawcett and Benjamin Corino. Staten Island, N.Y.: Center for Migration Studies, 1987.

Asian and Pacific Islander Center for Census Information and Services. *Our Ten Years of Growth—A Demographic Analysis on Asian and Pacific Islander Americans*. ACCIS, San Francisco, 1992.

Asian Women United in California. *Making Waves: An Anthology of Writing By and About Asian Women*. Boston: Beacon Press, 1989.

Avery, Donald H. "Strangers at Our Gates: Canadian Immigration and Immigration Policy, 1540–1990." *Canadian Historical Review* 75, no. 2 (June 1994): 303–6.

Bach, Robert L. "Recrafting the Common Good: Immigration and Community." *Annals of the American Academy of Political and Social Sciences,* November 1993, 155–70.

Badets, Jane. "Canada's Immigrants: Recent Trends." *Canadian Social Trends* 29 (summer 1993): 8–11.

Bald, Suresht Renjen. "Images of South Asian Migrants in Literature: Differing Perspectives." *New Community* 17, no. 3 (April 1991): 413–31.

Barkan, Elliott Robert. *Asian and Pacific Islander Migration to the United States: A Model of New Global Patterns.* Westport, Conn.: Greenwood Press, 1992.

Bennett, Bruce. *A Sense of Exile: Essays in the Literature of the Asia–Pacific Region.* Nedlands: University of Western Australia Centre for Studies in Australian Literature, 1988.

Bhabha, Homi. *The Location of Culture.* London: Routledge, 1994.

————. *Nation and Narration.* London: Routledge, 1990.

Bolaria, B. Singh, and Peter S. Li. *Racial Oppression in Canada.* Toronto: Garamond Press, 1985.

Bouvier, Leon F. and Anthony J. Agresta. "The Future Asian Population of the United States." Pp. 285–301 in *Pacific Bridges: The New Immigration from Asia and the Pacific Islands,* ed. James T. Fawcett and Benjamin Carino, Staten Island, N.Y.: Center for Migration Studies, 1987.

Bouvier, Leon F., and Robert W. Gardner. "Immigration to the U.S.: The Unfinished Story." *Population Bulletin* 41, no. 4 (1986).

Bouvier, Leon F. *Peaceful Invasions: Immigration and Changing America.* New York: University Press of America, 1992.

Brown, Judith M., and Rosemary Foot, eds. *Migration: The Asian Experience.* New York: St. Martin's, 1994.

Bryce-Laporte, Roy Simon, ed. *Sourcebook on the New Immigration: Implications for the United States and the International Community.* New Brunswick, N.J.: Transaction Books, 1980.

Carlson, Alvar W. "America's New Immigration: Characteristics, Destinations, and Impact, 1970–1989." *Social Science Journal* 31, no. 3 (1994): 213–36.

Castles, Stephan, and Mark J. Miller. *The Age of Migration.* London: Macmillan, 1993.

Champion, A.G. "International Migration and Demographic Change in the Developed World." *Urban Studies* 31, no. 4/5 (1994): 653–77.

Chan, Anthony B. "Born Again Asians: The Making of a New Literature." *Journal of Ethnic Studies* 11, no. 4 (1984): 57–73.

————. *Gold Mountain: The Chinese in the New World.* Vancouver, B.C.: New Star Books, 1983.

Chandrasekhar, S., ed. *From India to Canada.* La Jolla, Calif.: Population Review Books, 1986.

Cheung, Yuet W. "Asian Immigration: Assessing the Issues." *Ethnic and Racial Studies* 13, no. 1 (1991): 127–28.

Chirayath, Verghese J. "Asian Immigration to the United States: Some Preliminary Findings." Paper presented at the North Central Sociological Association Convention, 1979.

Cohler, Larry. "New Americans Who Keep Old Faiths Alive." *Scholastic Update* 117 (1 March 1985): 17–18.

Commonwealth Literatures and Language Conference (10th: Koenigsten, Germany). *Critical Approaches to the New Literatures in English.* Essen, Germany: Verlag die Blause Eule, 1989.

Contacts and Conflicts: The Asian Immigration Experience. Asian American Studies Center, University of California, Los Angeles, 1975.

Coppa, Frank J., and Thomas J. Curran, eds. *The Immigrant Experience in America.* Boston: Twayne, 1976.

Cornelius, Wayne, Philip Martin, and James Hollifield, eds. *Controlling Immigration: A Global Perspective.* La Jolla, Calif.: Center for U.S.–Mexican Studies, University of California, San Diego, 1994.

————. "The 'New' Immigration and the Policies of Cultural Diversity in the United States and Japan." *Asian and Pacific Migration Journal* 2, no. 4 (1993): 439–50.

Daniels, Roger. "The Indian Diaspora in the United States." Pp. 83-103 in *Migration: The Asian Experience*, ed. Judith Brown and Rosemary Foot. New York: St. Martin's, 1994.

————. "Westerners from the East: Oriental Immigrants Reappraised" *Pacific Historical Review* 35 (1966): 373–83.

"The 'Darkening' of America." *Asiaweek*, 27 April 1990, 50.

DeLepervanche, Marie. *Indians in a White Australia.* Sydney: Allen and Unwin, 1984.

Early, Gerald, ed. *Lure and Loathing: Essays on Race, Identity, and the Ambivalence of Assimilation.* New York: Allen Lane and Penguin Press, 1993.

"East Asian–Canadian Connections." *Canadian Literature* 140 (spring 1994).

Edmonston, Barry, and Jeffrey Passel. *The Future Immigrant Population of the United States.* Washington, D.C.: Urban Institute, 1992.

————, eds. *Immigration and Ethnicity: The Integration of America's Newest Arrivals.* Washington, D.C.: Urban Institute Press, 1994.

Fawcett, J.T., B.V. Carino, and F. Arnold, eds. *Asian–Pacific Immigration to the United States.* Honolulu: East–West Center, 1985.

Fawcett, James T., and Benjamin Carino, eds. *Pacific Bridges: The New Immigration from Asia and the Pacific Islands.* Staten Island, N.Y.: Center for Migration Studies, 1987.

Ferguson, R., et al., eds. *Out There: Marginalizations and Contemporary Cultures.* Cambridge, Mass.: MIT Press, 1990.

Ferraro, Thomas. *Ethnic Passages: Literary Immigrants in Twentieth Century America.* Chicago: University of Chicago Press, 1993.

Fisher, Maxine P. *The Indians of New York City: A Study of Immigrants from India.* Columbia, Mo.: South Asia Books, 1980.

Freeman, G.P., and J. Jupp, eds. *Nations of Immigrants: Australia, the United States, and International Migration.* New York: Oxford University Press, 1992.

Gabaccia, Donna, ed. *Seeking Common Ground: Multidisciplinary Studies of Immigrant Women in the United States.* Westport, Conn.: Greenwood Press, 1992.

Gardner, Robert. "American Immigration." *Asian Migrant* 2 (April 1989): 61.

Gardner, Robert, Bryant Robey, and Peter C. Smith. *Asian Americans: Growth, Change, and Diversity.* Washington, D.C.: Population Reference Bureau, Inc., 1985.

———. "Asian Immigration: The View from the United States." *Asian and Pacific Migration Journal* 1, no. 1 (1992): 64–99.

Gee, Emma, et al., eds. *Counterpoint: Perspectives on Asian America.* Los Angeles: UCLA Asian American Studies Center, 1976.

Gifford, Zerbanoo. *The Golden Thread: Asian Experiences of Post– Raj Britain.* London: Grafton, 1990.

Glazer, Nathan, ed. *Clamor at the Gates: The New American Immigration.* San Francisco: ICS Press, 1985.

———. "Is Assimilation Dead?" *Annals of the American Academy of Political and Social Sciences,* November 1993: 122–36.

Gurr, Andrew. *Writers in Exile: The Identity of Home in Modern Literature.* Atlantic Heights, N.J.: Humanities Press International, 1981.

Hesse, Jurgen, ed. *Voices of Change: Immigrant Writers Speak Out.* Vancouver, B.C.: Pulp Press, 1990.

Hewson, Kelly. "Opening Up the Universe a Little More: Salman Rushdie and the Migrant as Story–Teller." *SPAN: Journal of the South Pacific Association for Commonwealth Literature and Language Studies* 29 (October 1989): 82–93.

Hing, Bill Ong. *Making and Remaking Asian America Through Immigration Policy, 1850–1990.* Stanford University Press, 1993.

Hinnells, John R. "The Modern Zoroastrian Diaspora." Pp. 56–84 in *Migration: The Asian Experience,* ed. Judith M. Brown and Rosemary Foot. New York: St. Martin's, 1994.

Hiraoka, Jesse. "A Sense of Place." *Journal of Ethnic Studies* 4, no. 4 (1977): 72–84.

Hirschman, Charles, and Morrison Wong. "Asian Immigration to the United States: Recent Patterns, Trends, and Consequences." Association Paper, American Sociological Association, 1989.

Hongo, Garrett. "Asian American Literature: Questions of Identity." *Amerasia Journal* 20, no. 3 (1994): 1–8.

Hoyt, Edwin P. *Asians in the West.* New York: Nelson, 1974.

Hune, Shirley. "Opening the American Mind and Body: The Role of Asian American Studies." *Change,* Nov./Dec. 1989, 56–63.

Hune, Shirley, et al., eds. *Asian Americans: Comparative and Global Perspectives.* Pullman, Wash.: Washington State University Press, 1991.

"Immigration." *Canada and the World,* March 1993; 13–27.

Jacobs, Paul, et al. *Colonials and Sojourners.* New York: Random, 1971.

Japanese American Citizens League. *A Report on Anti-Asian Violence in the United States, 1985.* San Francisco, 1985.

Jensen, Joan. *Passage from India: Asian Indian Immigrants in North America.* New Haven, Conn.: Yale University Press, 1988.

Jussawalla, Feroza. "Chiffon Saris: The Plight of South Asian Immigrants in the New World." *Massachusetts Review* 24, no. 4 (winter 1988–89): 583–95.

Kessner, Thomas, and Betty Boyd Caroli. *Today's Immigrants, Their Stories: A New Look At the Newest Americans.* New York: Oxford University Press, 1981.

Kim, Bok Lim C. *The Asian American: Changing Patterns, Changing Needs.* Montclair, N.J.: Association of Korean Christian Scholars in North America, 1978.

Kim, Elaine. *Asian American Literature: An Introduction to the Writings and Their Social Context.* Philadelphia: Temple University Press, 1982.

———. "Asian American Literature and the Importance of Social Context." *ADE Bulletin* 80 (1985): 31–33.

———. "'Such Opposite Creatures': Men and Women in Asian American Literature." *Michigan Quarterly Review* 29 (1990): 68–93.

Kitano, Harry L. "Asian Americans: The Chinese, Japanese, Koreans, Pilipinos, and Southeast Asians." *The Annals of the American Academy of Political and Social Science* 454 (March 1981): 125–38.

Kitano, Harry L., and Roger Daniels. *Asian Americans: The Emerging Minority.* Englewood Cliffs, N.J.: Prentice–Hall, 1988.

Knoll, Tricia. *Becoming Americans: Asian Sojourners, Immigrants, and Refugees in the Western United States.* Portland, Ore.: Coast to Coast Books, 1982.

Koo, Hagen, and Eui–Young Yu. *Korean Immigration to the United States: Its Demographic Pattern and Social Implications for Both Societies.* Papers of the East–West Institute No. 74. Honolulu: East–West Center, 1981.

Labour Party (Great Britain). *Immigration and Racialism.* Researched by Liz Atkins. London: Labour Party, 1977.

Lamm, Richard, and Gary Imhoff. *The Immigration Time Bomb.* New York: E.P. Dutton, 1985.

Lane, David. "Race Relations in Britain: The Scene and the Prospect." *Contemporary Review,* 1978: 119–23.

Lee, Joann Faung Jean. *Asian American Experiences in the United States: Oral Histories of First to Fourth Generation Americans from China, the Philippines, Japan, India, the Pacific Islands, Vietnam, and Cambodia.* Jefferson, N.C.: McFarland, 1991.

Lee, Sharon M. "Asian Immigration and American Race-Relations: From Exclusion to Acceptance?" *Ethnic and Racial Studies* 12, no. 3 (July 1989): 368–90.

Leonard, Karen. "South Asian Immigrants: Then and Now." *San Jose Studies* 14, no. 2 (1988): 71–84.

Leong, Liew-geok. "Expatriates and Immigrants: Displacement and Americanization." Pp. 487–500 in *International Literature in English: The Major Writers,* ed. Robert Ross. New York: Garland, 1991.

Lesser, Jeff H. "Always 'Outsiders': Asians, Naturalization, and the Supreme Court." *Amerasia* 12, no. 1(1985/86): 83–100.

Levenstein, Aaron. *Escape to Freedom: The Story of the International Rescue Committee.* Westport, Conn.: Greenwood Press, 1983.

Lim, Shirley Geok-Lin. "The Ambivalent American: Asian American Literature on the Cusp." Pp. 13–32 in *Reading the Literatures of Asian America,* ed. Shirley Geok-lin Lim and Amy Ling. Philadelphia: Temple University Press, 1992.

Lim, Shirley Geok-lin, and Amy Ling, eds. *Reading the Literatures of Asian America.* Philadelphia: Temple University Press, 1992.

Lind, Michael. "Reinventing America." *World Policy Journal* 11, no. 4 (winter 1994): 77–84.

Lindsey, Robert. "The New Asian Immigrants." *New York Times Magazine,* 9 May 1982, sect. 9: 22–28.

Ling, Amy. "'Emerging Canons' of Asian American Literature and Art." Pp. 91-98 in *Asian Americans: Comparative and Global Perspectives,* ed. Shirley Hune, et al. Pullman: Washington State University Press, 1991.

———. "Whose America Is It?" *Weber Studies* 12, no. 1 (winter 1995): 27–35.

Liu, Zongren. *Two Years in the Melting Pot.* San Francisco: China Book and Periodicals, Inc., 1984.

Lyman, Stanford, ed. *The Asian in North America.* Santa Barbara, Calif.: ABC–Clio Books, 1977.

———. *The Asian in the West.* Social Science and Humanities Publication 4. Edited by Don D. Fowler. Reno, Nev.: Western Studies Center, Desert Research Institute, University of Nevada, 1970.

Mageli, P. D. *The Immigrant Experience.* Pasadena, Calif.: Salem Press, 1991.

Martin, Philip L. "Immigration and Integration: Challenges for the 1990s." *Asian Migrant* 7, no. 2 (April 1994): 46–51.

Massey, Douglas. "Dimensions of the New Immigration to the United States and the Prospects for Assimilation." *Annual Review of Sociology* 7 (1981): 57–85.

Maykovich, Minako K. "To Stay or Not to Stay: Dimensions of Ethnic Assimilation." *International Migration Review* 10 (1976): 377–87.

McGurn, William. "A Passage to Golden Mountain." *Far Eastern Economic Review* 156, no. 30 (29 July 1993): 28.

Melendy, H. Brett. *Asians in America: Filipinos, Koreans, and East Indians.* Boston: Twayne, 1977.

Michalowski, M. "Redefining the Concept of Immigration in Canada." *Canadian Studies in Population* 2, no. 1 (1993): 59–84.

Min, Pyong Gap, and Hyon Sook Kim. "The Post–1965 Korean Immigrants: Characteristics and Settlement Patterns." *Korea Journal of Population and Development Studies* 21 (1992): 121–43.

Morton, James. *In the Sea of Sterile Mountains: The Chinese in British Columbia.* Seattle: University of Washington Press, 1980.

Mukherjee, Bharati. "Immigrant Writing: Give Us Your Maximalists!" *New York Times Book Review,* 28 August 1988, sec. 7: 3, 28–29.

Muthuna, I.M. *People of India in North America.* Bangalore, India: Grangarams Book Distributors, 1982.

Minh-ha, Trinh T. *Woman, Native, Other: Writing Postcoloniality and Feminism.* Bloomington: Indiana University Press, 1989.

Nahal, Chaman Lal. *The New Literatures in English.* Delhi: Allied Publishers, 1985.

Namias, June. *First Generation: In the Words of Twentieth Century American Immigrants.* Boston: Beacon Press, 1978.

Nelson, Emmanuel S., ed. *Reworlding: The Literature of the Indian Diaspora.* Westport, Conn.: Greenwood, 1992.

Nhu Tran Tuong. "Vietnam Refugees: The Trauma of Exile." *Civil Rights Digest* 9, no. 1 (1976): 59–62.

Oehling, Richard A. "Hollywood and the Image of the Oriental." *Film and History* 8, no 2 (1978): 33–41; 8, no. 3: 59–67.

Okihiro, Gary, et al. *Shattered Windows: Promises and Prospects for Asian American Studies.* Pullman, Wash.: Washington State University Press, 1988.

Passel, Jeffrey, and Michael Fix. "Myths About Immigrants." *Foreign Policy* 95 (summer 1994): 151–60.

Peach, Ceri. "Three Phases of South Asian Emigration." Pp. 38–55 in *Migration: The Asian Experience,* ed. Judith M. Brown and Rosemary Foot. New York: St. Martin's, 1994..

Perrin, Linda. *Coming to America: Immigrants from the Far East.* New York: Delacorte Press, 1980.

Pfanner, Helmut, ed. *Exile Across Cultures.* Bonn: Bouvier, 1986.

Phillips, Andrew. "The Lessons of Vancouver: Immigration Raises Fundamental Questions of Identity and Values." *Maclean's,* 7 February 1994: 26–35.

Pido, Antonio J.A. *The Pilipinos in America.* New York: Center for Migration Studies, 1985.

Pooley, C.G., and I.D. Whyte, eds. *Migrants, Emigrants and Immigrants: A Social History of Migration.* London, New York: Routledge, 1994.

"Questions of Identity: Ethnicity, Apprenticeship, and the New American Writer." *New England Review* 15, no. 3 (summer 1993): 7–186.

Reimers, David. "South and East Asian Immigration Into the United States: From Exclusion to Inclusion." *Immigrants and Minorities* 3, no. 1 (1984): 30–48.

Renaud, Viviane, and Jean Badets. "Ethnic Diversity in the 1990s." *Canadian Social Trends* 30 (autumn 1993): 17–22.

"Rice Papers: Writing and Artwork by East and South Asian Women in Canada." *Fireweed: A Feminist Quarterly* 43 (spring 1994).

Rubenstein, Roberta. *Boundaries of the Self: Gender, Culture, Fiction.* Chicago: University of Illinois Press, 1987.

Rushdie, Salman. *Imaginary Homelands: Essays and Criticism 1981–1991.* London: Granta Books, 1992.

Rystad, Goran. "History and Future of International Migration." *International Migration Review* 26, no. 4 (winter 1992): 1168–99.

Said, Edward. *Culture and Imperialism.* New York: Alfred A. Knopf, 1993.

———. *Orientalism.* New York: Vintage Books, 1979.

———. "Reflections on Exile." Pp. 357-66 in *Out There: Marginalizations and Contemporary Culture,* ed. Russell Ferguson, et al. Cambridge, Mass.: MIT Press, 1990.

Salyer, Lucy E. "Records of the Immigration and Naturalization Service. Series A: Subject Correspondence Files, part 1, Asian Immigration and Exclusion." *Journal of American History* 81, no. 1 (June 1994): 361–62.

Samuel, T. John. "Asian and Pacific Migration: The Canadian Experience." *Asian and Pacific Migration Journal* 3, no. 2-3 (1994): 465–95.

Samuel, T. John, and Ravi B.P. Verma. "Immigrant Children in Canada: A Demographic Analysis." *Canadian Ethnic Studies* 24, no. 3 (1992): 51–57.

San Juan, E., Jr. "Filipino Writing in the United States: Reclaiming Whose America?" *Philippine Studies* 41 (1993): 141–66.

Saran, Parmatma. *The Asian Indian Experience in the United States.* Cambridge, Mass.: Schenkman Publishing Co., 1985.

———. *The New Ethnics: Asian Indians in the United States.* New York: Praeger, 1980.

Sarmiento, J.N. "The Asian Experience in International Migration." *International Migration* 29, no. 2 (June 1991): 195–204.

Sato, Gayle K., ed. "Asian Perspectives." *MELUS* 18, no. 4 (winter 1993–94).

Satzewich, Vic, ed. *Deconstructing a Nation: Immigrants, Multiculturalism, and Racism in the 90s Canada.* Halifax, Canada: Fernwood Publishers, 1992.

Schur, Joan B., ed. *In a New Land: An Anthology of Immigrant Literature.* Lincolnwood, Ill.: NTC Publishing Group, 1994.

Shahani, Roshan G. "In Quest of a Habitation and a Name: Immigrant Voices from India." *International Journal of Canadian Studies* 6 (1992): 87–98.

Sheehan, Teru Kanazawa. "Asian Americans Emerge." In *Without Ceremony, IKON #9* Asian Women United, 1988.

Sheth, Manju. "The New Asian Immigration and Immigrant in the United States: Implications for Research and Policy." Association Paper, American Sociological Association, 1989.

Shokoff, James. "American Cultural Literacy and Asian Literature." *American Studies International* 28, no. 1 (April 1990): 83–92.

Singh, Amritjit, ed. *Memory and Cultural Politics: New Approaches to American Ethnic Literatures.* Boston: Northeastern University Press, 1995.

Skeldon, Ronald, ed. *Reluctant Exiles? Migration from Hong Kong and the New Overseas Chinese.* Armonck, N.J: M.E. Sharpe, 1994.

"South Asian Connections." *Canadian Literature* 132 (spring 1992).

"Speaking of Imternational Migration." *Los Angeles Times,* 12 July 1994, H6.

Stafford, Tim. "Here Comes the World." *Christianity Today* 39, no. 6 (15 May 1995): 18–26.

Strand, Paul J., and Woodrow Jones, Jr. *Indochinese Refugees in America: Problems of Adaptation and Assimilation.* Durham, N.C.: Duke University Press, 1985.

Sue, Stanley, and Nathaniel Wagner. *Asian Americans: Psychological Perspectives.* Ben Lomond, Calif.: Science and Behavior Books, 1973.

Sugunasiri, Suwanda H.J. "The Literature of Canadians of South Asian Origins: An Overview." *Canadian Ethnic Studies* 14, no. 1 (1985): 1–21.

Sullivan, Rosemary. "Who Are the Immigrant Writers and What Have They Done?" *Globe and Mail*, 17 October 1987, E1.

Tachiki, A., et al., eds. *Roots: An Asian American Reader*. Los Angeles: UCLA Asian American Studies Center, 1971.

Takaki, Ronald. *A Different Mirror: A History of Multicultural America*. Boston: Little, Brown, 1993.

————. *From Different Shores: Perspectives on Race and Ethnicity in America*. New York: Oxford University Press, 1987.

————. *Strangers from a Different Shore: A History of Asian Americans*. Boston: Little, Brown, 1987.

Talwar, Ambika. "Transformations: Self and Community." *Rice Paper* (May 1993): 22–24.

Tenhula, John. *Voices from Southeast Asia: The Refugee Experience in the United States*. New York: Holmes and Meier, 1991.

Tepper, Eliot L., ed. *Southeast Asian Exodus: From Tradition to Resettlement; Understanding Refugees from Laos, Kampuchea and Vietnam in Canada*. Ottawa: Canadian Asian Studies Association, 1980.

Tradition and Transformation: Asian Indians in America. Williamsburg, Va.: College of William and Mary, 1986.

Tran, Qui-Phiet. "Exile and Home in Contemporary Vietnamese American Feminine Writing." *Amerasia Journal* 19, no. 3 (1993): 71–84.

Truong, Monique Thuy-Dung. "Vietnamese American Literature, 1975–1990: The Emergence of Voices." *Amerasia Journal* 19, no. 3 (1993): 27–50.

"Us and Them: Philosophical Bases of Political Criticism." *Yale Journal of Criticism* 2 (spring 1989): 1–31.

Vu, Nguyen Van, and Bob Pittman. *At Home in America*. Nashville, Tenn.: Broadman Press, 1979.

Wakil S. Parvez, C.M. Siddique, and F.A. Wakil. "Between Two Cultures: A Study in Socialization of Children of Immigrants." *Journal of Marriage and the Family* 43 (November 1981): 929–40.

Wickberg, Edgar. "The Chinese as Overseas Migrants." Pp. 12–37 in *Migration: The Asian Experience,* ed. Judith M. Brown and Rosemary Foot. New York: St. Martin's, 1994.

Wilson, Robert A., and Bill Hosokawa. *East to America: A History of the Japanese in the United States.* New York: Morrow, 1980.

Wong, Morrison. *The New Asian Immigrants.* Bethesda, Md.: National Institute of Child Health and Human Development, 1979.

———. "Post–1965 Asian Immigrants: Where Do They Come From, Where Are They Now, Where Are They Going?" *Annals of the American Academy of Political and Social Science* 487 (1986): 150–68.

Wong, Sau–ling Cynthia. *Reading Asian American Literature: From Necessity to Extravagance.* Princeton, N.J.: Princeton University Press, 1993.

Wong–chu, Jim. "Ten Years of Asian Canadian Literary Arts in Vancouver." *Asianadian* 5, no. 3(1984): 23–4.

"World on the Move: Special Report." *Los Angeles Times,* 1 October 1991.

Yu, Renqiu. "The Making and Remaking of Asian America Through Immigration Policy: 1850–1990." *Historian* 56, no. 4 (summer 1994): 751–52.

Yung, Judy. *Chinese Women of America: A Pictorial History.* Seattle: University of Washington Press, 1986.

Zaman, Niaz, and K.U. Ahmed, eds. *Migrants, Migration, and the United States.* Dhaka, Bangladesh: BAAS, 1992.

Zich, Arthur. "Japanese Americans: Home at Last." *National Geographic* 169 (April 1986): 512–39.

INDEX